Before Penn

An Illustrated History of The
DELAWARE RIVER COLONIES
1609 – 1682

Written & Illustrated by
HAL TAYLOR

© Copyright 2019 Hal Taylor
All rights reserved.

No portion of this book may be reproduced in whole or in part, by any means whatsoever, except for passages excerpted for the purposes of review, without the prior written permission of the publisher.

For information, or to order additional copies,
please contact:

Beacon Publishing Group
P.O. Box 41573 Charleston, S.C. 29423
800.817.8480| beaconpublishinggroup.com

Publisher's catalog available by request.

ISBN-13: 978-1-949472-87-5

ISBN-10: 1-949472-87-6

Published in 2019. New York, NY 10001.

First Edition. Printed in the USA.

The type is set in Minion Pro,
1669 Elzivir, and P22 Roanoke

✦ CONTENTS ✦

INTRODUCTION	*viii*
PROLOGUE	*x*
PART I • THE ENGLISH	
CHAPTER I	*1*
CHAPTER II	*7*
CHAPTER III	*12*
CHAPTER IV	*19*
PART II • THE DUTCH	
CHAPTER V	*26*
CHAPTER VI	*33*
CHAPTER VII	*43*
CHAPTER VIII	*52*
CHAPTER IX	*57*
CHAPTER X	*65*
PART III • THE SWEDES	
CHAPTER XI	*70*
CHAPTER XII	*76*
CHAPTER XIII	*85*
CHAPTER XIV	*89*
INTERMISSION	*92*
CHAPTER XV	*96*
CHAPTER XVI	*109*
CHAPTER XVII	*112*
PART IV • THE ENGLISH RETURN	
CHAPTER XVIII	*128*
CHAPTER XIX	*134*
CHAPTER XX	*137*
CHAPTER XXI	*141*
CHAPTER XXII	*147*
CHAPTER XXIII	*151*
CHAPTER XXIV	*159*
CHAPTER XXV	*165*
EPILOGUE	*172*
NOTES	*175*
BIBLIOGRAPHY	*181*
INDEX	*185*

To the Indians who didn't know they needed more, to the Dutch who convinced them that they did, to the Swedes and Finns, who found harmony with the land, and to the English, who gained the upper hand.

✦ INTRODUCTION ✦

There is an old maxim that goes: "Americans think 100 years is a long time, Europeans think 100 miles is a long way".

While the roots of the U.S. may not be as old as the rest of the world, they go much deeper than many Americans realize. We view our history as beginning with the landing of the Pilgrims, and then the revolutionary war happened. Not quite correct. Even before that apprehensive band of religious dissidents found themselves on the shores of Cape Cod, representatives of global corporations began probing the rivers of the northeast for resources. Instead of gold or other precious minerals, they found furs. Beaver in particular, that fed the fashion habits of Europe. The Dutch West India Company led the charge, which was eventually usurped by the Swedes, and English.

John Cabot claimed nearly all of North America for King Henry VII of England only five years after Columbus landed in the Caribbean. But Norse settlers had arrived and departed, long before Cabot, and there may well have been others long before the Norse. Henry Hudson recorded the first official finding of the Delaware Bay in 1609, but Giovanni Verrazano may have sighted it 85 years previously. It's even possible that Cabot himself may have happened upon the Delaware Bay. But it was Cabot's brief visit to Newfoundland in 1497 that eventually determined the fate of the entire eastern seaboard.

Lewes, Delaware, known mainly as the southern terminal of the Cape May-Lewes Ferry, uses as its motto "The First Town in the First State", because of a small settlement established there by Dutch whalers in 1631. It matters little to residents that the colony lasted less than a year. They celebrate the provenance rather than the details. Elsinboro Township in Salem County, NJ honors Swedish soldiers who manned a small fortress on the Delaware in the 1640s. It had to be abandoned because of mosquito infestation, but local inhabitants don't think of those who were stationed there as any less heroic. It gives them great pride to be attached to something so old in their own backyard.

Those early pioneers—the ones lucky enough to survive a grueling Atlantic crossing—arrived in a completely foreign landscape with next to nothing, lived on rat-infested, cramped sailing vessels while they built their own shelters, cleared land, grew their own food, prayed for good weather, and continued praying that they wouldn't be eaten by wildlife or besieged by hostile members of the native human population. They were a true cross section of humanity regardless of their nationalities; from hard working sod farmers to self-styled monarchs, to soldiers and sailors just doing their duty in a place that seemed like a distant planet. But each had a desire for a new and independent life. Throughout the tumultuous early days, as control of the region swung wildly, and often, from one governing body to another, the losers were given the option to stay put, or return to their homeland. Most decided to stay. It was from these tenacious settlers that the roots of an entirely new nation were grown.

William Penn was a late-comer to all this, appearing after much of the turmoil had settled. He arrived to find settlers who had been carving out rich lives for generations. The location for his "Greene country towne" was not even his first choice; that was already occupied. And when he stepped off the boat at what would become the City of Philadelphia, the Blue Anchor Tavern was there to greet him. He officially bought the city grounds from the Indians, who by this time were in the twilight of their ancestral existence. They had originally benefitted from European technology, but were now overwhelmed by it. It was the end of one era, and the beginning of another.

Before Penn is designed to give some clarity to the legacy of these earliest pioneers, and how they came to be here, but more importantly, to call attention to an underserved gap in the subconscious of the Delaware Valley. – HT

✦ PROLOGUE ✦

No man ever steps in the same river twice, for it's not the same river, and he's not the same man.

HERACLITUS OF EPHESUS

William Penn stepped gingerly from the ship *Welcome* and into the longboat that would take him to dockside. He had been at sea for two months in a cramped ship crammed with unwashed, seasick passengers, their belongings, crewmen, and livestock. Quaker leader and now real estate mogul, Penn had sailed from England to take possession of a land grant recently acquired through a debt owed his father. In fact it was named after him–Pennsylvania; a massive tract totaling some 45,000 square miles, the largest privately owned territory in the world.

Penn was a neophyte to this New World; European explorers and traders had combed the Delaware River Valley for years, and settlers began putting down roots long before he was even born. Much of his newly-claimed possession had already changed nationalities many times before he set foot in North America. Participating in this game of colonial musical chairs were the English, Indians, Dutch and Swedes. As we are well aware, the English captured the last chair. And it all came about with hardly a drop of blood being spilled–remarkable during a particularly violent era. What was even more remarkable was that in this age of exploitation, a pacifist would come to establish on the Delaware a community based on respect for basic human rights in a world ruled by monarchs and despots.

The *Welcome* was not nearly as crowded as when the voyage began. A passenger infected with smallpox had boarded the ship at Deal, in Kent, England. The disease spread through the ship during the Atlantic crossing and as a result the manifest was reduced by a third, the victims buried at sea. Penn was not a stranger to smallpox, having contracted the disease as a child. As the longboat made its way to the western shore of the Delaware River, his ever-present wig fluttered in the breeze like so many flags covering his bald head–an affect of the affliction.

The longboat finally reached the wooden dock to discharge its distinguished passenger at the little riverfront town of New Castle, where he was greeted by an enthusiastic and noisy crowd. The inhabitants had been anticipating this day for over a year. It was October 27, 1682.

✦ ✦ ✦

THE DELAWARE RIVER itself did not originally have appeal as an ultimate destination, but rather as a vehicle to spur the discovery of something else: a passage, a route to where known commodities lay. The commodities were the riches of the Far East: gold, gems, silk and perhaps the most precious of all—spice, the ingredient that just may have changed the world.

To many, spices were almost a religion; they could drive off evil spirits or summon good ones, enhance one's sexual prowess, and add extra prestige to any solemn event. (To honor the death of Nero's wife a year's supply of cinnamon was burned.) We also assume that spices were highly valued because food spoiled quickly without refrigeration and were a necessity to mask an unpleasant dining experience. But it has been known how to preserve foodstuffs from ancient times. Salting, smoking, pickling–all perfectly adequate methods of increasing shelf life; cheese is nothing more than preserved milk. Besides, spices were far too expensive to use as perfume for spoiled meat. But spices added, well…spice. It was the desire for that nearly unobtainable stuff that made it irresistible.

Cloves grew nowhere else on earth but on five tiny islands in today's Indonesian archipelago. And an even smaller group of neighboring islands were the only place where one could find nutmeg. Collectively, they were known as the Moluccas, but elsewhere in the world were reverently referred to as the Spice Islands. From these islands the spices made their way to India where additional aromatics like pepper, cinnamon, and cardamom grew. Add silk, gold and jewels to this mix and it would make up the collective exotic cargo that would wend its way over the Silk Road to the markets of Europe–Venice, London and the low countries, controlled most of the way by Arab tribesmen, each taking a cut for themselves like drug dealers. With each hand the precious commodities passed through, the price increased until by the final destination, it had inflated to an astronomical 1,000 percent or more. Then in 1453, Constantinople fell, the Ottoman Empire arose, and the flow of coveted goods slowed to a trickle. It was small wonder then, that trying to bypass the middleman spurred the Age of Discovery.

In medieval Europe, very few actually followed a flat earth theory; you could probably find more believers today. That the earth was round met with little doubt–everyone knew that you could go west to reach the east. But it took Columbus to actually *do* it. The problem was that he didn't do it far enough. Despite any tangible evidence, he lived to the end of his days convinced that he had found "ad loca aromatica", the place where the spices are. He confounded his miscalculation by trying to convince everyone else he had actually found what he set out for. He brought gold, parrots, natives (whom he dubbed "Indios"), and cinnamon back to Spain in 1493 for all to examine. And while the rest were real enough, the "cinnamon" presented in the form of twigs, looked a little like the real spice, but was more pungent and smelled something like cloves—or was it ginger? Another of his delusions was the discovery of the fruit of a plant that gave a piquant sensation when eaten, like black pepper from India. He called it "aji" or "child." German botanist and Columbus supporter Leonhart Fuchs later reaffirmed the misconception when he renamed it "Calcutta Pepper." But we, of course, now know it as the chili.

Portuguese explorer Vasco da Gama actually did find "ad loca aromatica", although it took over two years and 24,000 miles of ocean to accomplish the discovery. Setting out from Portugal, he passed the Canary Islands and swung down the coast of Africa toward the Cape Verde Islands. Sailing in a wide arc around the Gulf of Guinea he struck back for the coast and down to the very bottom of the continent. Rounding the Cape of Good Hope, da Gama was now in the Indian Ocean but still very, very far from the spices. It wasn't until May of 1498 that he finally reached the Malabar Coast of India and pay dirt. It was considered a navigational triumph, regardless of the fact that he had covered more than four times the distance of the Columbus expedition.

Because of the failure of Columbus

and the success of da Gamma, the Spanish realized they were going to be competing with Portugal for whatever else might be discovered and that they had better define who could claim what. In June of 1494, ambassadors from the two Iberian powers met to discuss the problem. What resulted was the Treaty of Tordesillas, which essentially divided the globe, like a melon that's been split down the middle. Spain would control all lands west of a line of longitude running about 320 miles west of the Cape Verde Islands, including the discoveries of Columbus. Obversely, the Portuguese would have possession of everything to the east including da Gama's passage around Africa. Not coincidentally, the Moluccan spice trade as well. (Which is why Brazilians speak Portuguese, while the rest of South and Central America use Spanish).

The Columbus west to east approach was also taken by another Portuguese navigator–Fernão de Magalhães, better known by his Spanish name—Ferdinand Magellan. Rejected by his own government, he offered his services to Spain who warily accepted. He left Spain in 1519 with five ships and close to 300 men and enough supplies and weaponry to furnish a globe-circling expedition. Almost three years later, only one of those ships, the *Victoria*, limped back into the Spanish port of Sanlúcar de Barrameda, with more holes than a colander and only eighteen survivors–Magellan not among them. In the leaking hold of this ship lay 53,000 pounds of cloves. And that small cargo was worth enough to pay the salaries of the remaining sailors, the loss of four ships, compensation to the families of the deceased, the outfitting of the ships, supplies, weaponry and ammunition–with still enough left over to make a profit of 2,500 percent.

The distances needed to travel for these exotic goods still made them expensive commodities. The Dutch were more than willing to endure the cost, and in 1602 they created the VOC, de Verenigde Oostindische Compagnie, the Dutch East India Company. The English were right on their heels, creating their own East India Company, both countries wresting the spice trade from the monopoly established 130 years earlier by the Spanish and Portuguese. But investors would grow impatient, the round-trip voyages taking sixteen months or more to complete. And some ships never returned, their precious cargoes seasoning the sea rather than their intended consumers.

The newly discovered land masses of North and South America had proved to be annoyingly massive obstacles. What was needed was a shorter path to the goods. Central and South America seemed impenetrable, but was there a passage through North America? There was no shortage of adventurers willing to look for it—English, Italians, Portuguese, Spanish, French, and more. And there were just as many promising rivers and estuaries begging to be explored.

The Delaware was one of them.

European Settlement in the

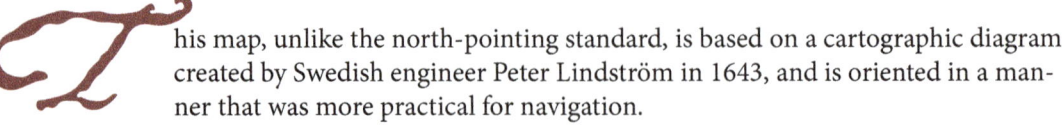

This map, unlike the north-pointing standard, is based on a cartographic diagram created by Swedish engineer Peter Lindström in 1643, and is oriented in a manner that was more practical for navigation.

Delaware Valley ✦ 1609-1682 ✦

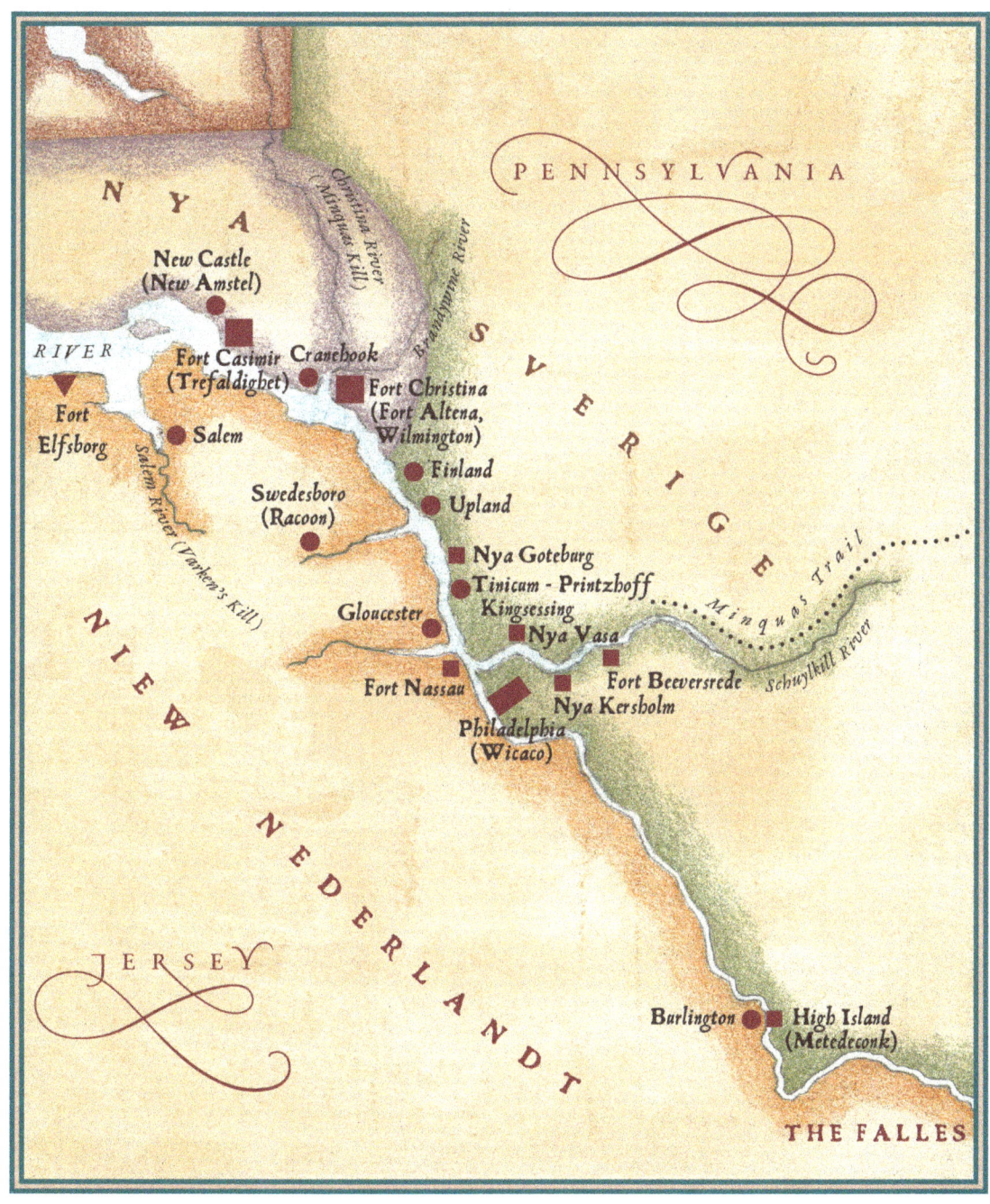

It depicts places and features as they would have been known in the time period as well as the contemporary era. Although the state boundaries as we know them did not yet exist, they are shown simply as points of reference.

◆ PART I ◆

The English

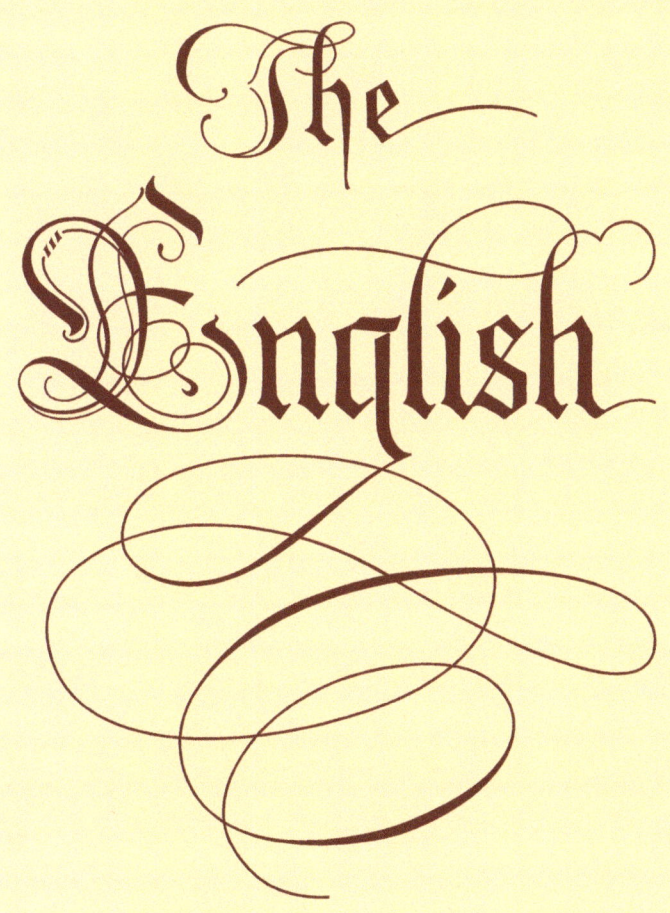

I

There is a general acceptance that the first Europeans to inhabit North America were Norsemen led by Leif Eriksson. He was the son of Eirik the Red, exiled from Norway for exhibiting intense homicidal tendencies, even by Viking standards. But Eirik was also a shrewd real-estate salesman. He was able to attract colonists to a barren, glacier covered island which he dubiously advertised as Greenland.

According to Norse historical records, or Sagas, (which are a composite of fact and legend) Leif eventually left the Greenland colony around 1000 AD with 35 men to investigate mysterious lands reported by a fellow Norse mariner who had become lost during a storm. They did find land to the west, and after preliminary exploring, Leif and company established a small foothold on the northern tip of Newfoundland in an area known as L'Anse aux Meadows. It is believed that this foothold served as a base camp for the Norse to explore a much larger area, including the Gulf of St. Lawrence and even venturing much further south. (A Scandinavian coin of the same approximate time period was found at an archeological site along the coast of Maine). In 2015 satellite imagery and excavation confirmed evidence of an iron working hearth and the possible remains of a turf wall at a site called Point Rosee, on the southwest coast of Newfoundland. The area yields an abundance of bog ore, material the Norse would have been well acquainted with. And somewhere in their travels (possibly New Brunswick), they discovered an abundance of wild grapes, a fruit they were not totally familiar with. Which may or may not account for this part of North America they mysteriously called "Vinland."

Despite Eirik's psychotic behavior, these people were not the brutal Vikings of legend. They were merchants, farmers, tradesmen and the like, looking for opportunities like

The Knarr, the norse work boat

any other businessmen. They did not even use the iconic dragon-headed long boats, but a short, squat vessel known as a knarr. These were much more practical for hauling cargoes of passengers, livestock, and supplies on the open seas. There were as many as four different voyages made to L'Anse aux Meadows, but it was not to be a permanent colony. Establishing a pattern that would be repeated over and over again for the next thousand or so years, the settlers clashed with the native population. General misunderstandings and distrust kept the two cultures at length. But unlike what was to occur in the future, the native population won this battle. The Norse left Newfoundland after only a few years–never to return. And no Europeans visited North America again for the next 500 years...that we know of.

Apparently, the Norse Sagas were not shared elsewhere in Europe, only rumors and speculation which percolated for years about lands to the west, like the mythical 'Island of 'Brasil' also known as 'Hy-Brazil.' These may have derived from the Gaelic Uí Breasail, 'descendants of Breasial', or 'Isle of the Blest'. This would make sense as the island was reputed to be located somewhere to the west of Ireland, which at times could appear to be the very edge of the known world.

It could also account for the legendary story of Saint Brendan, an Irish monk credited with a possible visit to America some four hundred years before the Norsemen. As described in the eighth century tome Navigatio Sancti Brendani Abbatis, or The Voyage of Saint Brendan the Abbott, one of his fellow monks returned from a long sea voyage emotionally describing in glowing detail the discovery of an island he called the Promised Land of the Saints. Brendan was so impressed by the tale that he and his brothers constructed a currach-like boat made of butter-softened hides to sail to this alleged land. Brendan was indeed a real person, but his described nautical escapades may not have been. On one adventure, the party landed on a small island, but when they made a fire, the island began to move. It was discovered they had grounded on the back of a whale.

More parts of the tale have them visiting an island inhabited by birds which sang psalms, and they venture far north where they find a "coagulated" sea. But there are also allusions to a place where "great demons threw down lumps of fiery slag from an island with rivers of gold fire" and "great crystal pillars", which could have been references to volcanoes and icebergs. (In his book *Made in America: An Informal History of the English Language in the United States*, Bill Bryson makes the very astute observation that by island hopping across the north Atlantic, it is possible to travel no more than 250 miles between stops.) All this meandering took seven years, at the end of which they finally arrive at the Promised Land of the Saints. The monks explore the island for forty days, then sail home, where Brendan passes satisfied into the next life. Not only is it a highly fanciful and entertaining tale, but in true Irish fashion, has also been put to music, describing St. Brendan's adventures with his jolly monks. It has been recorded by many different musicians, including native Irishman and longtime Philadelphia legend Mick Maloney.

The Voyage of Saint Brendan the Abbott, which also enjoyed wide popularity during the Middle Ages, was translated into a variety of languages and encouraged geographers to include St. Brendan's Isle in their descriptions of the known world. Columbus himself was undoubtedly familiar with Brendan's story, scouring it for navigational clues to assist him in his upcoming expeditions.

✦ ✦ ✦

Atlantic Cod

IN HIS SUPERB BOOK *Cod*, Mark Kurlansky speculates that Basque fisherman may have reached the Grand Banks and beyond, sometime before Columbus' famous voyage. Sailing to the west and remaining away for weeks or months at a time, they would return with dried cod. As there was not enough room on their boats for this procedure, they would need large areas of dry land to process the fish. An account dating from 1481 describes an unusually large amount of salt being stowed for an exploratory expedition. But their lips were sealed. They wouldn't give up their secret fishing spots any more than modern fisherman.

There were others eager to explore to the west, particularly from Bristol in England, itself an island that had been somewhat isolated from the rest of Europe, except for the occasional invasion. These were merchant pioneers and fishermen who ventured to colonies on Iceland and Greenland, trading wool and searching for fishing grounds. It was there that they may have gotten wind of lands even further in the direction of the sunset. And eventually, they did discover the same grounds that the Basques were tight-lipped about–near where the Norse had landed so long ago. The discovery was helped along by war in Europe that in 1475, blocked the Bristol fishermen from their traditional catches off Iceland. But somehow, they still managed to procure loads of cod, until in 1490, when the grounds were again opened and they were invited to return, the Bristolmen said thanks, but no thanks.

In the late fifteenth century, the Bristol fishers were joined by other Europeans, making yearly trips to the Newfoundland cod-laden waters, and by 1578 it was reported that fifty English and Portuguese, one hundred Spanish, and one hundred more French vessels, plus twenty or thirty whalers were plying the icy Canadian waters. By 1604, there were at least 600 French ships working the Grand Banks.

Unlike the Basques, the Bristol merchants shared their discoveries during trading voyages to Spain. It was there that a fellow tradesman from Venice listened intently to their tales. The merchant, known as Giovanni Caboto began to develop his own theories about their discoveries. Obviously, Columbus had been entirely off base in his claims, never having found any trace of spices, but Caboto reasoned that if he were to sail to the north-west, a much shorter route, and hug the coast, the mysterious East and all of its glorious riches would be revealed. A contemporary of Columbus (and the two may even have met, being fellow countrymen), Caboto also propositioned King Ferdinand to back an expedition. But by this time the King had had enough of Italian explorers and flatly refused.

Disappointed but not defeated, Caboto decided to try his luck in the land of the Bristol Merchants. His sales pitch involved the impending discovery of an island he called "Cipango", 'where he believes all the spices of the world have their origin, as well as the jewels.' King Henry VII must have been impressed enough, as he granted Caboto an official license (although with only modest support) to make discoveries for England in 'the eastern, western, and northern sea.' He was presented with a new ship; the *Matthew*, and a new name; John Cabot, the Angli-

PART I

cized version of his original Italian. In May of 1497 (the same year that de Gama sailed for India) he set out from England along with his son Sebastian and reached the coast of Newfoundland, but did very little exploring on land, only staying long enough to plant the banners of St. George for King Henry VII, and St. Mark for Venice.

Cabot returned to England to great fanfare claiming that 'he has discovered mainland 700 leagues away, which is the country of the Great Khan', which was of course adventurers' smoke, raising many a skeptical eyebrow on the faces of people who had heard this tale before. But he did also report, without secrecy, of the cod fisheries and vast natural resources. It was reason enough for King Henry to consider everything Cabot had found as now belonging to England—a single assertion that would have far-reaching consequences for the eventual history of the New World—more than King Henry, Giovanni Caboto or anyone else could have possibly imagined.

And for a reward, King Henry gave Cabot £10 "to amuse himself." It is said that he spent most of it on wine, women and natty apparel. The rest he squandered. It was also observed that while on this binge disposing of his new-found fortune that he would promise new friends he met in taverns that he would name islands for them.

Having had barely time to bask in his accomplishment, Cabot was asked to undertake a second voyage. This time he was given five ships manned by three hundred men. Leaving England in July of 1498, he reached North America again, but this time pack ice impeded a northerly course, forcing him to turn south where he explored the coastline, possibly as far as Cape Hatteras. If so, Cabot could well have been the first European to view the New York, Delaware, and Chesapeake Bays. But this is only speculation. Cabot and four of the five ships disappeared on the voyage, the last limping back to Ireland, badly damaged. But he will always be memorialized as the man who discovered North America.

And here's a small tidbit of barely useful information: it has long been assumed that the Americas have taken their name from Italian merchant and explorer Amerigo Vespucci, whose name appears for the first time on the Waldseemüller world map of 1507, but one of Cabot's backers was the sheriff of Bristol, Richard Amerike. Some would claim that it is his name that appears on early maps identifying the lands of the New World.

PART I

◆ I I ◆

Despite the discovery of a new continent, its value continued to lay hidden in plain sight. Gradually acknowledging that North America was indeed *not* China, explorers and opportunists grudgingly viewed it as a frustrating obstacle to reaching the Orient. It became known to geographers and cartographers as The Fourth Part of the World. For hundreds of years previously, the earth had been neatly compartmentalized in T-O maps: Europe and Africa separated by the main stem of a "T", with Asia resting on top, surrounded by a circular frame representing the oceans of the world.

And so began the search for the legendary Northwest Passage that would continue for hundreds of years. The next to give it a shot was none other than John Cabot's son Sebastian, also sailing under the English flag, who in a voyage that began in 1508, may have reached the Hudson Strait, but his reports were so vague, it was unclear exactly where he had sailed. But upon his return the next year Henry VIII took next to no interest in the expedition. He was far too preoccupied in dealing with problems at home (his love life, presumably), Ireland, and on the European mainland.

As far as anyone was concerned, North America was still a blank slate. Frustrated, Cabot offered his services to Spain. Englishman John Rut set out with two ships in 1527 for the same purpose. A yeoman of the crown, Rut was relieved of his normal duty of transporting Bordeaux wine to Henry and given command of the king's ship *Mary Guildford* and another named the *Samson*. His mission was to find a passage around or through North America and engage in trade when he reached Asia, a straightforward assignment. Almost immediately upon setting off from Plymouth, the two ships lost contact, but Rut continued on across the North Atlantic, touching the coast of Labrador and then south to St. John's, Newfoundland. In the first known letter sent from North America, he reported to King Henry of finding fishermen of Norman, Briton, and Portuguese origins. In another first, Rut sailed south from the Canadian provinces briefly exploring the Chesapeake Bay and possibly Florida. Despite Rut's far-reaching explorations, Henry was unhappy that the Northwest Passage remained undiscovered, and like his father, also lost interest in the New World. Upon his return to England, Rut was returned to his old position as royal wine hauler.

Realizing that Henry VIII was not interested in expansion, privately funded expeditions began to be organized. English dandy Robert Hore set out in 1536 with thirty gentlemen and no plan other than to seek "strange new things." After their food supplies ran out, they were forced to dine on each other until they were rescued by a French fishing vessel.

Meanwhile, the Spanish didn't seem to care about the Northwest Passage. They were doing quite well plundering Mexico and Central and South America, as well as establishing settlements in Florida and the southwest of North America. This left the English and French in direct competition for dominance of North America. France had more money, more ships, more people and more coastline from which to launch–which they did. They sent fishermen to the cod banks of the North Atlantic and explorers like Jaques Cartier and later Samuel de Champlain. And since Spain and England had both commissioned Italian navigators to search for the Indies, France just had to have one as well. They found their man in Giovanni da Verrazano.

Verrazano was a gentleman explorer, coming from a noble family in Tuscany whose ancestral estate was an actual castle complete with stone defense towers. (Although the Verrazano family became extinct in 1819, the estate still survives as a winery, in the heart of the Chianti Classico region). Between 1524 and 1528, he made two voyages in search, like most preceding mariners, for the route to what he termed "the happy shore of Cathay." He explored a vast amount of coastline, from South Carolina to Newfoundland, including what would become New York and New Jersey, naming various islands, rivers and other geographic features after

his investors and their family members.

Landing for fresh water and food the Verrazano party would often encounter the native inhabitants. He generally described them in glowing terms as being "well featured in their limbs, sharp-witted and nimble." The biting irony should not be overlooked that he was killed and eaten by these same folks after rowing ashore for an innocent visit. Finding no route through the new land and meeting an untimely and gruesome death, Verrazano's name is nonetheless remembered with a body of water–and the longest suspension bridge in the country spanning it; more than other failed explorers can claim.

✦ ✦ ✦

ELIZABETH I, THE DAUGHTER of Henry VIII, took the throne in 1558. She was only slightly more receptive to improving England's overseas prospects than her father had been, but was concerned that too many English sea ventures might upset her delicate relationship with Phillip II of Spain. However, she didn't mind a bit of discrete privateering by seamen such as John Hawkins. The queen even provided him with a ship called *Jesus of Lûbeck* and a knightship. But possibly best known was Hawkins' cousin, Sir Francis Drake, another pirate-adventurer who led only the second circumnavigation of the globe in 1579 with his ship the *Golden Hind*. English sea power began to improve through increased weaponry and innovative design, allowing them to literally sail rings around the Spanish galleons. Queen Bess' coffers (and privateers' pockets) were becoming filled with gold and silver collected from treasure ships, as well as "black ivory"–profits resulting from the slave trade. Since Spain's hold on the New World was now becoming suspect, the Queen was gradually encouraged to pursue opportunities in North America.

Not everyone who sought expansion was a seafarer. Richard Hakluyt, a lawyer, heartily endorsed settlements through his chronicles of voyages and adventures such as "Divers voyages touching the discovery of America," and "The Principle Navigations Voyages Traffiques and Discoveries of the English Nation." These publications were a compilation of Hakluyt's and many other's scourings of log books and journals compiled by pre-seventeenth century explorers.

As the hunt for the Northwest Passage continued, privateer Martin Frobisher made three attempts, returning with rock samples from one expedition which were analyzed as containing a large percentage of gold. The Queen fronted him £1,350 for another expedition which consisted of a fleet of fifteen vessels. They returned with 200 tons of worthless rock. The earlier samples, upon further examination, were found to contain only mica and iron pyrite–fool's gold. Still no Northwest Passage, and no riches. Most reasonable peoples would have given up the quest by now, but the English were known for their tenacity, if lacking in common sense. It has been said that "an Englishman is both afraid and embarrassed by abstraction, but fears no visible obstacle." Despite his geologic failings, Frobisher did manage to discover a bay in Baffin Island which now bears his name, and Resolution Island.

Tracing Frobisher's route was explorer John Davis, who in 1585 searched for open water to the North West. Halted by melting ice, he mounted two more attempts during the next two years, and did in fact chart what is now known as the Davis Strait off the coast of Labrador. Each of these discoveries would add more and more accuracy to the ever expanding map of this unknown corner of the planet.

The next willing participant was Humfrey Gilbert, half-brother of the famous Walter Raleigh, of whom we'll hear more of shortly. Gilbert was granted a royal patent to explore North America, which was left intentionally vague as to any specific location. The only instructions were to discover, possess, and colonize "heathen lands, not in the actual possession of any Christian prince." This of course referred to Spanish claims. Using the motto *Quid non*–Why not? as his philosophical guide, Gilbert set out in 1578 with seven ships, one captained by Raleigh, but the expedition ultimately failed due to conflict of interests and uncooperative weather, costing him nearly his entire fortune. To recoup, he sold large tracts of unseen North American real estate to unwitting investors. Gradually replenishing his capital, he was able to outfit five ships for another attempt in 1583. This was composed of a complement of about 260 men that included masons and carpenters. He also brought musicians, Morris dancers, "Hobby horsse, and Manylike conceits to delight the Savage people, whom we intended to winne by all faire meanes possible." This time he was more successful, establishing the first English colony in North America at St. John's, Newfoundland. Upon landing, a formal ceremony was performed with Gilbert officially taking possession of Newfoundland for England. This was a repeat of Cabot's arrival in 1497, but since it had taken place so long ago, was all but forgotten. Gilbert then performed the ancient ritual livery of seisin, in which he was given a piece of turf with a twig placed on it. (William Penn would repeat the same rite one hundred years later upon taking possession of Pennsylvania). Tragically, Sir Humfrey was lost in the Azores on the return trip aboard the ship *Squirrel*. His final words were "We are as neere to heaven by sea as by land."

✦ III ✦

With Gilbert's passing, Walter Raleigh now took possession of his half-brother's royal charter. And this time, instead of becoming yet another glory seeker in the futile search for the nearly-mythical Northwest Passage, he concentrated efforts to "plant" a profitable colony in a more southerly clime. Also to establish a permanent base from which to stage attacks on Spanish shipping. He enlisted Arthur Barlowe and Phillip Amadas to search for a suitable location, which they found in the Outer Banks of the Carolinas, in particular an island called Roanoke. They returned to report of their venture with furs and plant samples. They also brought two native inhabitants named Wanchese and Manteo who were fussed over, dressed in English garb and placed in the care and tutelage of a young scholar, Thomas Harriot. He was to teach them English and in turn learn their native Algonquian. This early reconnaissance was a resounding success, the result being that Raleigh's English claim now extended north and south from the Carolinas to Maine and to infinity to the west. He called the territory "Virginia" in honor of Elizabeth I, the Virgin Queen who apparently was more than a bit smitten with Raleigh. It seems that like his half-brother, Gilbert, Walter Raleigh had chosen his own motto well: Amore et Virtue–By love and virtue. The queen knighted him for his compliment.

A much larger colonial expedition was now organized under the command of Sir Richard Grenville, naval commander, former sheriff of Cornwall, member of parliament, aristocratic relative of Raleigh's and all around badass. Sir Walter had wanted to command the voyage, but it was not to be as Queen Elizabeth forbade it. That and the fact that he was prone to seasickness. A little over one hundred men were recruited for the trip including the scholar Harriot, a highly skilled and well-traveled artist and cartographer named John White and Wanchese and Mateo, who were to be returned to their homeland. There was also a group of "gentlemen", who had no idea what they were in for and proved to be an unwelcome burden. The rest of the party was comprised of soldiers. After being deposited on the shores of Virginia by Grenville, who then sailed off eagerly in pursuit of Spanish treasure ships, the colonists built a fort, tried to grow a little corn, and in about a year, managed to wipe out much of the native population through the spread of disease. In 1586, the colony, facing starvation while they waited for Grenville to return, were suddenly and miraculously visited by none other than Sir Francis Drake, on his way back to

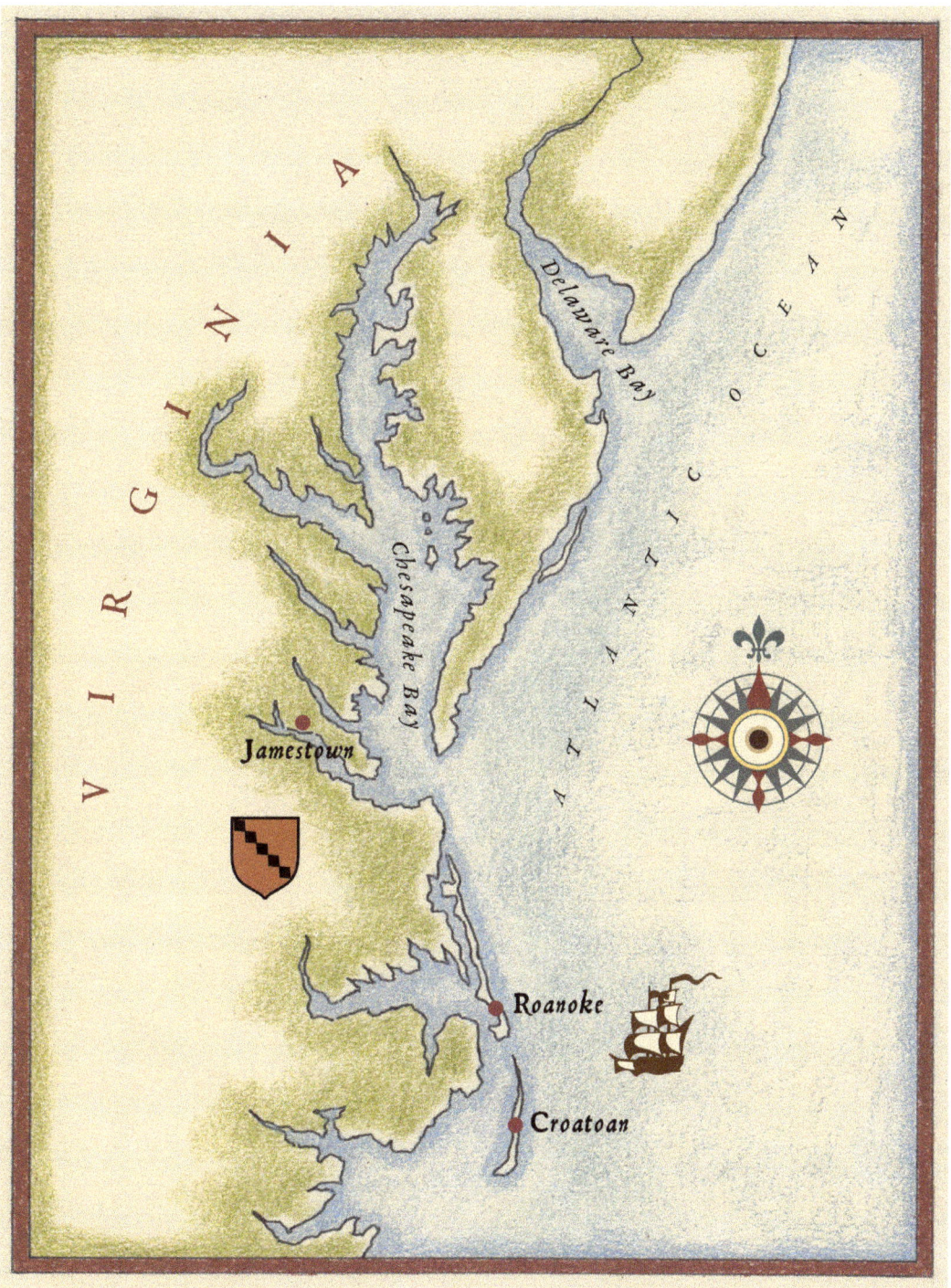

The 16th century manifestation of the Virginia Territory which Walter Raleigh named in honor of Queen Elizabeth I, referred to as the "Virgin Queen." It's boundaries were vague as it had yet to be explored, let alone surveyed.

England after raiding Spanish ships and colonies. Most of the recruits had had all of Virginia they cared for, and begged for a ride home. Grenville finally returned shortly after their departure. He left eighteen men to hold the fort and followed Drake back to Britain.

Despite its short existence, the Roanoke attempt did provide a few hopeful opportunities. Tobacco was introduced to Europe and immediately became immensely popular. Sir Walter himself developed quite a fondness for the stuff and the story is told that while smoking one of his first bowls, was doused with a bucket of water by a servant, who assumed his master was on fire.

The fur trade showed great promise, and perhaps not the least success was the discovery of the abundance of sassafras, the roots of which were believed to be a cure for syphilis, as well as just about any other human ailment. Now a small group of families, farmers and craftsmen were incorporated as the "Cittie of Raleigh in Virginia." John White, the artist from the previous voyage would be in charge as its governor. His daughter Eleanor and son-in-law Ananias Dare would be among the colonists, and would give birth to the first English child born in the New World, appropriately naming her Virginia.

And so begins one of the oldest mysteries in North America: The Lost Colony of Roanoake. I will not go into great detail as there have been volumes written about it. But basically, it goes like this: The original plan for the City of Raleigh was to establish it along the deeper waters of the Chesapeake Bay to accommodate large merchant and naval vessels. But when the colonists arrived in North America they first stopped at Roanoke to retrieve the soldiers left behind by Grenville. All they found were the soldiers' remains, and the fort which was now in ruin. Then the Portuguese pilot in charge of the expedition refused to take them to the Chesapeake location for reasons not exactly clear. He may have been impatient to return to privateering; it was too late in the season to travel farther to the north, etc. The settlers sensed trouble brewing and convinced Governor White to return to England for more support. Reluctantly, he agreed. It was the last time he ever saw them.

When White returned to England, all ships, military and otherwise, were commandeered by Her Majesty in anticipation of an attack by the Spanish Armada. He would be unable to return to the New World for another three years, and then only for a very brief visit to Roanoke. All 113 colonists had vanished leaving only the word "Croatoan" carved on a post of the old stockade.

Some speculation suggests that the colonists moved to Croatoan Island, south of Roanoke, while other sources maintain they crossed west over Croatoan Sound to the mainland. And still more think they traveled north to the Chesapeake after all. As so little evidence remains after more than 425 years, we will probably

PART I

never know with certainty. What does remain is branding: Virginia Dare this, Lost Colony that, even a play depicting a fanciful version of the story and so on.

Despite disastrous beginnings, Raleigh's intentions were not without some positive results. It has been said that the first white potato was brought from Virginia to Britain where Raleigh cultivated it on his Irish estate. This would lead to an entirely new food resource that would transform the economy of large portions of Europe. And since the decline of the Spanish empire following the defeat of its Armada, Britain was becoming overwhelmed with desire for more serious colonization in the New World–a land whose time had come.

Ambitious English merchants set about creating two business enterprises: the Virginia Company of London, and the Virginia Company of Plymouth, both incorporated in 1606. They were each to choose a region to exploit, from the Cape Fear River in North Carolina to the forty-fifth parallel in Maine. The Plymouth Company chose the northern part, and the London Company, the southern.

The London Company would have no problem recruiting enterprising young adventurers–there were tales in abundance touting the riches of the Americas: gold, silver, and other precious metals and gems practically laying in plain view waiting to be plucked like ripe melons, and plenty of elbow room, which was becoming a scarcity in London. Late in December of 1606, the *Susan Constant*, the *Godspeed*, and the *Discovery* under the command of Captain Christopher Newport set sail from London loaded to the gunwales with supplies and over 105 passengers, all men, to seek their fortunes in a virgin land named for a virgin

The Jamestown settlement

queen. They found a convenient spot on an island in a river some thirty miles inland from the ocean, and began to settle in, building fortifications against possible attacks by the Spanish or Indians, temporary shelters and tried planting crops. They called their settlement Jamestown, in honor of the current monarch. Likewise, the river was also christened the James.

But there seemed to be a pattern emerging: this latest endeavor at colonization by the English proved just as clumsy as the previous attempts. Crossing the often dark and moody Atlantic took them over five months, and in the process a mutiny took place, which resulted in its alleged leader, John Smith, being clapped in irons for the remainder of the voyage. This was hugely ironic as he would eventually emerge as the leader of the failing colony.

Captain John Smith; this is a man for whom the term swashbuckler was invented. At least, that is what he would have everyone believe. Fond of spinning hair-raising, ripping yarns of his exploits, he did not merely arrive in the New World, he pounced on it. His most famous tale was the legend of his rescue by Pocahontas, as he was about to have his head clubbed in by Powhatan, the most powerful native chief on the eastern seaboard. Earlier tales were told (by himself) of how he had de-

capitated three Turks in consecutive duels, been captured and sold into slavery in Transylvania, broke free after killing his master, escaped to Muscovy, traversed the whole of the Holy Roman Empire, and wound up on a pirate ship off the Barbary Coast. All before his twenty-fifth birthday.

He did, however, instill a modicum of discipline and kept the colony on an even keel during his command. He led expeditions along the rivers of Virginia and was the first to map the Chesapeake Bay. After a suspicious "accident", he returned to England to recover, but returned in 1614 to map the coastlines of Maine and Massachusetts Bay. He called it by a name that has been used ever since: New England.

After Smith's departure, the Jamestown Colony deteriorated. Lack of fresh water and food, an unfriendly climate, and hostile encounters with the native population greatly reduced the colonist's numbers. There were power struggles, starvation and apparent cannibalism. They did manage to hang on for three years, with occasional reinforcements, but 500 colonists had been reduced to just sixty. The survivors eventually decided to abandon their venture and sail for Newfoundland to find aid from the fishing fleets. Just as they were heading down the James with thirty days' worth of supplies, they were met with unexpected visitors coming upstream–an advance party from the supply fleet of Thomas West, Lord De La Warre. Their new governor had arrived, ordering them to immediately turn around and head back to Jamestown.

✦ IV ✦

In charge of one of the previous reinforcing missions was Samuel Argall. In 1609, he was assigned, under great secrecy, to find a new route to the Chesapeake, "by leaving the Canaries to the East, and from thence, to run in a straight western course." Basically following the thirtieth parallel, this was to avoid as much as possible the Spanish presence in the Caribbean. The Jamestown Colony was in a delicate state and the London Company wanted to protect their interests. Following Argall's path would be nine ships carrying, among others, Sir Thomas Gates, slated to become the temporary governor of the Jamestown Colony until Lord De La Warre arrived.

The last of eleven children, Argall was to the manor born in East Sutton, county of Kent. Experience in his younger years as a soldier, sailor and merchant prepared him for a career as an expert sea captain. His newly discovered northern

route across the Atlantic brought him to Jamestown in just a month, a far shorter voyage than had been previously imagined. Upon his arrival at Jamestown, Argall found the colony in an appalling condition populated by weak and hungry settlers, battered from a hardscrabble fight for survival. An unpleasant but apparently factual tale paints an entrepreneurial Argall selling his stores of food to the colonists, but generously supplying them with freshly caught sturgeon, free of cost. The caviar from the fish, however, he retained for private sale back in London. One can find this not so far-fetched as a result of a merchant's inherent nature, but more so from having to survive as the last of eleven children.

Despite the arrival of the rescue fleet carrying acting Governor Gates and supposedly enough supplies to sustain not only existing colonists, but the new arrivals as well, very little relief actually occurred. The nine ships had been reduced to only four, their supplies all but depleted. Their crossing had been a hellish affair, battling a particularly fierce Atlantic hurricane. The survivors escaped from the terrors of the sea only to face a different misery on land.

Captain Argall found himself back in the same situation less than a year later, leading yet another errand of mercy, this time with the official "Governor for Life of Virginia", Lord De La Warre. But more bad timing and planning ensued. De La Warre's party arrived on June 10, 1610, too late in the season to plant corn, nor did they bring any other seeds for planting the following spring. They had sufficient stores such as oatmeal, butter, and salt, but little to no meat. All previous livestock had been either consumed or stolen by the Indians. It was decided to send out two ships on a foraging expedition to Bermuda to fetch hogs and fish to nourish the colony. Argall would set out in the *Discovery*, while Commander Sir George Somers would take the *Patience*.

But the Atlantic weather refused to cooperate and they were unable to reach Bermuda. Forced to turn north, they sailed as far as the currently named Kennebec River catching "near one hundred Cods and a couple of Hollybuts." They also encountered a different type of weather that the seas off New England are famous for: pea soup fog. When it eventually lifted, the *Patience* was gone.

After searching in vain for Somers, Captain Argall sailed south again towards Jamestown, hugging the coast. On August 27, 1610, the *Discovery* dropped anchor "in a very great Bay." Argall had no way of knowing that one year previously, almost to the day, this same body of water had been entered by fellow countryman Henry Hudson. Hudson's visit was for an entirely different purpose, however, as we will find out shortly.

As the *Discovery* lay calmly at anchor, she was visited by Indians who paddled out in dugout canoes to see the "floating house with white wings." This was probably not their first encounter with European sailing vessels, or Europeans, but they

still displayed a great deal of curiosity. They were also quite hospitable, promising to bring corn in the morning. Argall was overjoyed at the prospect of returning to Jamestown with fish and a supply of corn, but that night the wind shifted from southwest to east-northeast, and like any good sailor, he was forced to take advantage of a fair wind.

We have no way of knowing what Samuel Argall was thinking, but since he had not encountered this large bay before, or was even aware of its existence, he gave to it the name of his governor. It may have been a gesture designed to divert attention from the fact that he would not be returning with pork, or it may have been a genuinely respectful tribute to His Lordship. He also referenced in his journal "a great many of shoals, about twelve leagues to the Southward of Cape La Warre." We're not sure if he was referring to what is now known as Cape Henlopen or Cape May. It is quite clear, however, that Thomas West, the 12th (or 3rd) Baron De La Warre never set eyes on the estuary that now bore his name. (The obfuscated title comes about due to the fact that the original barony, created in 1299 for Roger la Warr, was removed in a legal squabble in 1570 and was later reinstated. Therefore, loyalties are divided between the uninterrupted lineage or the newly restored version. In case you're interested, the title still exists).

In 1613, Argall wrote in a letter describing his exploits in Virginia of "the De la Warre Bay." This was the first recorded use of an English name for the bay. The bay and river attached to it, however, would not be recognized by its present name for some time to come. It would have many more visitors in the following years, and had unknown numbers previously—possibly as far back as Cabot and Verrazano, and most certainly Spanish and Portuguese explorers and fishermen as well. It was even given the name of St. Christopher's by Lucas Vasquez d'Ayllon in 1525. And there was a rumor that circulated of a number of Dutch sailors wintering there in 1598. Early maps crudely define the coastlines of the Carolinas, Virginia, the Chesapeake; but where the Delaware Bay (and other waterways) ought to be is simply an interruption of the inked line. The map makers knew something was there, but did not have enough cartographic evidence from mariners to commit to its depiction.

A prime example is the controversial "Velasco Map", which is a chart allegedly drawn in 1610 by an anonymous English cartographer depicting much of the coastline of the northeastern seaboard of America. It was pilfered by Spanish ambassador to England, Don Alonso de Velasco in 1611 and sent to King Phillip III of Spain. Along with the map, he sent encoded information clandestinely gathered, regarding activities of the English in the Virginia territory. And there the map resided until it was discovered by historian Alexander Brown in 1887, who published it along with a commentary in The Genesis of the United States in 1890.

The immediate reaction to the publication was that it was too accurate to be authentic, especially when compared to other maps of the era. It seems to correspond to Henry Hudson's navigational descriptions, especially the Hudson River and Chesapeake Bay. But as you can see, what is probably the Delaware Bay gets no respect—it is simply a void.

Eventually, the Jamestown Colony would right itself, the English would expand into Maryland and begin new settlements in Massachusetts and then Connecticut, leaving a vast area in between. The Delaware River Valley, one of the richest areas in resources on the Atlantic seaboard was left as a sort of buffer zone, its geography unknown even to the London Company or the Plymouth Company. But they had already laid claim to it, anyway.

The empty void on the map was examined further in small expeditions by navigators such as Thomas Dermer, who twenty years after Argall's visit, seems to have been the first Englishman to realize the existence of the river that emptied into the bay. But the details of his expedition were sketchy…not even much was known about Dermer himself. In 1632, Sir John Harvey, the governor of Virginia, sent a sloop with approximately eight men to prove the existence of said river. Also

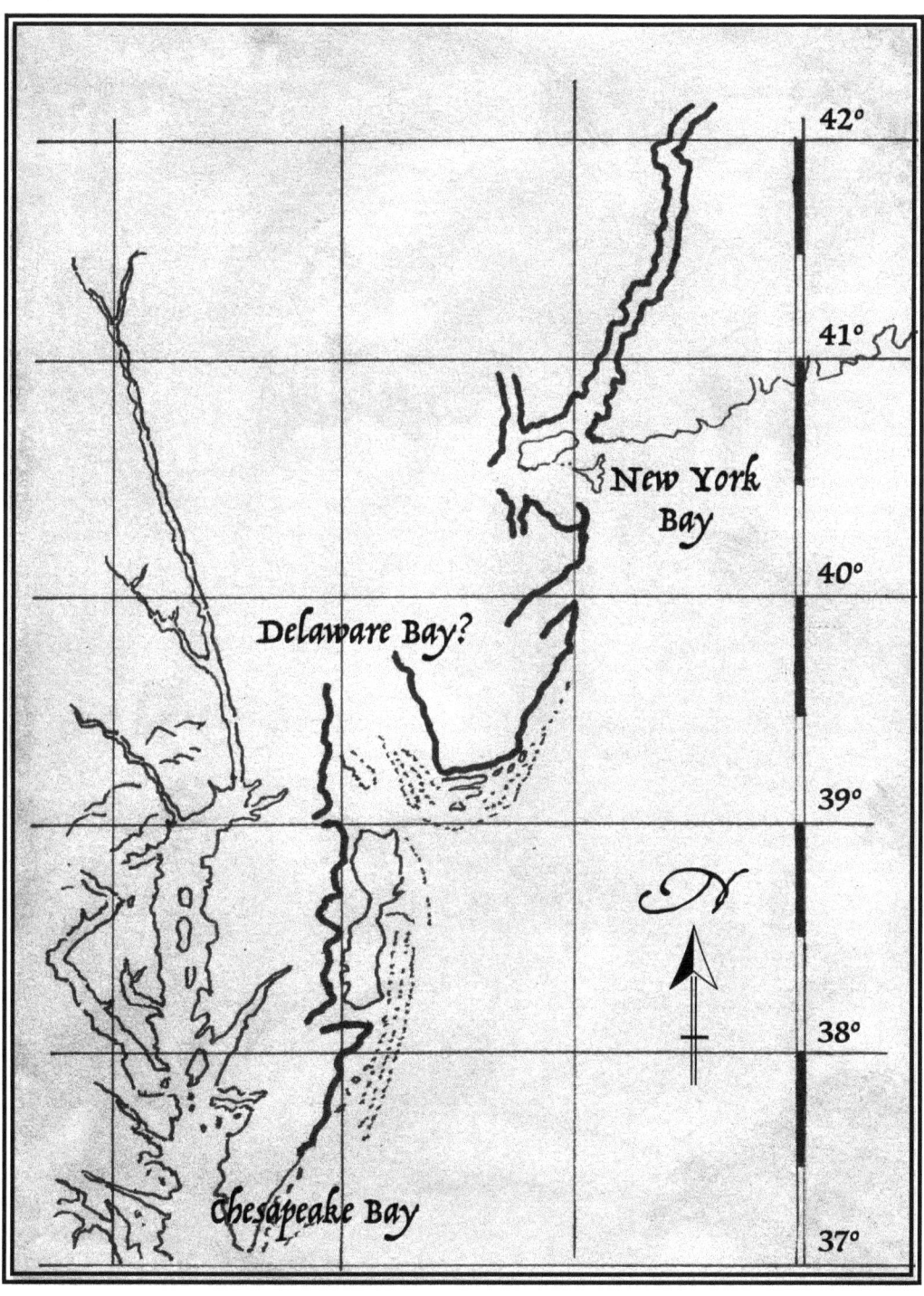

A portion of one of the earliest depictions of the Atlantic coastline from the controversial Velasco Map, circa. 1610-1611. The Delaware River is completely unknown in this time frame.

to see if it might prove a passage through the continent and into the Pacific. The party never returned.

The following year an independently wealthy Londoner named Thomas Yong convinced his monarch Charles I to allow him to lead an expedition to America to discover, occupy and exploit uninhabited lands. Yong would foot the bill himself. Stories and tales abounded about passages and lakes in the interior of America, which would lead to the Orient, and Yong fell prey to one such fable. It concerned the existence of a Lake Laconia, said to be far inland that could possibly be accessed from the Delaware. This bit of speculation may have been based on old Algonquian legends of the far distant Great Lakes which the Europeans adapted to suit their own purposes. The name "Laconia" resulted from the European love of classical civilizations, referring to a region of ancient Greece. Another river exited the lake from the western end, leading to the treasures of the East. This ambitious undertaking proved yet another dud. Yong could navigate the river no farther north than "the falles", at the present site of Trenton. He then decided to call it a day, blissfully ignorant of Dutch navigators and traders who were already exploring, mapping, and doing business right under the very nose and the bejeweled crown of Charles I.

The English would leave the Delaware for a while, to return some years later with more serious intentions. But it was already inhabited by people whose grandfather's grandfather's and grandmother's grandmother's had lived for eons.

• PART II •

The Dutch

✦ V ✦

When Europeans first set eyes on the Delaware River Valley, it was as if they were encountering a virtual Garden of Eden, covered with pristine, virgin forest–enormous oaks, tulip trees, beeches, sycamores, chestnuts, walnuts, hickories, maples; all elbowing each other for open sky. Tall, straight pines and craggy cedars perfumed the air. It has been said that a squirrel could travel from the East coast to the Mississippi River and never need to touch the ground.

Below the forested canopy was a lush, nearly impenetrable thicket of an unimaginable variety of smaller trees, low-lying shrubs, bushes, and ground cover–everywhere festooned with vines, many of them loaded with red, white, muscadel, and fox grapes. And beneath it all in many places were swamps and bogs, filled with dark umber water sprouting grasses and marsh plants. This all emptied into the Delaware River, which in turn flowed seamlessly into the Delaware Bay.

The bay abounded with vast colonies of oysters–one could literally scoop them up with a shovel–eight foot sturgeons scoured the bottom along with flounder and blue crabs. Dolphins and whales vied with each other for krill, shrimp, and massive schools of shad and sea trout. Along much of the shoreline were marshes–essential nurseries for hatchling fish and crabs, and muskrats that made mound-like homes among the cattails and salt hay.

The land was also filled with abundant wildlife of every species; from amphibians to water fowl, birds of prey, fifty-pound turkeys, elk, deer, and the wildcats

and wolves that hunted them. Flocks of pigeons darkened the sky for hours on end.

And in the streams and creeks that fed the Delaware were beaver and otter, whose pelts would play a crucial role in the upcoming clash of cultures. Side by side with all these wild things lived a people whose lifestyle varied so dramatically from the Europeans that the two might as well have come from different planets.

The original inhabitants of this land migrated from the west and spread out along the Delaware which they called 'Lenapewihittuck'. Some of the land they called 'Scheyechbi', which William Paterson, one-time secretary of the New Jersey Historical Society says was pronounced Shay-ak-bee, and that it means "long land water," referring to the Cape May peninsula. Most of the rest of their territory, however, was named 'Lenapehoking.'

They called themselves Lenni-Lenâpé (Lenny-LenApAy) which translates as Men of Men, Manly Men, or translated further, Original People, or in yet another translation–Common People. Part of the Algonquin Nation, they were composed of three main regional groups that straddled nearly the entire length of the Delaware and part of the Hudson: the Minsi or Munsi, who lived along the Upper Delaware, whose ancestors were the Shawnee-Minisink, the first human inhabitants in the north-eastern U.S.–down to the confluence of the Lehigh River (which they called "place where there are forks in the stream"); the Unami who dwelt along the mid-river area, and the Unilachtigo, who lived along the lower portions of the river, bay, and the ocean. As far as is known to this point, the Shawnee-Minisink seem to have arrived with the passing of the last Ice Age. According to evidence collected by one of the country's earliest students of Paleo-Indian civilization, former Civil War Army surgeon Charles Conrad Abbott, they probably arrived between 10,000 and 12,000 years ago.

Divided and subdivided into many tribes and communities, they lived in groups as large as two to three hundred people, but most existed in more clannish arrangements that contained no more members than a large family. Of these were the Andastakas, Assunpinks, Naraticons, Kechemeche, Nanticoke, Mantes, Rancocas, Siconese, Sankikans, and countless others. It must be noted that these names may vary greatly in spelling and pronunciation since the ears of translators and scribes were not always attuned to the same interpretation. And each band, although sharing the same base language, had their own dialects. The farther they traveled from their own tribes, the less they could understand the speech of others. In Lenape land, there was a river known as Susquehanna, but to a more distant tribe–the same river was Kanastoge. (Later on, Kanastoge became Conestoga, which had a freight wagon and a type of cigar named after it). It's fairly simple to see the evolution of some words; seganku became skunk, wampumpeag was condensed to wampum. But some have taken a far more circuitous route. An Algonquian word for tribal leader went from the nearly unpronounceable cawcawwassoughes, to the slightly easier coucorouse, to one that still refers to its original intent, as well as being kinder to the tongue–caucus. And of course, more words that needed no refinement: tomahawk, raccoon, opossum, moccasin, powwow, wigwam, etc.

Perhaps because of these many variants of speech, Indians thought carefully before speaking, and were known to be frugal with their language–one word could take the place of three. When Penn finally met with these people, he glowingly praised their speech: "I know not a language spoken in Europe that hath words of more sweetness or greatness in accent and emphasis than theirs." Physical descriptions from as far back as Verrazano's documentation describe them as particularly handsome folks: "well-fashioned; comely; slender and straight as a candle; without blemish."

The Lenape's long lineage afforded them great respect from their peers, who referred to them as the "grandfathers" or "ancient ones." Because of their provenance and generally amicable nature, they often assumed the role of diplomats in negotiating disputes among other tribes. Quite often, the women performed the delicate duty of mediation, so the men would not appear weak and lose face. Occasionally though, their peaceful attitude could work against them as more aggressive tribes would taunt them as "grandmothers." But they were by no means pansies. If wronged in any way, they were quite skilled in exacting revenge rigorously—usually served cold as the old saying goes.

The Lenape lived not so much right on the banks of the Delaware, but in carefully placed villages along the fresh water streams and creeks that flowed into it, where they found better protection from the winds that blew across the river. Some of the encampments were described by Europeans at Wickquakinick (later shortened to Wicaco, the future site of Philadelphia), along the Schuykill, Neshaminy and Ridley creeks in Pennsylvania, Brandywine and White Clay creeks in Delaware and Big Timber Creek and the Salem and Maurice Rivers in New Jersey. The populations were described in some accounts as having 100 or fifty or forty souls, but it's not as if these figures were compiled by professional census takers, traipsing around the countryside, poking their heads in wigwams and asking for the number of residents. Estimates of the total Lenape population in the Delaware Valley in 1600 seem to agree on about 20,000 people. A more accurate approach is to say that there were approximately 45 inhabitants per one hundred square miles for agricultural communities. In regions that were populated more by hunter-gatherers in the mountainous areas, it was probably far less. Incredibly, we find that by the time this book reaches its conclusion in 1682, the number of Lenape had been reduced to around 4,000.

✦ ✦ ✦

THEY SLEPT UNDER the sky when the weather was good, and constructed wigwams covered with bark, skins, or rushes for the cold months. They also made use of their ever-present dog population when winter set in. Botanist Peter Kalm warned that "visitors who slept with the Indians were in danger of being squeezed to death by a dozen or more dogs which lie round and upon him." Small, windowless one-room structures, the wigwams were generally large enough only for one family, arranged wherever they happened to be built. There was no grid or layout to a Lenape village.

The men provided the bulk of the natural diet by hunting whatever game was available, usually deer, elk, rabbit, bear, turkey, pheasant, and squirrels. And living by the water naturally, fish and other types of seafood were to be had in abundance. The Unilatchtigo especially had a fondness for oysters. Large piles, or middens, of ancient shells have been found all along the bay-shore area.

Whenever available, they picked wild huckleberries, blackberries, cranberries, and strawberries, and fruit from trees laden with cherries, plums, crab apples, and from nut trees as well. In fields close by their homes, the woman cultivated maize, beans, and squash, which they called the "three sisters." The rigid corn stalks acted as natural trellises for the beans, and the oversized squash leaves provided shade and kept the weeds at bay. A popular dish making use of the vegetables was called by a name we still use today: succotash. Cooking was done in clay pots on open fires which could create problems when the vessels became brittle and started to crack. Iron pots would have solved the problem of course, but despite the abundance of bog ore which was found throughout much of the swamps of the pine forests, the Indians never discovered the art of smelting, leaving them perpetually in the stone age. They were able to work small amounts of copper, mostly from ore that was found in surface deposits, but this was used mostly for ornamentation or currency–alloys were beyond them. Most of their tools and weapons came from existing natural materials such as deer or elk antlers, bones, wood, and from stones and rocks. (To this day, arrowheads are still to be found almost anywhere along the river, and far inland as well). Their clothing was fashioned from animal hides, furs, and feathers, yielding mostly functional, yet often exquisitely crafted apparel. And though they were able to weave baskets and containers from reeds and straw, they had no flax, wool or cotton from which to create any type of cloth.

The Lenape, as well as many of the native people, possessed a vast knowledge of herbs which was interwoven between medicinal and health applications and spiritual uses. Bark from the tulip tree was said to relieve stomach distress, while willow bark was known for its anti-inflammatory quality, which would one day be discovered as the pain killing ingredient in aspirin.

Tobacco, an entity unto itself, was regarded with reverence by just about all native people. A Huron Indian legend goes like this: In ancient times when the land was barren and the people were starving, the Great Spirit sent forth a woman to save humanity. As she traveled over the world, everywhere her right hand touched the soil, there grew potatoes. And everywhere her left hand touched the soil, there grew corn. And when the world was rich and fertile, she sat down and rested. When she arose, there grew tobacco.

An all-purpose plant, it was dried and cured, then ground and smoked in clay or stone pipes. Occasionally mixed with other ingredients such as sumac, it could be used as a curative like an herb, shared socially during a casual get-together, or become the focal point in a more formal ceremony. Recreational smoking was enjoyed in silence, the imbiber contemplating the swirling smoke, thinking deep thoughts, and bonding with the spirits.

Even though their agricultural methods were adequate, the Lenape did not have large farm animals to produce fertilizer, and were consequently unable to replenish the soil. When it was spent, they simply moved on to another location, usually about every ten years. The same applied when the game became scarce. Rarely did they live their entire lives in one place.

Balanced as they were within the natural world, close association with the spirits explained the workings of it, much like belief in the ancient Greek gods.

PART II

Those beings responsible for the changing of the seasons and the weather were "Our Grandfather where the daylight begins", or "Our Grandfather where it is winter." The nourishment of people and animals was taken care of by "Our Mother the Earth"; and one who presides over all vegetation: "Mother Corn." There were spirits attached to just about every aspect of their lives.

The deep forest was a particularly ethereal place for spirits–a place for visions. It was there that many a Lenape boy entering puberty would hope to acquire a spirit guide or internal presence that would help him over the rough spots through his life. He would venture out into the primeval alone in hopes of communicating with a supernatural being who could appear in the form of a bird, wolf, or even an inanimate object such as a rock or tree. Girls could have spiritual experiences as well, but since they did not hunt or engage in warfare, it was thought they didn't really need one. Having his own personal protector would give the young man a tremendous sense of security; (As if teenagers didn't already feel immortal). In this way, any Indian imbued with this magical internal force would have no fear of death itself, only the fear of a shameful death.

Not every Indian male was enthusiastic about gaining a spiritual advisor; some had to be encouraged rather forcefully into the wilderness to find his special guiding force. And still others might not have a spirit vision until late in life or if some personal tragedy finally brought about one. And some might have none at all, in which case they would feel rather rejected. But those who were successful would often create an amulet or totem, worn on their person, which was so sacred to the individual that no one else would be allowed to touch it–one of the only things an Indian would not share.

Life could be harsh–the general life expectancy was only about thirty-five–but the Lenape took it in stride. None took more than they needed, and none went needy. All they owned was freely given; food, the comfort of their dwelling–even their women. The concept of individual ownership, particularly land ownership, simply did not exist for them, it was shared by all. The only notion remotely resembling a claim was the right to hunt, fish, and trap in a particular area, handed down through generations, and was usually upheld by only loosely enforced rules. If someone was caught accidentally hunting in another's territory, it was not a big deal.

Each group, or tribe, or community was a democracy, guided by a Sachem, chosen by election. Generally, he was the person with the most sewan, or money, not unlike the white man's politicians. It was his duty to affix fines for criminal or anti-social behavior, and to decide if a stranger should be welcome into their midst.

The Lenni Lenape lived in this manner for millennia, virtually undisturbed except by each other. But their world was about to change…drastically.

◆ VI ◆

The twenty-eighth day of August, 1609 found an eighty-five foot sailing ship, the *Halve Maen* (Half Moon), slipping gingerly into the Delaware Bay. On the poop deck stood its captain, Henry Hudson, intently observing the proceedings. The ship's mate, Robert Juet shouted out orders and carefully took note of the location and soundings: "wee found the Land to trend away North-west, with a great Bay and Rivers. But the Bay wee found shoaled; and in the offing wee had ten fathoms, and had sight of Breaches and dried Sand." Juet later recorded the episode in great detail, describing how long they had stayed in the bay and when they left. Hudson was the latest in a long line of English explorer-navigators whom we've met previously, like Frobisher, Davis, Gilbert, Drake and others, but his situation was different—Hudson was working for the Dutch.

How that came to be goes something like this: Hudson worked previously for the Muscovy Company, an English concern that was established when yet another explorer, Richard Chancellor, also looking for the elusive passage to the Orient, found his way to Russia. The exploration was abandoned, and in its place, a lucrative agreement was established in which the English would trade their wool for hemp, whale oil, and most importantly, furs from Russia. But as time passed and business began to fade, the resumption of a search for a new trade route to Cathay came back to the forefront.

Henry Hudson seemed a reasonable candidate to take on the challenge. He was a well-seasoned and experienced seaman armed with extensive charts, maps and plenty of navigational savvy. He already had ties to the company as his grand-

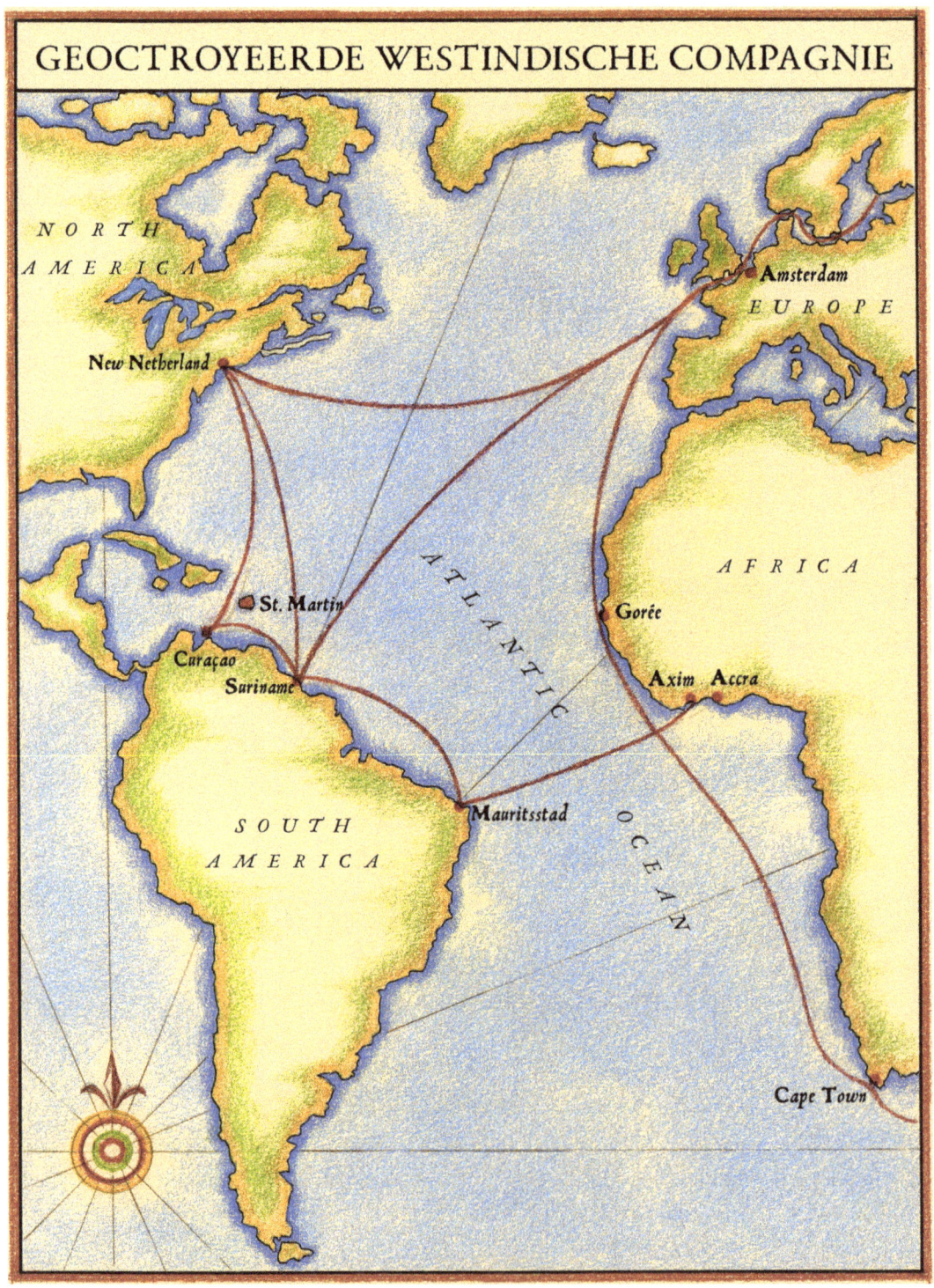

Trade routes of the Dutch West India Company, Est. 1621

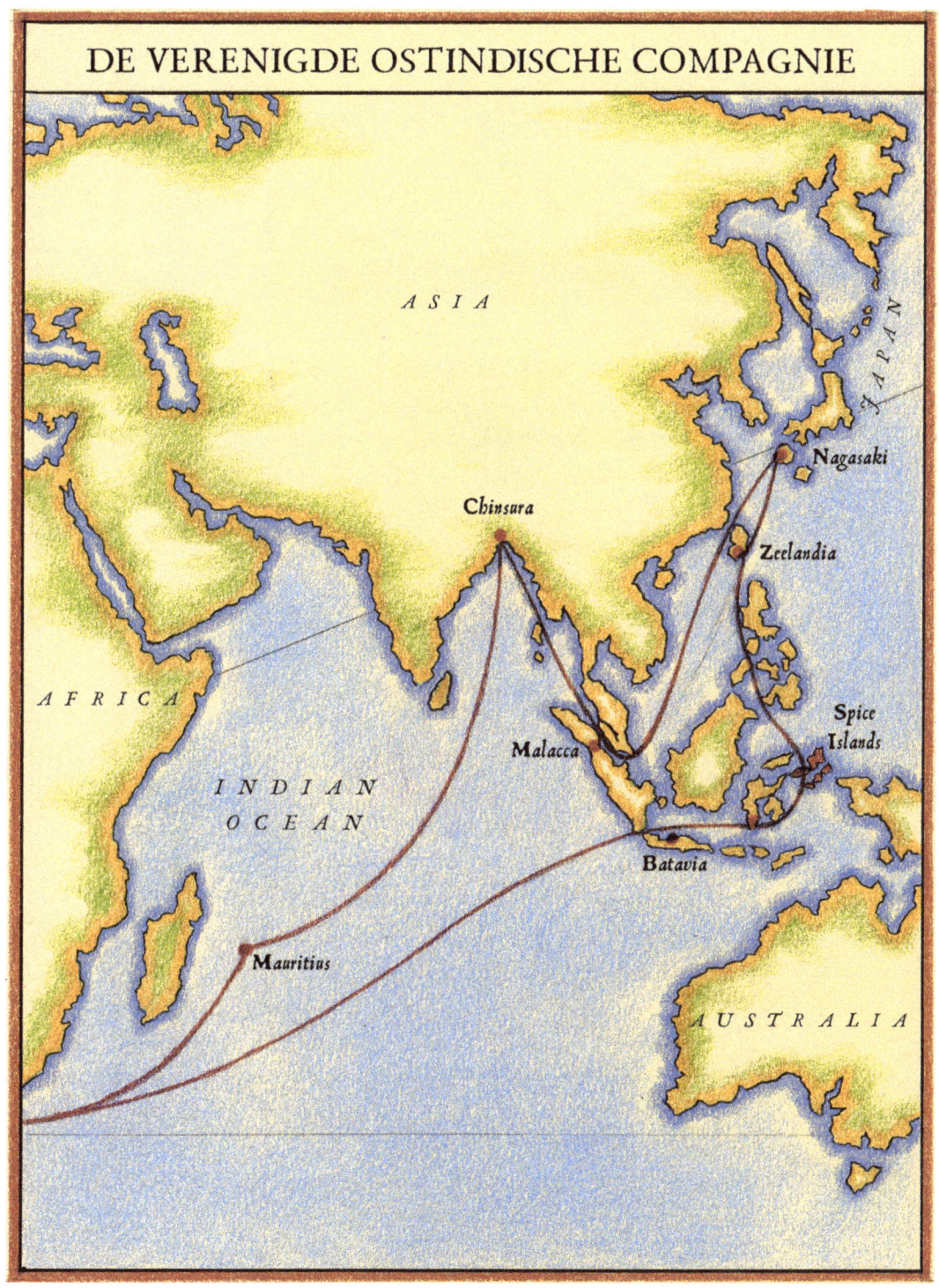

Trade routes of the Dutch East India Company, Est. 1601

father (also named Henry) and an uncle were previous employees, so it did not take much to persuade the Muscovy Company to outfit him for a crack at the passage that everyone was so desperate for.

The first voyage proved just short of a complete failure. He attempted to sail over the top of the world, crossing the North Pole, and down again to the Orient. There was a wildly mistaken notion at the time that the closer one sailed to the North Pole the less ice one would encounter–the pole itself being totally clear. (Mapmakers and topographers were notorious for vivid imaginations, and not adverse to doling out erroneous information, not with malicious intent, but more to glorify their products). He found out before long that this theory was far from correct. Barely surviving, living on bear and seal meat and battling horrendous weather, he returned to his backers telling them there was just too much ice. There was an upside to this disappointment, however—by process of elimination, he had discovered another route that was impassible and could be dismissed. He had also discovered an abundance of whales near Spitzbergen Island that spawned a temporary industry until the whale population was depleted.

Slightly encouraged, the company set him up for another voyage. This time Hudson, who seemed to have a high tolerance for cold, would try a northeast passage, around the islands of Nova Zembla in the Russian Arctic. Once again–ice. He wrote, "it is so full of ice that you will hardly thinke it." Still not quite defeated, he backed up and set a course for the northwest. But after ten weeks in the bitter arctic with a mutinous crew, Hudson was forced to return to London, admitting to another expedition that came to naught.

A dark and brooding man, Hudson often retreated within himself but refused to accept failure. After recovering his confidence, he began to prepare for another assault. On this expedition he would attempt to find a route through North America. Reinforced by encouragement from Richard Hakluyt, and more maps and charts supplied by Captain John Smith, he again approached his directors for another try. But they flatly refused this time. They had lost faith in Hudson, not to mention money. But he had barely time to let the shock of this denial sink in, when he was approached by Emanuel van Meteren, the Dutch consul in London. If his abilities and experience were lost on his former employers, there were certain Dutch merchants who appreciated them. Hudson's reputation remained sound as a navigator who was a well-informed risk taker and could lead an expensive expedition without undo loss of life…or his investors' money.

He arrived in Amsterdam in the fall of 1608 in the midst of a changing climate. The firm grip that Spain and Portugal had on the world and its resources for the past one hundred years was loosening. The Lowlands of Europe in particular had been under the thumb of the Spanish Catholics for far too long. Now the Dutch Protestant movement gained enough momentum to unite the Northern provinces and issue a declaration of independence. Known as the Dutch Revolt, it resulted in the Eighty Years War; eight decades of occasional warfare with Spain. But in the midst of such turmoil, the rest of Europe began clamoring for Dutch products: furniture, utensils, woolen goods, and fish from Dutch waters. And so began the dawn of Europe's Golden Age.

It was also about this time that Dutch ship builders began to establish a substantial edge in technology by coming up with the fluyt, a merchant ship that was better designed, cheaper to construct, and needed a much smaller crew than their competitors–namely the English. Other northern European neighbors actually found it cheaper to buy Dutch ships than build their own. The Dutch began expanding their horizons, trading in the Mediterranean and more ambitiously, sending ships across the Atlantic to the Caribbean, and Brazil and Venezuela in South America. They brought in cargoes of slaves to work the plantations, and returned with sugar and salt. They established outposts in Guiana, and Curaçao and other islands on the Spanish Main. Then in 1588 the Spanish Armada was destroyed, resulting in an unexpected and remarkable victory for England. But it was the Dutch who benefitted nearly as much as the English, eliminating much of their Spanish opposition on the seas.

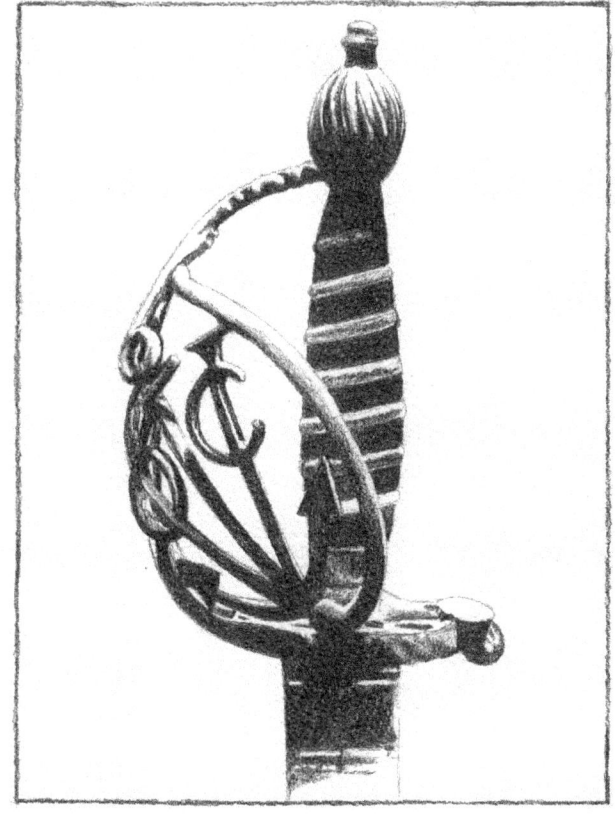

The treasures and spices of the East Indies began beckoning even more than the West. Finding a northeast passage had proved futile, as Hudson had shown, and the route pioneered by Magellan was far too dangerous. Rounding the Cape of Good Hope proved long but functional as exhibited by a voyage completed in 1599. Dutch ships returned after a fourteen and a half month absence with 600,000 pounds of pepper and 250,000 pounds of cloves as well as smaller amounts of nutmeg and mace. Church bells sounded in Amsterdam expressing the joy of the investors whose profits exceeded 400 percent.

Two years later, the Dutch East India Company was founded; a monopoly created by consolidating import-export concerns sanctioned by the States-General. Before anyone had invested a penny, shares were selling on the Amsterdam Exchange for 15 percent. The company, known in Dutch as de Verenigde Ostindische Compagnie (hereafter referred to as the VOC, one of the world's earliest acronyms) was an immediate success. During its first seven years of operation, the VOC sent fifty-five ships to the Far East, compared to England's twelve. Even by today's standards, it was embarrassingly lucrative. At its zenith, the VOC was worth more than any private company ever, with assets totaling approximately 7 trillion dollars in today's market. It employed upwards of 50,000 workers and sailors, 10,000 soldiers and owned 150 merchant ships and forty warships. It was very nearly a state unto itself.

By 1610, the VOC had taken over Batavia in today's Indonesia, and established their headquarters on the island of Java. By 1641, Malacca had been wrested from the Portuguese, giving the VOC complete control of the spice trade. The company eventually branched out from dealing primarily in spices to include coffee, textiles, porcelain and other luxury goods, continuing to make whopping profits for nearly 200 years.

Both England and the Netherlands become powerhouses of commerce and military might. But the Netherlands were vastly different from Britain and the other monarchies of Europe: they were a republic ruled by a board of directors. Their High Mightinesses (as they were addressed) represented the seven provinces: Holland (the most prosperous and influential), Zeeland, Guelderland, Utrecht, Overyssel, Friesland, and Groningen, known collectively as the United Netherlands. Boldly, the Dutch took advantage of the declining Spanish sea forces and started to arm their merchant ships with the latest in naval weaponry.

Which brings us back to Mr. Henry Hudson. Although the Dutch now had an established route to the East Indies, they were still desirous of a short cut. The Dutch explorer Willem Barentsz (for whom the Barentsz Sea is named) had tried fifteen years earlier on three separate occasions to find a north-eastern passage, and frozen to death on the last. But enthusiasm was still high. They believed that this time, Hudson was the man to find that ever-elusive course to Southeast Asia. They quickly signed an agreement, lest some other nation should steal him away.

Manned with a crew of sixteen, half Dutch and half English, Hudson set off from Amsterdam in the *Halve Maen* on his newest quest on April 6, 1609. A number of crewmen from previous voyages signed on again, including first mate Robert Juet. Rather than Hudson, it is from Juet's journal that we learn the details of the 1609 expedition.

Hudson's new employers, like those previously, ordered him to find a northeastern route. And once again, he totally ignored his orders. He began well enough

sailing along the coast of Norway towards Russia, but was soon facing a fierce gale. Rather than battle against the winds, he turned the *Halve Maen* 180 degrees to carry the ship far to the west.

Eventually sailing past the southern coast of Newfoundland, he continued a westerly course, bouncing along the coast of Nova Scotia, and on to what is now Maine, where he turned south, following the lead suggested by John Smith's data. This was what Hudson had wanted to do all along. Smith implied that he would find a route not in the northwest, but a southwest course that would plunge through the middle of the continent somewhere around the fortieth parallel, and out to its west coast. After six weeks of hugging the North American coastline, he came to within ten miles of the Jamestown settlement. Believing he would not be welcome in the fledgling English community, he gave the Virginia waters a wide berth, continuing south to Cape Hatteras Island where he reversed his settings for the north. It was not long before we find him entering the Delaware Bay.

By the amount of shoals encountered, and other indications which a well-traveled navigator would recognize, Hudson determined that this great bay would not lead to an inland waterway, but that it was more than likely an estuary. Spending only one night, he left the bay next morning, brought the *Half Moon* to starboard, and continued his northerly course.

Hudson continued to hug the coastline of the future Jersey Shore until, on September 3, with high hills on his left, he followed the length of a narrow spit of sand that seemed to beckon like a long bony finger. It led the *Half Moon* into another very large bay with more tributaries leading into it. This was not shoaled as the Delaware had been, and Hudson chose to maneuver into the broadest of them. The shoreline was studded with massive oaks, from whose shadows emerged a group of local inhabitants; the Munsees of the northern branch of the Lenape. The *Half Moon* anchored and a party was cautiously sent ashore to make contact. This first of many encounters was civil and without incident. Goods were exchanged on both sides: green tobacco from the Indians and beads and knives from the Europeans. But further meetings often turned sour, including one in which English crewman John Colman was killed by an arrow through his neck.

The explorers sailed further upriver, stopping occasionally for more trading sessions which became increasingly tense, the crew not knowing if they were going to be treated cordially or with hostility, as word spread up-stream of the strange intruders. But each encounter yielded more and more information about the local natural resources, including the abundance of fish, and especially of beaver and otter pelts. Oysters, beans, pumpkins, maize, and tobacco were also offered by members of who were probably Mahican and Catskill tribes in exchange for what Juet termed "trifles." They were impressed with the apparent fertility of the land,

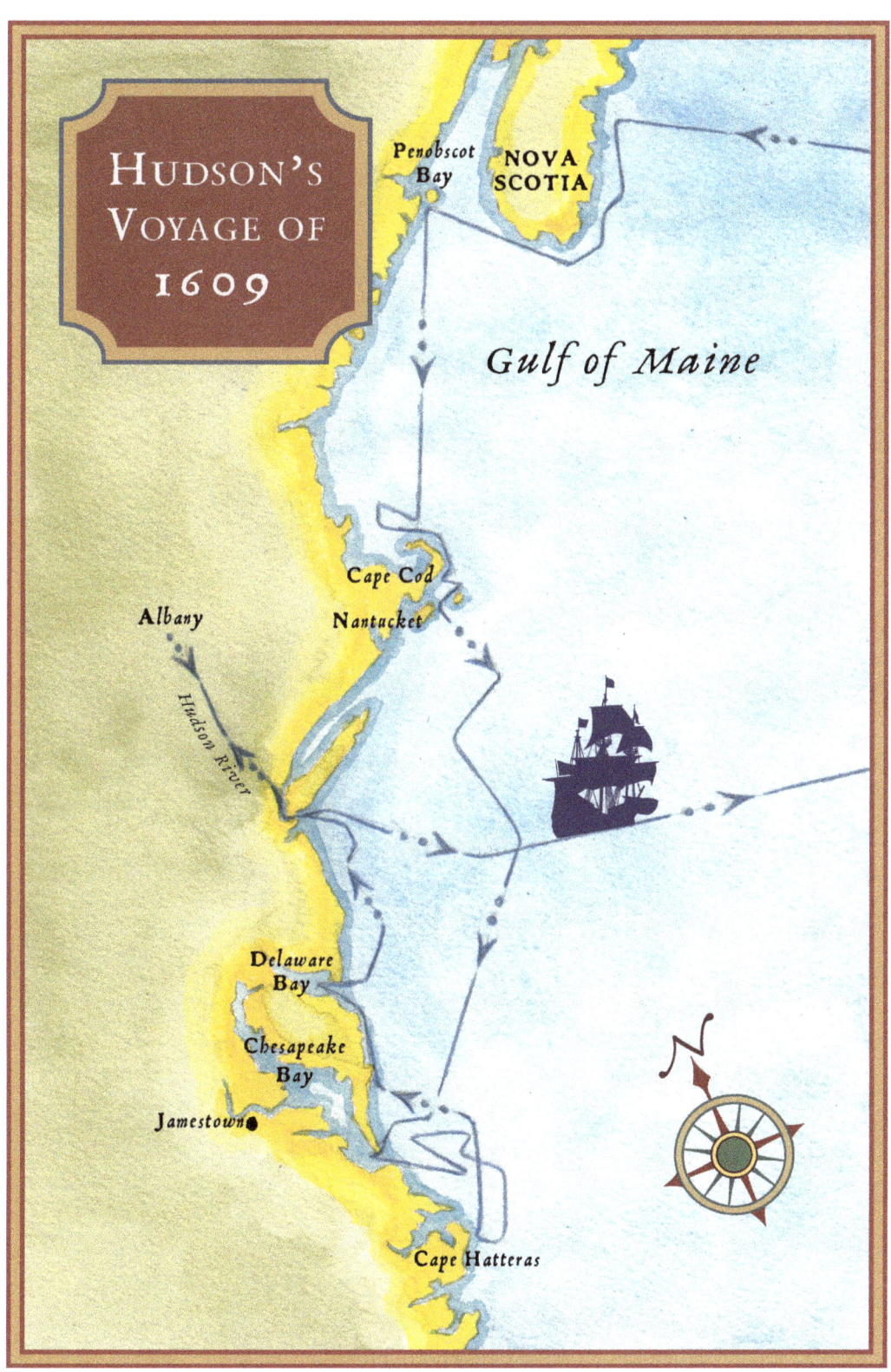

the first mate noting of one spot, "This is a very pleasant place to build a town on." Speculation led them to believe that there could be an assortment of minerals in the surrounding mountains.

Nearing the end of September, Hudson began to suspect that the river they were following might be one more extensive dead end. He sent a small crew further upstream to investigate, and upon their return learned that indeed, the waterway became more narrow and shallow to the north. They were now near present-day Albany when the decision was made to reverse course. The downstream voyage became more hazardous as many of the inhabitants seemed to be waiting for them. One incident involved a man who paddled up to the *Half Moon* in a canoe, jumped onto the ship's rudder, and then climbed into a window and attempted to escape with a prize of some of Juet's belongings. He was shot and killed for his efforts. The ship ran a gauntlet of skirmishes during the rest of the return voyage until they reached a place the locals called Manna-hata. On October 4, they again entered the Atlantic Ocean, whose mood seemed to match that of Hudson's.

With nothing but speculation about the new lands he had explored, he made the trek back to Europe, once again unable to declare the fabled passage. For all his effort, Hudson would be paid the tidy sum of eight hundred guilders, about $320 in today's money–his wife to receive $80 if he did not return. But for reasons not entirely clear, he did not sail to Amsterdam, but to Dartmouth in England. He may have been convinced by his English crewmen to let them off on their homeland. Whatever the reason, he immediately found himself in waters almost as deep as those he had just left. He was contracted to release all his logbooks, charts, and related information to his Dutch employers, but English authorities thought otherwise. Hudson was detained while his findings were reviewed. Fortunately, for the East India Company, he was able to smuggle his logbook to the Dutch consul Van Meteran who helped it find its way to Amsterdam.

In his records, Hudson did have high praise for the deep water harbor and the lands surrounding the waterways, the people that inhabited them, and information detailing the possibilities of new trade partners. He described them as offering "many skins and peltries, martins, foxes, and many other commodities." This caused a flutter within the hearts of the Dutch merchants. Not only was praise heaped upon the river that would take on the name of its discoverer, but there were also two other rivers that would become highways leading into virgin territory: the Connecticut, and the Delaware.

But Hudson cared more about what he didn't find; to him it was another failed venture. In the next year, after procuring private funding, he continued to search, going ever further north until, in yet another very large bay, Hudson met a frozen and bitter end, set adrift by a crew who had finally been pushed past their limits.

✦ VII ✦

The Nonesuch House, one of the world's first pre-fabricated structures c.1579

The Netherlands blossomed in this Golden Age. They introduced the microscope, tulips, the stock exchange, and Rembrandt. Dutch-built ships were the most advanced vessels of their time, used throughout the world for both merchant and military purposes. Their architectural and building innovations led to other projects as well. The Nonesuch House was fastidiously designed and built in the Netherlands—then taken apart and reassembled on London Bridge in 1579. It was the first prefabricated building ever recorded. Each timber of the structure was marked for later joining–using only wooden pegs–no nails, mortar, or iron fasteners. When assembled, it graced the principal approach to London in the center of the bridge. The house had two sundials on top of the south side, one of which sported the adage: "Time and tide stay for no man."

✦ ✦ ✦

TRADE EXPANSION in the New World seemed eminent. English writer Daniel Defoe summed up the Dutch psyche: "The Dutch must be understood as they really are, the Middle Persons in Trade, the Factors and Brokers of Europe…They buy to sell again, take in to send out, and the greatest Part of their vast Commerce consists in being supply'd from All Parts of the World, that they may supply All the World again."

Hudson had been absolutely correct; the resources along the waters of North America were rich indeed. Dutch merchants began to look past the seemingly nonexistent Northwest Passage and concentrate on what was much more tangible: timber and other raw materials, gold, silver, precious metals—and furs. The manufacture of fabric had been taken to extravagant heights–satin, silk, tightly woven cotton garments and exquisite lace creations, but to the European eye, nothing could take the place of the natural beauty of animal fur. Status was identified by how much ermine or fox or mink a person could adorn themselves with.

Beaver was also very much in demand for making coats and wildly popular felt hats, in vogue for much of the seventeenth and eighteenth centuries. It took as many as eight pelts to fashion one of these monstrously brimmed hats, resulting in the eventual extinction of the animal in Western Europe. But there were plenty of *castor canadensis* (North American beaver) whose skins the native inhabitants were more than willing to provide. Not only was it stylish, the pelts consisted of two workable layers used for different purposes making it extremely warm, versatile, and durable.

Beaver fur had been processed since the time of the Romans for a variety of uses: from padding worn under armor to capes and shoe lining, so a new source was well received. In the brief period from 1626-1632, over 50,000 pelts were shipped from North America to the Netherlands. The demand steadily increased until 1656, when it was reported that 80,000 pelts a year were crossing the Atlantic to Holland.

Obviously, the States-General were very pleased, forming the New Netherland Company, a monopoly giving willing merchants from Amsterdam and Hoorn a pass to conduct four voyages, for the purpose of discovering "any new Courses, Havens, Countries or Places." They were so encouraged by the prospect of fantastic revenues from the beaver fur trade that they incorporated the animal into the seal of New Netherland. They knew the value of branding.

But to be able to exploit the resources as they expected, they would have to establish outposts, or footholds, no matter how impermanent they might be in order to justify their intrusion. The Dutch were aware that Britain laid claim to a vast area of the eastern seaboard, from Virginia to Maine, but they had only a ragged settlement in Jamestown that was hanging by a thread, and the Plymouth Colony was far in the future. The void in between seemed to be up for grabs. For the next ten years Dutch traders and navigators combed the Hudson and Delaware waterways exploring, mapping and setting up small outposts that would serve as convenient trading centers where the Indian trappers could bring pelts to exchange for much coveted European manufactured products: hatchets, cheap jewelry, mirrors, and one of their more favorite items–"duffels"–wool cloth named for Duffel near Antwerp. They named this land New Netherland, the same as the trading company. It would stretch from the Connecticut River south to the mouth of the Delaware Bay and include what would eventually become New Jersey, and parts of New York, Connecticut, Pennsylvania, and Delaware.

Ambitious sea captains were dispatched out of Amsterdam: Adriaen Block in the *Tijger* (Tiger), and Hendrick Christiaensen in the *Fortune of Amsterdam*. From Hoorn, another Dutch seaport that was an important staging area for the VOC, sailed Cornelius Jacobsen Mey in a ship named *Fortune of Hoorn*. Block did not fare well on his first visit to America. The *Tijger* caught fire soon after he landed at the island of Manhattan where he and his crew were forced to spend the winter of 1613-1614 in makeshift shelters on the shore. There they set about building a new craft with material salvaged from the *Tijger* and gathered from their surroundings. The result was the *Onrust*, or Restless. It was the type of vessel the Dutch called a yacht, a 40-foot long, shallow-draft affair fitted with a single sail, ideal for exploring streams and inlets. It was the first craft built by European hands in America. Block would continue voyages to America, exploring the Hudson River, Long Island Sound, and the coast of Rhode Island.

The Onrust

Christiaensen would make at least ten trips to North America, serving for a time as the director of the Manhattan outpost. His fate was far worse than Block's, however, for while trading in the Hudson, his ship was attacked by the very Indians he was attempting to do business with. He and most of his crew were murdered.

The *Onrust* soon came under the command of another Dutch navigator: Captain Cornelius Hendricksen of Utrecht. Hendricksen sailed south into the Delaware Bay and began exploring the river that emptied into it. Some sources claim that he sailed all the way up the river to "the falles" at present day Trenton, where navigation becomes nearly impossible. But it is very plausible that he did reach the mouth of the Schuylkill. It is also highly probable that he entered the Minquas Kill or Christina River, where he met and traded with a band of Minquas Indians, not only for furs, but also for the release of three fellow Dutchman. The men had apparently been stationed at Fort Nassau, one of the small trading posts set far up on the Hudson near present day Albany. For some unexplained reason, they had left their post, wandering far inland and been captured. To show their gratitude, the men gave Hendricksen notes and sketches they had made of the region. He incorporated the findings in a report and a "Figurative Map" which he submitted to Dutch merchants on August 19, 1616. In it he claimed to have discovered "certain land, a bay and three rivers situated between 38 and 40 degrees." One of the rivers was undoubtedly the Delaware, and the other two were probably the Christina and the Schuylkill. The map still exists today in the Royal Archives at The Hague. It was closely guarded when first presented, no doubt to keep it hidden from the prying eyes of potential competitors such as the English. They would not even include any of the new information on existing maps.

Hendricksen continued exploring, this time along the coastline of New Jersey, eventually entering an inlet that was given the name Barende-gat, meaning an inlet with breakers. The name was recorded as Barndegat on the first maps of the coast, then gradually involved into today's Barnegat, home of the beloved light house "Old Barney."

As for Captain Mey, he hove into Delaware Bay and River on his ship *Blijde*

Boodschap (Joyful Message) sometime after Hendricksen for further exploration. Mey noted the two capes at the mouth of the bay, naming the southern cape Hindloopen, in homage to the old seaport town in the province of Friesland. The Northern Cape took on Mey's own name, but it's unlikely he actually named it for himself, rather, it began appearing on charts as Mey's Cape and eventually Cape May.

The bay itself went through an identity crisis early on, appearing for a time on Dutch maps as Nieuw Port Mey, (which Mey christened it), Godyn's Bay (after a Dutch investor whom we'll meet presently), and Zuyt-Baye or South Bay among others. But the Dutch seemed to agree on calling the Delaware River the Zuyt, or South River. This was because it defined the southern boundary of New Netherland. Also in a bit of naive reasoning, they felt it would be of a more tropical climate since it was further south than the Hudson, which they of course named the Noort Rivier. This may have also been wishful thinking as a year-round navigation system free of ice would be of great advantage. It was also referred to early on as the Mauritius River, the name given it by Hudson in honor of Prince Maurice of Nassau.

After exploring much of the bay and environs, Mey also sailed upriver, mapping and naming various tributaries in the process, although just how far he traveled is not known. He returned to Amsterdam to report his findings of "new and fruitful lands." In a few years he would find himself back in New Netherland, although for a far different assignment.

The West India House, Amsterdam

✦ ✦ ✦

THE CHARTER FOR THE New Netherland Company expired in 1618, so now a new company was proposed by an influential Amsterdam merchant by way of Antwerp, Belgium named Willem Usselinx (also spelled Usselincx). It would be modeled after the East India Company and be called appropriately enough, the West India Company. The Dutch were poised to control trade literally on a global scale.

The company was born June 3, 1621 when it was granted a charter by the 19 members of the Board of Directors of the United Netherlands. It would have as its place of business practically the whole western hemisphere—from Brazil to the far north, including the West Indies, North America, and West Africa, which included the Atlantic Slave trade—also parts of the Pacific. The GWC, (Geoctroyeerde Westindische Compagnie), like previous Dutch enterprises, would be a monopoly, intended to eliminate English, Spanish, and Portuguese competition. Dutch merchantmen would be heavily armed, not only with weapons, but privateering licenses granting them the right to raid Portuguese shipping some of the time and Spanish shipping all the time, with whom they were still engaged in the Eighty Years War. And they did it in the grandest pirate style, capturing the Spanish silver fleet in Matanzas Bay, Cuba in 1628. The taking of sixteen Spanish ships not only made Dutch Admiral Piet Hein a national hero, but netted over 11 million guilders in booty; enough to fund the Dutch army for eight months, and present investors with a fifty per-cent dividend for the year.

Up to this time, the Dutch intentions had been primarily to trade, not to colonize. But after the formation of the GWC it was now time to legitimize their claim in North America by bringing in permanent settlers. But finding people willing to abandon their ancestral homes, spend several months at sea in a cramped, stinking sailing ship packed not only with other unwashed passengers, but stressed barnyard animals as well, and then attempt to put down roots in a totally unfamiliar wilderness would be difficult at best. The Dutch were quite comfortable in their homeland with nearly as much in the way of creature comforts as anyone in today's world. And it seemed the good times were there to stay.

But the Directors eventually found warm bodies in the people known as Walloons, thousands of French-speaking protestant refugees from Wallonia, (which to certain ears, may sound like something from the fertile mind of Dr. Seuss, or a fictitious country from a Marx Brothers movie.) This was a region to the south of Holland, still in the grip of the Spanish Inquisition. Today, it is part of Belgium. The Walloons were promised their own land in exchange for six years of service to the GWC and allegiance to the Dutch government.

The Netherlands seemed to be a magnet for the throwaways and refugees of Europe, drawn to a land that maintained a national air of tolerance. For twelve years about four hundred families of English Separatists had sought asylum in Holland. Now that the Netherlands were actively recruiting colonists for the New World, the English petitioned their host country to allow them to join the party, but the States-General politely refused. Determined as they were to create a new colony for themselves, they humbly returned to England and were able to procure two vessels. Unfortunately, one of the ships proved unseaworthy, so one hundred of the would-be pilgrims boarded the other ship, which was named the *Mayflower*. Sailing from Plymouth in September of 1620, they set a course for "Virginia", the name given not only to the land where Jamestown was situated, but the entire Eastern Seaboard, from North Carolina to Maine. (The location of the New World colonies was so vague to some that they simply referred to any settlements across the Atlantic as the West Indies).

There is some school of thought that believes the pilgrims may have actually been headed for the Delaware Bay. If that is the case, their first winter may not have been quite as harsh.

Late spring of 1624 found Captain Mey back in North America in command of a different ship than his last–this one named appropriately enough *Nieu Nederlandt*. He was also appointed the first Director of the new colony. Onboard were 30 of the newly recruited Walloon families, some of whom would be let ashore at Fort Amsterdam, the trading post on Manhattan Island. More were taken far up the Hudson to the post known as Fort Orange near present day Albany. (Named for William, Prince of Orange, also known as William the Silent). More families were taken to an outpost on the far northern edge of New Netherland on the Connecticut River, and the rest sailed with Captain Mey down the North River, out into the sea, south along the coast of New Jersey and up the Delaware. An island in the middle of the river had been scouted a year or two previously, probably by Mey himself, and was recommended as a favorable spot for settlement. Since it was an island, it was still accessible to the potential Indian traders, but easily defended against any European intruders.

Onboard were Catalina Trico and Joris Rapalje, aged eighteen and nineteen respectively. Many of the refugee settlers were of the same ilk–young, separated from families and willing to start a new life in a new land. Some of the young couples were married during the voyage, but Catalina and Joris were joined four days before the ship left Amsterdam. It seemed doubtful the union would last, cast as they were between the hazards of an Atlantic crossing and trying to establish a home in a wilderness. But last it did. They were among the first colonists in what would eventually become New Jersey. Much later, in her eighties, Catalina, who became a Manhattan land-owner and mother of eleven children, was recruited to give testimony during the infamous legal battle between William Penn and Lord Baltimore, as proof of "Christian" occupation in the long standing border dispute. Her first child Sarah, would long claim to be the "first born Christian daughter of New Netherland." The island where they landed was known as Meteneconk by the local Indians, now known as Burlington Island. It sits about 85 miles from the mouth of Delaware Bay, across from today's City of Burlington. The Dutch had a few other names for it: Prince's, Murderers, but more impressive, Hooghe Eylandt, or High Island.

The following year, 1625, the West India Company sent Willem van der Hulst to be the new commander of New Netherland. His instructions stated he was to have "his usual place of residence on the South River", where with a number of underlings "he shall deliberate and act upon all matters of importance". It would seem clear that High Island was intended as the seat of Dutch government in New Netherland. A typical palisaded fort was also constructed to be used as a trading post or factorij, named Fort Wilhelmus, another reference to William of Orange.

✦ ✦ ✦

Whenever one tries to piece together events from hundreds of previous years, some of those pieces are bound to go missing. The history of the New Netherland colonies is no exception; in fact, even more so. In 1821, much of the East and West India Company records from the seventeenth century were sold at auction in Amsterdam as scrap paper. Some of the records may have been damaged by mold and vermin and destroyed, while others were simply described as "lost." But some, known as the Van Rappard Documents, were recovered years later and indicate that not all Dutch colonial activity took place on the Hudson. Still, it is not known if van der Hulst, or Verhulst (an informal surname), ever actually inhabited High Island. He may have gone directly to Manhattan instead. But it is certain that Walloon refugees settled there, even though they were eventually re-situated to Manhattan. It is also certain that van der Hulst was removed from his position in the fall of 1626 and sent back to Holland for behavior unbecoming a governor– most likely for overstating his position, much like the biggest fish in a small pool.

To add to the frustration of missing records, what remains of writings on New

York's beginnings rarely mention the Dutch settlement on High Island, and to be sure, there is very little physical evidence. Most of that evidence was uncovered in the 1890s by New Jersey's first archaeologist Charles Conrad Abbott, while searching for Native American artifacts. What he did find lay forgotten for a century in the University of Pennsylvania's Museum of Archeology and Anthropology, and in the Peabody Museum at Yale University. Abbott's findings included hundreds of clay pipe stems and bowls, glass beads, fragments of glass bottles, iron nails, and most importantly of all, pieces of yellow bricks and roof tiles which are typical seventeenth century Dutch building materials. Abbott referred to the collection as the remains of a "Dutch trader's house."

The island continued to be used by European colonists in a variety of ways including a retreat for vice director of New Netherland, Alexander d'Hinoyossa, and later as farmland by the English. In the early twentieth century, an amusement park was established, burned down, and then in 1955, a gravel mining operation excavated a large basin, effectively removing any further chance for archeological explorations.

Typically, a clay pipe's worth of tobacco would be purchased, and when finished, the next customer would break off the end. This would continue until the stem was but a nub. This illustration also shows one of the many styles of beaver hats, so popular in Europe at the time. These were the two most lucrative products exported from North America in the seventeenth century.

VIII

Upon van der Hulst's departure, New Netherland was left without a governing leader. He was eventually replaced by Peter Minuit, from the German town of Wesel. But it seems that Minuit may have stumbled into the position by chance.

Originally of French Huguenot extraction, Minuit, pronounced Min-wee, was destined to play a key role not only in the history of New Netherland, but later in the upstart colony of New Sweden as well. We do not know enough about him other than coming from a widely divergent background that also included French, Walloon, Dutch and German ancestry.

He was said to be a highly motivated, educated man with energy, good business sense, and the command of at least three languages. Abandoning his early training as a diamond cutter, which he found exceedingly dull, he approached the GWC when he learned of the French-speaking Walloon venture to the New World and offered his services as a volunteer businessman. The directors took him up on his offer, giving him instructions to scout the condition of the lands along the river–basically to look for trading and business opportunities as well as the presence of minerals or precious metals. His observations would serve him well in future exploits along the Delaware. He explored the tributaries along the river, observing the flora, fauna, and natural resources of the region, and established good relations with the native peoples as well. Minuit returned to Amsterdam for a short time to report his findings, no doubt punctuated with plant, vegetable and mineral samples. But when he returned to Manhattan, it was to find that he and Verhulst would be trading places. Although not his intention, Minuit had so impressed his fellow pioneers that they petitioned him to be their new director.

He accepted readily and immediately set to work transferring the settlers at High Island, Fort Orange, and the Connecticut River post to Fort Amsterdam on Manhattan. Due to Van der Hulst's incompetence, relations with the Indians were in a deteriorating state. Too few settlers were spread out over too large an area; it was far better to consolidate the population and strengthen the colony. Fort Amsterdam then became New Amsterdam, the epicenter of the New Netherland Colony.

Minuit's next act upon taking over on Manhattan was to buy it from the Indians in order to further legitimize the Dutch claim. The far-too-familiar tale is told that it was purchased with sixty guilders worth of trade goods–the period equivalent of $24, or in today's currency, about $1200. As with many legendary events that have become embedded in the national psyche, there may be nothing more than a tiny grain of truth involved with the incident.

While it's quite true that Europeans did make many land purchases from the natives, the Indians didn't view the transactions in quite the same way. The whites expected them to leave once the land was bought, but the Indians continued to hang around, much to the annoyance of the new owners. To the Indian's way of thinking, they would simply continue with their ways, content to share the land in exchange for some gifts. In fact, the Indians might sell the same land over and over again, to many different buyers.

The Manhattan transaction is mentioned only briefly in the surviving Dutch records, none of which mention Minuit, but in a letter addressed to the States General in The Hague dated November 5, 1626, it states that "They have purchased the Island Manhattes from the Indians for the value of 60 guilders; it is 11,000 morgens in size." The letter was written by Dutch official, Peter Schaghen, apprising his superiors of the contents of a departing ship, the *Arms of Amsterdam* of its contents and pertinent news of the colony. That being said, it's difficult to say if the sale

actually took place or not. Many other important records have failed to survive. But it remains a part of modern folklore as one of the most absurdly lop-sided real estate deals in history.

✦ ✦ ✦

COMMERCE WAS STILL the main purpose of the West India Company (hereafter referred to as WIC), and with the colonists firmly rooted on Manhattan, the company felt that a fortified storehouse was needed to complete their very lucrative fur monopoly on the South River. A typical Dutch stockade was built: a palisaded outer wall constructed of vertical logs surrounding a house-like structure of brick or wood, often called a blockhouse. It was named Fort Nassau—not to be confused with the fort of the same name on the upper Hudson, which was destroyed by flood...or fire, we're not sure which.

Other than that, the murky shadows of history creep in again: Disputes over the date of its construction–1623-1626? Who oversaw the construction–Cornelius Jacobsen Mey, Peter Minuit, or someone else? Where was it located–at the confluence of Big and Little Timber Creeks, or of Newton Creek? Was it on the site of present day Gloucester City, or Fairview? A joint effort by both the New Jersey and Pennsylvania Historical Societies could not come to an agreement after a search was conducted in 1852. Even the name Nassau cannot be agreed upon. Some claim it was named after a town on the Upper Rhine in Germany. Other, and probably more feasible sources, cite the origin as coming from the name of the by now familiar Dutch sovereign, the Prince of Orange.

The only point of total agreement is that it's not there anymore. Most also agree that the fort was on the east side of the Delaware, oddly placed since most of the trappers brought their furs from the west side. You can almost picture a misty morning on the river, quiet for the most part except for the songs of birds, and then the muffled splunk of paddles becoming more pronounced and slowly, out of the ether, a dugout canoe emerging, occupied by one or two men sporting feathers in their topknots, beaver furs piled high in their dugout canoe.

These men would have been Minquas (Mink-wass) from the Susquehannock, a tribe far unlike the Lenni Lenape. The furs they were offering came from animals trapped as far away as one hundred miles, in the Susquehanna River valley in southeastern Pennsylvania. They were carried over a route that became known as the "Great Minquas Path", one of a network of Indian trails used to transport furs to the ready outposts of the European traders.

Part of the Iroquois Nation, their language group was distinct from Algonquian. They also exhibited much more aggressive tendencies, which, as it turns out, made them excellent trappers, but terrified their more passive neighbors. Captain John Smith, while exploring and mapping the Chesapeake Bay during his tenure as leader of the Jamestown colony, was even a bit startled by their mannerisms and impressive weaponry. More formally, they were known as the Mingwe, who were also part of the cast of characters in the novels of James Fenimore Cooper known as "Mingo." The Algonquian name Minquas meant "treacherous", giving an idea of what the Lenape thought of them.

Even before the Dutch arrived, there were complicated conflicts between the various factions of the Iroquois and Algonquins. Now that the Europeans had created a market for furs on the Delaware and the Hudson, a new element was added to the hostilities. The most aggressive tribes tried to drive away the more benign groups in an effort to eliminate the competition.

But the Dutch traders were a rough and unsophisticated bunch and did not concern themselves with the intricate cultural disagreements of their business associates. The Directors of the WIC preferred it that way–the traders were supplied with implicit instructions to treat the natives, if not with a certain modicum of respect, at least with a simple policy of live and let live. (This was in direct contrast to the Spanish, whose contact with local populations in the Americas was too often of a brutal nature. Rather than seeking trade, their objective was plunder—instant riches of gold, silver, gemstones—or the promise of them, procured by slaughtering the natives who resisted and enslaving those who surrendered.)

The Indians were far better at trapping beaver than the Dutch, especially in large quantities. However, the trade agreements were almost always stacked unfairly on the side of the Dutch buyers. The Indian trapper would be overjoyed with the simplest of household utensils, clay pipes, jewelry, combs, glass beads and the like. Anything made of iron was valued in even greater esteem, especially knives, hatchets and iron pots. Metal tools were not always completely understood–a Lenape trapper was given an axe head on one trading session, but was later seen wearing it around his neck like an amulet. Even after a handle was attached by a Dutchman, he still preferred his original usage. The Indians too were known to try and pull a fast one on occasion. A Lenape brave tried selling a buzzard to a Swedish man of the cloth, telling him it was a turkey. The preacher would have none of it, and asked why the brave tried to cheat him. "I didn't think you knew the difference between the birds of this country" was his reply.

The cloth known as duffel, also held in high esteem, was sold by the arm length. The Dutch would stretch the cloth as far as they could before cutting off a length. But their customers would often counter by sending their largest and tallest tribal member to make the purchase.

Eventually, firearms and liquor were added as desirable trade goods. Originally, the WIC forbade alcohol as payment, but the traders ignored the rules as they found the Indians were even easier to take advantage of when they were as Benjamin Franklin described "among the Philistines." This would often lead to problems of tragic proportions. Liquor had never been part of Indian diet or culture and often produced unpredictable results. A drink "to your health" to celebrate a deal was not understood by the Indians as being a social nuance. They simply drank until all the available alcohol was gone. If there was not enough liquor for every member of a group of Indians to get fully "beschonken", then one would be appointed to represent them all in becoming one with the spirit. Even after the chosen one fell unconscious, they would continue to pour liquor down his throat until it was gone. There were undoubtedly many cases of death by alcohol.

Dutch money was, of course, no use to the Indians. However, there was a native currency in use when the Europeans arrived. The Dutch knew it as sewan or sewant, and in New England it was called wampum, or peake. It was different to the Indians than money, as it had ceremonial and spiritual value. Cockle shell beads were carefully worked using bone and stone and then strung together in various increments. Four beads on a string or six loose beads counted as one stuiver–about two cents, twenty stuivers were worth a florin, and one beaver pelt would be worth seven or eight florins–about eighty cents.

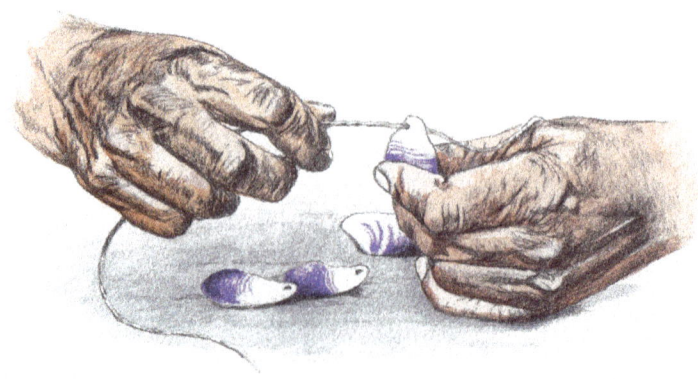

✦ IX ✦

On January 13, 1629, two representatives from the WIC were dispatched to New Netherland to buy prospective real estate from local Indians. Gillis Hossitt, a sailor, and Jacob Jansz, described as a cooper, did not seem likely candidates for the job other than that they had possibly been in the New World before. Nothing previous is known of them.

They were sent by three directors of the WIC with the intention of establishing a start-up colony that would make money from whaling and sustain itself by farming. The directors, who were also prominent Amsterdam merchants, were Samuel Blommaert, Kiliaen van Rensselaer, and the mastermind behind the plan, Samuel Godyn, the president of the Amsterdam Chamber. They were given permission by other members of the States General through a document entitled the Charter of Freedoms and Exemptions to establish patroonships, which allowed them to establish colonies at their own expense. This was a concept unique to Dutch colonization. It was basically a feudal system that allowed the patroon the authority to recruit settlers, appoint officials and collect rents. However, the WIC required the patroons to establish a settlement of at least fifty families within four years. (Van Rensselaer would in a few years become the owner of Manor Rensselaerswyck, the largest patroonship in New Netherland, involving hundreds of acres along the Hudson River that included present day Albany. He would, however, never visit his immense holdings in the New World, as would many of the patroons).

The spot chosen was "South Hook", a section of the southern coast of the Delaware Bay near Cape Hindlopen. It would be along a fresh water stream that ran through an area named "Zwaanenndael", Valley of the Swans. The mouth of the bay was a rich soup of nutrients that drew dolphins, pilot and sperm whales, and especially humpbacks to feed voraciously during the winter months. So close would they come to the shoreline that harpooners stationed on the beach could spot them easily, then launch small whale boats and row out for the kill. They would be towed back to shore and butchered for their oil which in turn would be exported to Holland where it could be sold for up to sixty guilders a hogshead. Fur trading, however, was unmentioned—which may seem odd at first since it was the first and foremost Dutch money maker, but it would mean that the WIC would have been competing with the patroons, which meant basically, they would be competing with themselves.

The land at Zwanenndael was purchased from an Algonquin-speaking tribe the Dutch called the Great Siconese. Their chief, or sachem, at the time was only a boy, and since Hossitt requested the sales agreement to be finalized in Manhattan, he was accompanied by two adult members of the tribe: Quesquakous and Eesanques. There they all appeared before Director-General Peter Minuit who confirmed both the land transaction and the establishment of the patroonship. Shortly after, another WIC director, Albert Conraets Burgh registered an additional colony, this one to be situated on the east side of the bay, on the southern portion of Cape May. It was then decided to admit ten more members to the group as sub-patroons, the chief among them being David Pietersen de Vries, a spirited adventurer and skilled seaman who, though only thirty-seven years old, had already experienced more than his share of naval activity. Recently returned from the East Indies, he had been in command of a fleet of seven ships sailing under the French flag. When propositioned with a sub-patroonship by Godyn though, he demanded to be granted a full patroonship, which was issued with little grumbling.

On December 12, 1630, after recruiting prospective settlers, the Godyn venture sailed out from Holland with a manifest of eighty passengers, and a cargo of lime, bricks, tiles, four horses, a dozen cows, ammunition, provisions, trade goods, tools and several whaling boats. The ship carrying all of this was a private vessel appropriately named the *Walvis* (the Whale), captained by Peter Heyes of Edam, an experienced Greenland whaler. In charge of the colony would be the aforementioned Gillis Hossitt. Little could any of this expedition imagine what was in store for them.

✦ ✦ ✦

AFTER DROPPING OFF passengers in the West Indies, the *Walvis* set a northerly course until she entered the shoal strewn Delaware Bay. It would now become known as Godyn's Bay and retain that name for many years on Dutch maps and journals. Twenty-eight men were deposited at Zwanenndael with their supplies and livestock, including one very large mastiff dog. They began construction on a large house with a storage loft made of the familiar yellow bricks which would serve as barracks for the men, a smaller cook house, and a palisaded log wall surrounding the property. Since it was now spring of 1631, cultivation began on cleared land around the fortification. Godyn and company had obviously recruited well, for they were a self-sufficient bunch, capable of becoming as needed, bricklayers, carpenters, masons, and farmers, not to mention experienced whalers.

Once the settlement was under way, Captain Heyes returned his empty ship to Holland, much to the consternation of the patroons, who had expected him to return with whale oil, or at least some profitable merchandise from the West Indies. Heyes explained that they had arrived in the bay too late for the whaling season, which normally ran from December to March. After calming the disappointed investors, Godyn convinced them to outfit a ship and a yacht to return in 1632 for the next whaling season. They would also carry provisions to re-supply the new colony. In charge would be the venerable David Pietersen de Vries.

As the next expedition was making ready, news arrived from New Netherland that the Zwanenndael colony had been destroyed and all the men massacred by Indians. Both Godyn and De Vries were furious and demanded immediate revenge. However, the Company would not permit punitive action, claiming peace must be kept with the Indians. On May 24, 1632, De Vries continued with the plans they had previously arranged and set sail from the Texel (an island at the mouth of the Zuyder Zee, in Holland) in the *Walvis*, accompanied by a yacht called *Teencoorntgen* (Little Squirrel).

De Vries kept a journal of his experiences which were later published in Holland in 1655. He gave it the gargantuan title:

Korte Historiael Ende Journaels Aenteyckeninge van versheyden Voyagiens in de vier deepen des Wereldts-Ronde, als Europa, Africa, Asia, end Amerika sedan, Door D. David Pietersz. de Vries, Artillerij-Meester vane Ed: M: Heeren Gecommitteerde Raden van Staten van West-Vrieslandt end 't Noordenquartier. Waer in verhaelt werd watt Batailjes hy te Water gedaen heft: Yder Landtschap zijn Gedierte, Gevogelt, wat soorte van Vissen, end wat wilde Menschen near 't leaven geconterfaeyt, end van de Bosschen end Ravieren met haer Vruchten. t' Hoorn. Voor David Pietersz. de Vries, Artillerij-Meester van 't Noorder-quartier. Tot Alckmaer, by Symon Cornelisz. Brekegeest, Anno 1655.

Many book titles of this era were of epic length. Translated to English, it goes like this:

Short Historical and Journal-Notes of various Voyages performed in the Four Quarters of the Globe, viz., Europe, Africa, Asia, and America, by David Pieterszoon de Vries, Artillery-Master to the Noble and Mighty Lords the Council of West Friesland and the Northern Quarter [of the Province of Holland], wherein is set forth what battles he delivered on the Water, Each Country, its Animals, its Birds, its Kinds of Fishes, and its Wild Men counterfeited to the Life, and its Woods and Rivers with their Products.

In it he described what was found at Zwanenndael and the aftermath. He wrote of smelling the land as they approached the South Bay before it came into view: "This comes from the Indians setting fire, at this time of year, to the woods and thickets, in order to hunt; and the land is full of sweet-smelling herbs, as sassafras, which has a sweet smell." On December 5th, 1632, they came upon the ruins of Zwanenndael. There they found the skeletal remains of the settlers as well as heads of the horses and cows that were brought with them. There appeared to be no survivors, so the task at hand was to try and extract an explanation from the local Indians. They sailed into the creek on the *Squirrel* and managed to coax one of the Indians aboard with a cloth dress. He stayed the night, and in the morning revealed what had happened.

The Dutch pioneers officially staked the claim to their newly acquired property by setting up a wooden column to which they fastened a piece of tin painted with Holland's coat of arms. One of the Indian chiefs removed the tin, perhaps thinking it was a gift, with the intention of using it to make tobacco pipes, unaware that he was defacing the symbol of the fatherland. The Dutch made quite a fuss about it when confronting the accused—so much so that the Indians left, but returned with the culprit's head to compensate for the insult. This only made things worse as the Dutch felt the punishment far exceeded the crime. They had just wanted to reprimand the unfortunate chief and warn him against such acts in the future. Now the Indians were thoroughly confused, which quickly turned to anger. De Vries described them "as they are a people like the Italians, who are very revengeful—to set about the work of vengeance."

They waited until most of the settlers were working the fields when three of the tribe approached the house with beaver pelts as a ruse, and asked to come in for a trading session. Once in the house, they planted an axe in the head of Gillis Hossitt as he was about to pay them. There was a sick man lying in a bed whom

they quickly put out of his misery. The mastiff, who they were all terrified of, was chained in the house and was no doubt quite upset over the grisly activity. They dispatched him as well, needing twenty-five arrows to finish the job. They and the rest of their war party then made their way out to the fields and under the pretense of friendship, murdered the remaining Dutchmen, one by one. De Vries did not seem to convey much emotion when recording the event in his journal, only that it was a "serious loss." Perhaps he realized it was just a deadly misunderstanding, or that the specter of an untimely death was always lurking for strangers in a strange land.

The next day de Vries and company were paid a visit by some of the Indians and their chiefs, and sitting in a ring, they conducted a peace ceremony. Presents of duffels, bullets, hatchets and trinkets were then handed out, with the Indians promising to return the favors in the future as they had been hunting. It was agreed that the Zwanenndael incident should be put behind them as there was no proper route of revenge. Ironic that such a tranquil image would be so tainted by tragedy.

Despite the failure of the colony, it would play an important role in determining the future makeup of the entire Delaware Valley.

✦ ✦ ✦

THE 1ST OF JANUARY, 1633, de Vries left the *Walvis* and the majority of the men at Zwanenndael to set up a shelter so that the original intent of the colony could continue: the catching and processing of whales.

De Vries and the remainder of the party set off up the South River in the yacht *Squirrel* to forage and try to barter with the Indians for beans or corn as their supplies were running dangerously low. They came upon Fort Nassau, which was at the time unoccupied by Dutch traders, and tried to barter for food with a local tribe. About forty of them came aboard the Squirrel offering to sell beaver furs, but the Dutchmen had already exhausted their supply of trade goods at Zwanenndael. The Indians were cordial enough and even brought some of their native instruments to provide a little entertainment. But De Vries became suspicious when they began urging him to sail his yacht up Big Timber Creek. Some of these men, whom De Vries described as Mantes, were wearing English-made jackets which added to the gravity of their situation. De Vries suspected they may have been acquired from the Harvey expedition from the same year. He ordered them off, threatening to shoot them all, and they quietly obliged. The entire trip was fraught with tension, as the Dutchmen feared attack at almost any moment. They had picked a very inopportune time to forage; the Minquas were invading Lenape lands, burning their fields of corn and wreaking havoc in general. Pickings were slim.

After the trappers left, a lone Indian woman managed to sneak onboard and reveal to Commander De Vries the real reason for the Indians "friendly" visit. They wanted the Dutch to sail up the narrow creek where it would be easier to dispatch the lot of them. She didn't want any of her tribe to be killed in the process. She also told them of an English shallop that had ventured into these waters and whose occupants had been slaughtered by her kinsmen. It now became clear that the Harvey expedition had indeed come to a bitter end. Grateful for the information, de Vries presented the woman with a cloth garment. He and the crew were now more wary than ever, in case they were paid another visit.

De Vries returned to Zwanenndael, re-supplied, and sailed up the river again. And once again they were able to acquire very little. De Vries was surprised to come upon a whale north of the Minquas Kill (Christina River). He seemed to be equally surprised by the amount of ice encountered, which locked them in for a time, even though it was the dead of winter. He wrote: "no pilot or astrologer could conceive, that in a latitude from the thirty-eighth and a half to the thirty-ninth, such rapid running rivers could freeze." There was still the vague notion among navigators that the climate on the "South" river should be more like Florida than New England.

Finally, after failing to procure enough food, and fearing the worst from the warring tribes, the De Vries expedition left the South Bay and River to visit the "English in Virginia." Once there he related to Governor Harvey the sad truth about the Englishmen who had met an unfortunate end on Big Timber Creek, as well as the Dutch tragedy at Zwanenndael. The Virginia governor gladly re-supplied de Vries and company and they returned to their homeland.

Even though the Zwanenndael venture had been a complete failure, De Vries continued to live the life of an adventurer, returning to New Netherland and establishing a colony known as "Vriessendael" in Bergen County, as well as a farming settlement on Staten Island. He also acted as a negotiator in disputes between the Lenape and director-general Willem Kieft, and was instrumental in Keift's eventual dismissal and recall to the Netherlands for trial. Returning to Holland for good in 1643, he wrote of his adventures in his generously titled journal.

✦ ✦ ✦

As a result of the massacre and finding that the whaling was not up to expectations, the Godyn patroons were forced to take a bath on the whole venture. In 1635 with their charter about to expire, they sold both the Zwanenndael and the proposed Burgh tracts to the WIC for 16,500 guilders. The company made no attempt to re-start the colony or the whale fishery. An occasional fur trading deal between Dutch and Indians took place, but the only thing that changed was the name. Zwanenndael now became Hoornkil.

There is much dispute over the origin of the name, but the most logical explanation is that someone simply attached the name of the city of Hoorn in Holland to the Dutch term for a body of water—kill. This may even have been attributed to David de Vries himself, who spent most of his youth in Hoorn, a port city renowned for its shipbuilding; in particular, the revolutionary fluyt. The city is also responsible for lending its name to Cape Horn, the southernmost tip of land in South America.

Unfortunately, Hoornkil was eventually misinterpreted to mean Harlot's Creek, and degraded further in English to "Whore Kill". There was no doubt much tittering overseeing the location spelled out on a map or document for the first time. The name eventually came to refer to a large portion of southern Delaware. Embarrassment and humiliation finally got the best of the local inhabitants, and in 1680, just a few years before Wm. Penn's arrival, the justices of the court begged then Governor Andros "to give Whorekill some other name." He evidently took pity and renamed the town and county "Deale." This didn't last very long, for in 1682, Penn changed the name again–to the town of Lewes, in the county of Sussex. In today's Lewes, the tragic, early Dutch settlement is commemorated in the form of the Zwanenndael Museum, a scaled down replica of the town hall of Hoorn. It was built in 1931 in honor of the unfortunate settlers and its leader, David Pietersen de Vries, whose likeness stands atop the highest point on the building.

After the patroons sold their interests to the WIC, the Indians began to drift back onto the tract, not that they'd ever really left. Sensing a possible threat to business interests on the South River from English trespassers, the governing powers in New Amsterdam felt that the area should be occupied again or even fortified. But the Siconese, who were becoming more disagreeable, would have to be appeased. In 1659 The Dutch sent vice director Alexander d'Hinoyossa and William Beekman to southern Delaware, along with twenty soldiers and trade goods, and for the second time in less than thirty years, bought the same land from the Indians.

Later that year, a fort was built, simply called "the Company's fort", the company naturally being the WIC. But business was on the downturn for the WIC, and in 1656 they sold a large portion of the west side of the river to the city of Amsterdam. In 1663 the city bought their interests on the entire river including the bordering lands and the fort at Hoerenkil.

The old port city of Hoorn, Holland

PART II

✦ X ✦

In 1633 an agent of the WIC named Arent Corssen paid a visit to Fort Nassau. From there he crossed the South River, sailed up the Schuykill, and landing at a place called Armenveruis, purchased a small parcel of land from the Passayunk Indians. This was at the terminus of the Minquas trail used to bring furs from far up in the countryside. There he constructed a temporary shelter to act as a trading post when the Indians came calling with their products. It was so small and insignificant that it wasn't even afforded a name, but it was the first indication that the Dutch were aware of the need to have a receiving point for Indian trappers on the west side of the river. They now had two spots on the South River to continue their monopoly of the beaver trade. But that was about to change.

In the summer of 1634 two boats sailed into the South Bay from the Virginia territory. Aboard were fifty-four-year-old Thomas Yong, the gentleman explorer from London whom we met previously, and his nephew Robert Evelyn. Accompanying them were a small group of men hired by Yong to do no less than help him take control of the entire Delaware Bay and River territory. Armed with a royal commission from Charles I, it gave Yong the authority to "take possession of all such Countries, Lands and Territories, as are yet undiscovered or not actually in the possession of any Christian Prince, Country or State, and therein to erect our Banners"…etc., etc.— the standard formal decree issued regularly by the British Crown to erstwhile explorers cleverly worded to avoid stepping on anyone's toes—just in case. He also was equipped with the not-so-original goal of searching for a passage through the country to the Orient.

Sailing upriver, which he named the Charles, undoubtedly to gain points from his beloved monarch, the group came upon Fort Nassau. But he failed to mention it in his "Relation", a journal that he kept of his expedition as it would have been at odds with the terms of his commission. His men took possession of the outpost rather easily with little loss of blood and no casualties—it was unoccupied at the time.

After leaving a portion of the company at the fort, Yong continued sailing north on the river where he made friends with a variety of tribesman, including one terrified Lenape man whom he hid on his ship from a marauding band of Minquas. Sharing hospitality and gifts, he questioned his newly-made friends as to how far it was to the fabled passage. All gave him differing accounts of distance and direction, but there was a general acknowledgement that "the falles" at Sankikan (Trenton) would present a problem.

When he did reach them, he encountered a Dutch shallop manned by "poachers." He had the men brought to his ship and sternly demanded "what they made here?" to which they meekly replied that they were only trading. He then questioned if they were in possession of a charter from King Charles, which they of course were not. But they did have a commission from the Governor of New Netherlands, at which Yong fumed "I know no such governor, nor no such place as New Netherlands!" To further clarify his position, he told them that the country they were trespassing on belonged to the Crown of England, which his Majesty now intended to colonize. As if to minimize their indiscretion, the Dutchmen replied that they had traded there before, which only gave Yong further cause to boast of the authority of the King, and that it would be "good manners in them to desist."

The cowering Dutchmen then humbly asked to see the commission, and it was at this moment that Yong, with all the regal complacency that he could muster, proudly pulled out his document, affixed with the royal seal and signature, proclaiming that he could "take possession thereof." The Dutchmen were forced to concede that the commission was much better than theirs, one of them admitting "indeed they had not seen a larger commission."

If Yong had been able to get past the falls and follow the river north to the foothills of the Appalachians, he might have come upon more Dutchmen engaged in a different sort of "poaching". There had always been rumors of gold, silver and other precious metals to be found throughout New Netherland. In fact, the whole of North America. Since the WIC felt they had the fur market cornered, scouts were sent out to probe the countryside and see if the rumors were true. And indeed, at a place known as Pahaquarry, deposits of low-grade copper ore were found. It was along the river's floodplain just north of what would eventually be called the Delaware Water Gap. Using an old Indian game trail, they built an access road from the agricultural community of Esopus on the Hudson River 104 miles south to the mines. That town is now called Kingston, and the road is known as The Old Mine Road–the oldest continuously used route of its kind in the country. Strangely, the Dutch miners had no idea about the river by the mines–its name or where it ran to. They could have shipped their ore down the Delaware instead of hauling it all the way up to the Hudson, and then to New Amsterdam.

Coming to the realization that a waterway through the country was not to be found by following the Delaware, Yong and company departed, sailing back down the river, to pick up the men at Fort Nassau. They were, however, quite surprised to find a much larger and well-armed group of Dutch tradesmen waiting for them. They were then taken to New Amsterdam, where then governor Wouter von

Twiller recruited David de Vries to take the group of Englishmen back to Virginia. Thus ended an early English invasion of the Delaware, but there would be more and larger such incidents in the years to come. The British colonies in Virginia and New England were growing and gradually closing in on New Netherland. But in just a few years would come a direct intrusion from a much more unlikely source.

The great seal & "signature" of Charles I

• PART III •

The Swedes

✦ XI ✦

On a nondescript, but well-traveled road just a few miles south of the Delaware River in the small hamlet of Gibbstown, New Jersey, sits an old house. And attached to that old house is a structure that is older still. Fashioned from white oak, it is reputed to be the oldest log dwelling of its kind in the world. It is known simply as the Nothnagle Cabin. Built by a Finnish immigrant, it seems to date to the mid-seventeenth century when the area was part of the New Sweden colony. Lovingly cared for by its owner Harry Rink, former mayor of Gibbstown, it has remained in a remarkable state of preservation. The day I visited and met Harry he was replacing some of the decayed chinks between the logs with clay he digs himself from the banks of the Delaware, not far from Salem. He then stores it in various stages of consistency in covered plastic tubs. A man in his mid-eighties, Harry knows every square inch of this old cabin including the ax and adze marks created by its original builder. Remarkably, those tools still survive within the cabin. One of the unique features of the structure is the squared shaping of the logs and the hand-hewn full dovetail joints on its corners; cracked and worn, but still very visible. The original brick and plaster fireplace straddles a corner, the chimney built inside the cabin for extra warmth. The Finns perfected the art of building log dwellings. It was their humble gift to the New World.

I had come to snap a few photos of the exterior and be on my way, but Harry graciously invited me to step inside. When we did, everything changed. Harry said "doesn't the atmosphere feel different? It can be really hot and humid outside, but in here it's very comfortable and quiet". He was absolutely correct. But there was something else besides the climate that was very unusual. I have toured many historic buildings, but when I stepped into this old cabin, it was like nothing I have ever encountered before. It was like entering a different dimension. There was nothing eerie or paranormal–more of an ethereal, dreamy, sensation. Everything appeared soft-edged and slightly out of focus—as if we were inside an ancient security blanket. The precise age of the cabin is unknown. As of the printing of this book, a tree ring analysis has not been performed, but it is a very safe bet that it was well over one hundred years old by the time the American War of Independence began.

Hundreds of years before the Nothnagle Cabin was created, and after their brief, failed incursion on the North American continent, the Norse retreated back to their Scandinavian roots, weary from their adventures for a long nap. They

PART III

*Harry Rink and a newly repaired section of the
Finnish-built Nothnagle House*

Coat of arms of the House of Vasa

eventually awoke from the Viking era to find their old gods had been replaced by Christianity, and the more sedate life of farming was now preferred over raids of plunder on foreign shores. All of Scandinavia now found itself on equal footing spiritually, except for the ancestral builders of the Nothnagle Cabin, the Finns. The neighboring Swedes then set about mounting a series of crusades during the 12th and 13th centuries until the Finns also converted, their country gradually absorbed by Sweden.

Over the years, seemingly endless squabbles, wars, and general chaos involving religion, politics and border disputes were commonplace throughout Scandinavia; in fact, through most of Europe. To avoid a sweeping comprehensive history of Sweden describing its involvement in the Hanseatic League, the Union of Kalmar, the Stockholm Bloodbath and many other events, let's leap forward to the reign of the Vasa dynasty. It began with Gustav I on June 6, 1523, and continued with his son Erik XIV, Erik's half-brother Johan III, Sigismund III, Gustav's youngest son Charles IX, and finally to his son Gustav II Adolph, crowned in 1611. Remembered

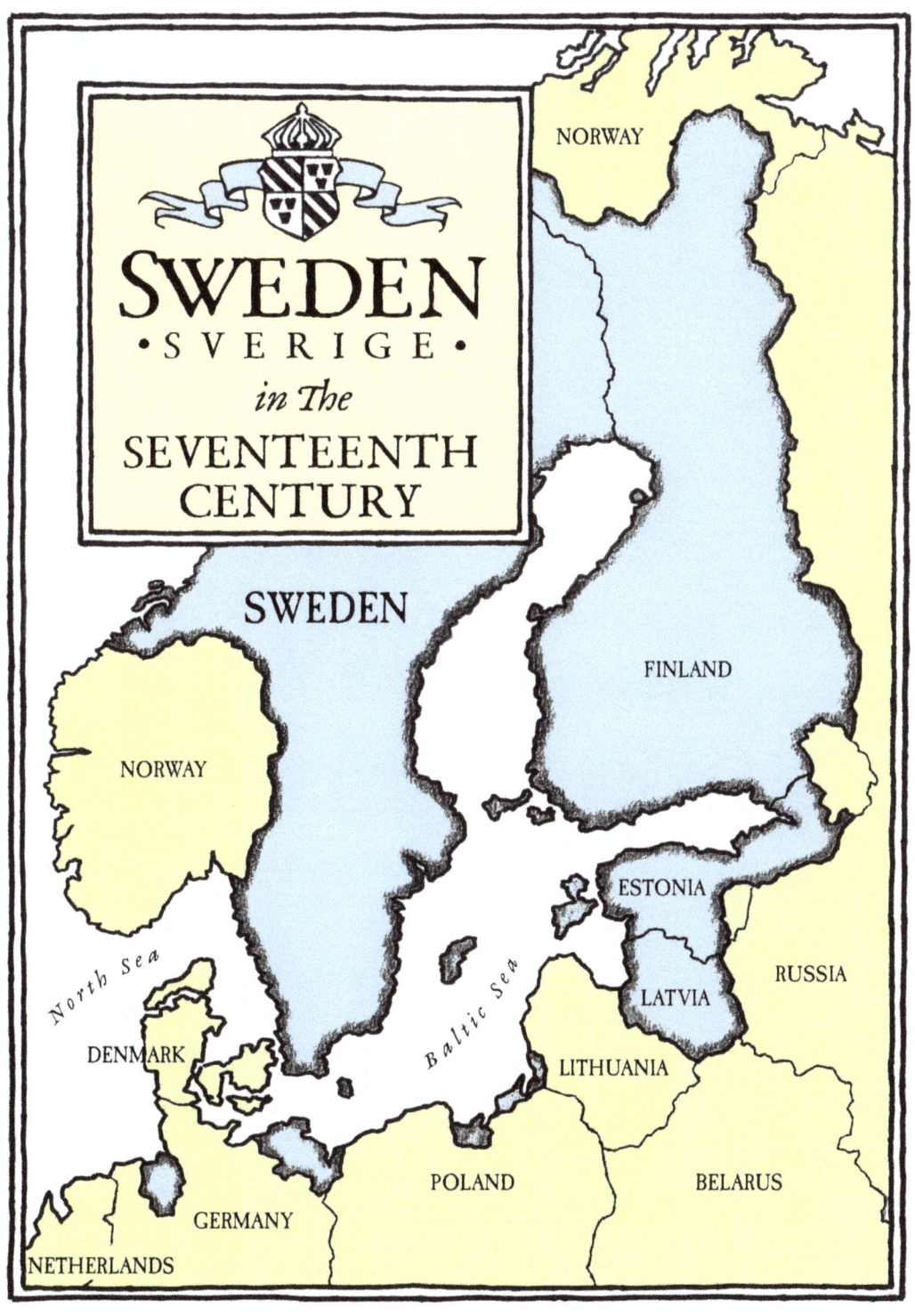

formally by his Latin title Gustavus Adolphus, he was also known as "The Lion of the North" referring to his extraordinary military skills. In fact, he has also been called the "father of modern warfare." Upon taking the throne at age seventeen, Adolphus found Sweden a small, underpopulated country with little capital and at war with Denmark, Russia and Poland. Within ten years he had completely turned the tables, bringing Sweden to prominence as the most admired and feared world power in the 17th century.

A neutral country since before the First World War, it is difficult today to conceive of Sweden, whose most compelling contribution to modern culture is affordable self-assembled furniture, as once controlling much of the Baltic region including Finland, Estonia, Latvia, parts of Norway, Poland, Russia, Germany, etc., and all due to the military genius of Gustavus Adolphus.

To maintain its military dominance, Sweden also had an abundance of natural resources to draw on. Copper and iron were mined and used to manufacture high quality cannons, muskets, pistols, and other weaponry. They also made naval equipment such as anchors and tackle, as well as extracting tar and lumber from its vast forests. But all these products were used extensively to fund Sweden's military efforts, and not much thought was given to organized commerce on the world market, like their contemporaries the English, and especially the Dutch. The Dutch so dominated the trade of the Baltic Sea that during the 16th century, 55 percent of their ships entering the Baltic carried 75 percent of the cargoes. They even retained ten of eighteen members of the first city council of Gothenburg (Göteburg), a city founded by Adolphus in 1619 to provide Sweden with a port on the Atlantic. Dutch was spoken there as frequently as Swedish.

While Gustavus Adolphus was absorbed in conquest, other European powers were focusing on expansion of a different sort in the New World. Spain held much of South and Central America, France claimed a large portion of Canada, England was planting colonies on the Atlantic seaboard and the Netherlands were involved in a booming fur trade on the Hudson and the Delaware. As it is with human behavior, these ventures had been going on just long enough for dissatisfaction to set it. One instance in particular found Flemish business man Willem Usselinx at the door of the Swedish king. He was the Amsterdam merchant we met earlier, largely responsible for the formation of the Dutch West India Company. Things had taken a sour turn, however. Usselinx felt he was being under-compensated for his involvement, especially since he had poured much of his own money into the company, so he decided to put some distance between himself and his ungrateful business associates. Enamored with Sweden's unprecedented success, Usselinx felt that he could persuade the Lion of the North that it was time to join the rest of the European powers in foreign commerce.

In 1624, during an unusual lull between wars, Usselinx was able to procure an audience with Adolphus while in Gothenburg for other business. It resulted in a six hour meeting during which Usselinx related his desire to create a "General Trading Company for Asia, Africa, America, and Magellanica" (an archaic name for Australia), which would be modeled after the DWIC. The King, to Usselinxs' great relief, proved a willing supporter and was impressed enough with the proposal that he signed a charter for a foreign trade enterprise to be called The South Company. Excitedly, Usselinx set about launching his scheme, recruiting investors and establishing conditions and terms.

But the plan languished over the next several years as potential subscribers were slow to respond, side businesses took attention away from the original intentions, and management of the whole affair was sub-par. Usselinx didn't need to read the script to see that the venture was doomed. He left Stockholm in early 1629. Discouraged but not defeated, he still had hopes for his elaborate trading company and shopped it all over Europe. There was minor interest, but the investment of his time and resources had left him financially ruined. His efforts were not completely in vain, however, for the South Company would evolve into a new and unique enterprise.

✦ XII ✦

Europe seemed to be perpetually involved in lots of wars dating to pre-history. One would almost think the participants enjoyed the wars very much since many of them dragged on for generations. There was the Hundred Year's War involving the two traditional rivals, England and France, the Eighty Years War between Spain and The Netherlands, and a war that involved the next set of players that included Sweden, Denmark, France, Saxony, England and a host of other nations. It was also one of the deadliest, resulting in eight million casualties: the Thirty Years War.

A general who believed in leading his troops literally, Gustavus Adolphus was killed in the Thirty Years War, in a battle at Lützen, Germany in 1632, one of the war's most decisive. Leading a cavalry charge astride his horse Streiff, he galloped into thick fog and gun smoke. It was the last he was seen alive. After the battle, his body was recovered, which had been stripped of his jewelry and the buff moose hide tunic he was wearing for protection. Years later it was returned to Sweden, a bullet hole clearly visible on the right side.

PART III

The Lion of The North was the last male heir in the Vasa dynasty. Left behind was his daughter Christina, who at six years of age became the Queen of Sweden. Obviously too young to head a household, let alone a country, the leadership role was left in the very capable hands of Lord High Chancellor, Count Axel Oxenstierna. Highly regarded as one of the most important men in Swedish history, Oxenstierna took on the responsibilities as the country's head of state. He had originally been hired at the age of twenty-eight by teenager Gustavus Adolphus as his prime minister.

After the king's demise, Oxenstierna re-opened interest in the foreign trading company proposed years earlier. And once again, Dutchmen were involved–not one this time, but two. Samuel Blommaert, the investor in the failed Zwaanendael venture–also a disgruntled WIC director–and Peter Minuit, former governor of the New Netherland colony. It was not unusual for the Dutch to be involved in Swedish affairs, as hundreds had resettled from Holland eager for positions in the newly prosperous empire. Minuit had been recalled to company headquarters in Amsterdam to face charges that among other things, he was accused of favoring the interests of the Patroons over those of the WIC and that he had performed underwhelmingly at recruiting new settlers. There is very little evidence that he was guilty of either.

His accuser, the first official man of the cloth to come to New Amsterdam, was

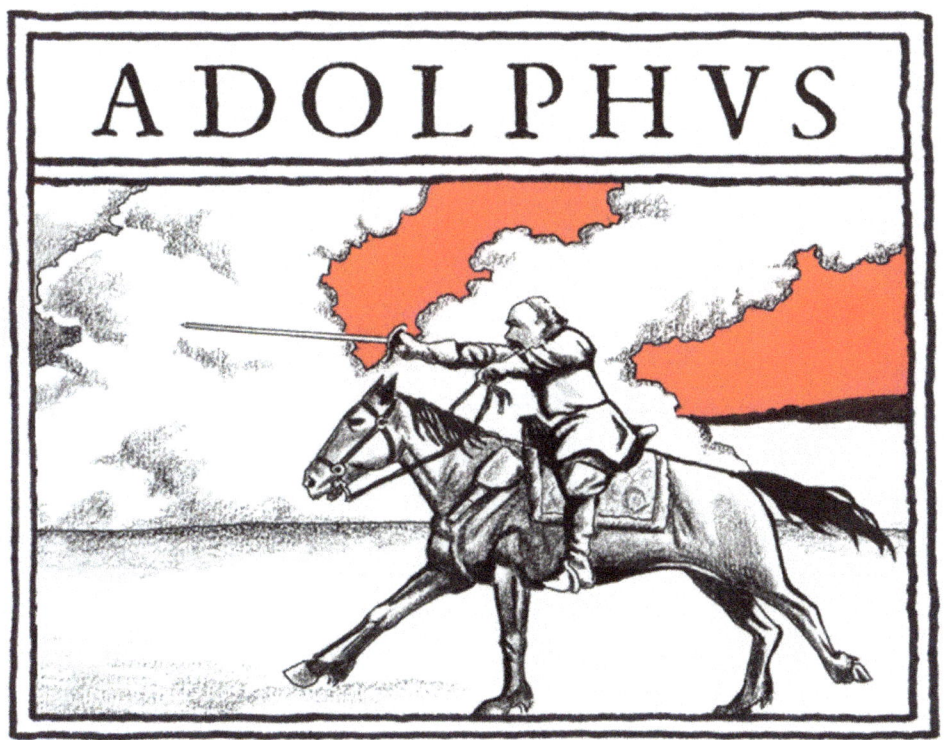

the Reverend Jonas Michaelius; by all accounts a nasty and spiteful individual. He had barely arrived in Manhattan before firing off bitchy missives grousing about the settlers, the climate, the natives, and the food, not to mention the voyage itself. He seemed to develop an immediate dislike for Minuit and sent letter after letter back to Amsterdam, complaining of his ineptitude. Somehow convincing the directors of the WIC that Minuit was cheating them, both men were recalled to Holland to settle the matter in person. Minuit was livid. Not only at the charges, but at having to endure two months shipboard with his accuser. (Ironically, the ship they sailed on together was named the *Unity*). He had spent five years in the New World and accomplished much, including keeping peace with the native inhabitants, itself a major achievement, and now all that he had been responsible for was in danger of coming undone.

Even worse events were about to unfold. The *Unity* was caught in a storm off the coast of Plymouth and forced into port where the entire ship, crew and passengers was taken into custody. It was a political gesture by the English, trying to protest the existence of the New Netherland colony, which was ludicrous, since they had known about it for years.

After skillful negotiations by both the Dutch and English, the ship was released and continued on its journey to Amsterdam. Appearing before the Directors, Minuit now had to hear the astounding verdict handed down—he was to be dismissed from his position as Governor of New Netherland on the charges that not enough settlers had been recruited for the colony. Flabbergasted, Minuit was beyond words since he had repeatedly asked for more immigrants.

✦ ✦ ✦

OXENSTIERNA HAD THE support and approval of the equally powerful Klas Fleming, admiral of Sweden's navy, and Peter Spiring, born in Holland to a wealthy Dutch merchant who enriched his name to Peter Spiring Silfverkrona as a nobleman in Sweden. The original course of action decided upon would be to create a new company to develop an overseas outlet for Sweden's copper, in particular, Guinea on the coast of West Africa, where Blommaert had considerable experience. (Blommaert's involvement may have been an attempt to recoup his losses from the Zwaanendael disaster). But when Minuit came aboard, he would speak of nothing else but developing a fur trade and a colony under the noses of his former employers. Furs certainly sounded appealing to men who knew more than a little about cold weather, and a new world colony would improve their status among the other European powers. A bonus was that Minuit was already very familiar with the territory selected–the South River.

An excerpt from a letter by Minuit to Chancellor Axel Oxenstierna in which he makes a compelling argument goes:

PART III

As navigation makes kingdoms and countries thrive and in the West-Indies (North America) many places gradually come to be occupied by the English, Dutch, and French, I think the Swedish Crown ought not to stand back and refrain from having her name spread widely, also in foreign countries; and to that end I the undersigned, wish to offer my services to the Swedish Crown to set out modestly on what might, by God's grace, become something great within a short time.
Firstly, I have suggested to Mr. Pieter Spiering to make a journey to the Virginias, New Netherland and other places, in which regions certain places are well known to me, with a very good climate which could be named Nova Sweediae...
   Your Exellency's faithful servant, Peter Minuit
   Amsterdam, 15 June 1636

A charter was now drawn up for the the New Sweden Company: *Nya Sverigekompaniet*. It was given exclusive rights to trade on the Delaware for twenty years. Fleming was made director of the company, Blommaert was commissioned to buy merchandise and trade items in Holland and Peter Minuit would be chief of the first expedition. It would seem that despite the high ideals expressed, the New Sweden Company was born as corporate revenge against the WIC as much as a Dutch-dominated joint business venture with the Swedes.

A hunt was now initiated to find ships, sailors, and potential settlers to get the venture started. The obvious dealers in vessels would be the Dutch, the most technically advanced boat builders of their day. They chose a "Pinnace" that had been built about 1625. Around 100 feet long with a displacement of 298 tons, she was designed to serve as either a small warship or an armed merchant vessel. She was equipped with twelve six-pounder cannons and two smaller swivel guns attached to the quarterdeck rails. She also carried a disassembled sloop that could be re-assembled and used for exploring the shallows. The ship was neither too small, nor too large. Just about right to carry the amount of people and goods for the first expedition. Which was the outlook of the Swedish portion of the venture, known as *lagom* (pronounced: law-gum). It can only be described as a "Goldilocks effect"—all things appropriately in the middle. The Dutch attitude was simply one of efficiency, and together they seemed to mesh.

The New Sweden Company was not the first owner of this ship, rather the cities of Kalmar and Jönköping had originally purchased her from the Dutch to augment the protection of Kalmar harbor, and gave her the name *Kalmar Nyckel* (Key of Kalmar). The Swedish Navy became the next owner for a short while, until she was finally purchased by Minuit and company in 1637. An extremely sturdy ship, she would make the Atlantic crossing four times, more than any other ship of her era.

Today, a remarkable reproduction of the *Kalmar Nyckel* sails out of her home anchorage on the Christina River in Wilmington, DE. The modern version, built in 1997, serves as a floating museum, classroom and Goodwill Ambassador: www.kalmarnyckel.org.

The Kalmar Nyckel

To accompany the pinnace, the company purchased the *Fogel Grip* (which loosely translated means Flying Griffen), another Dutch vessel. The *Fogel Grip* gets very little attention in descriptions of the first voyage, other than her name. But some sources describe her as a yacht, which if so, demands at least as much credit as the *Kalmar Nyckel*, because this type of vessel is rarely thought of as large enough to handle a trans-Atlantic voyage. But you have to consider the *Half Moon* in the same context, as Hudson's ship was not much larger, and survived an incredible coastline battering. Further proof of the Dutch boat builders' skill.

The two ships were captained by Dutch skippers: Captain Jan Hindricksen van deer Water, and Captain Adrian Jöransen respectively. Despite an extensive sea-bound coast, the Swedes never quite developed the same capacity for navigating as their Netherlands allies. Added to the fact that Swedish sailors were hard to come by at this time, about forty to fifty Dutch sailors were recruited. The expedition's personnel were rounded out by twenty-three Swedish and Finnish soldiers under the command of Captain Måns Nilssen Kling. There were also a few Germans and a Scot or two to keep things serious.

From Minuit's previous experience on the Delaware, he knew exactly what to bring in the way of supplies and trade goods, supervising the loading himself, right down to the 500 bricks purchased in Gothenburg to be used for fireplaces and chimneys. Duffel, iron axes and blades, tobacco pipes, mirrors, and gilded jewelry trade items would all be necessary for a successful start to the colony. For protection, thirty muskets and one and a half tons of gunpowder were also provided.

The expedition got under way in November of 1637 from Gothenburg and was immediately slammed by a raging North Sea storm. The two ships became separated, but eventually both limped into the Texel, an island staging area near Amsterdam. Repairs were made and the two ships put to sea again on New Year's Eve. Since it was winter, it took the ships two-and-one-half months to make the trip from Holland to the Canary Islands, then south-west across the Atlantic to the West Indies, and finally up the North American coastline.

Even though Minuit knew where he was going and what he would find there, he was given very specific instructions by Blommaert as to how to proceed in establishing the vanguard of the New Sweden colony. It consisted of thirty-two articles outlining everything from obeying the commander to the forbidding of drunkenness and playing games of chance. He was also given the option of first making landfall at Ille de Sable, approximately 100 miles southeast of Nova Scotia, weather permitting. If not already occupied by anyone of European ilk, he was to explore the possibility of making it both a stop-off for sailing vessels and a fishing station. If it should prove satisfactory, he was to take formal possession, erect a stone monument bearing the Swedish coat of arms and name it Christina Island, after the young Swedish Queen. The weather, however, did not cooperate, and he was forced to abandon the option.

The two ships then continued on to their main objective, finally entering Godyn's Bay, or South Bay, in March of 1638. After so long at sea they anchored at a spot where "The land was so grateful and agreeable to them." They thankfully named the place Paradise Point, which was not far from the site of the Zwaanendael tragedy. After a well-earned rest, they carefully proceeded up the Delaware,

The Kalmar Nyckel *and the* Fogel Grip *running before a storm upon entering what was then known as Godyn's Bay*

keeping an eye out for any sign of Dutch or English ships and shoals, to a tributary that Minuit had explored some years previously. It was called the Minquas Kill by the Dutch after the native trappers who brought furs there to trade. The ships entered the kill and sailed about two miles to an outcropping of blue gneiss rocks that formed a nearly perfect wharf for docking.

Aside from an excellent harbor, Minuit had also chosen this spot because it was slightly off the beaten track of the Delaware. It offered a nearly perfect defensive position between two rivers, was located on a major Indian trading path, and the Dutch had never legally acquired any land on the west side of the Delaware.

There was no doubt in the minds of any of the members of the New Sweden Company that they would be challenging the Dutch and their established fur trade, but it was unlikely there would be any form of retribution. Even so, Minuit sent the *Kalmar Nyckel's* sloop further up the river to make sure there were no Europeans lurking in the vicinity. When none were found, the sloop returned and fired a ceremonial two-gun salute, to signal their intent to take possession of the land. The cannon's roar also brought the Indians, which was convenient, because Minuit's next order of business was to purchase their land. Through Minuit's interpreter, Andres Lucassen, it was conveyed to the curious Indians the European's intentions. Before long, the *Kalmar Nyckel's* deck was crammed with Dutch, Swedes and five sachems.

It is unclear whether the Indians actually understood they were selling their land or just receiving gifts, or if the Europeans were communicating well enough with the Indians. Obviously, they could not read the document presented to them, which was later related in a deposition by four sailors who had returned from the expedition:

> The parties were therefore agreed with one another, and thereupon, on the twenty-ninth of March [,1638] appeared and present themselves before the above mentioned ship's council, in the name of their nations or people, five sachems or princes, by the name of Matterhorn, Mitot Schemingh (Mitasemint), Eru Packen (Elupacken), Mahamen, and Chiton…and in the presence of the whole ship's council…ceded, transported, and transferred all the land, as many day's journeys on all places and parts of the river (Minquas Kill) as they (the Swedes) requested; upwards and on both sides.

After the pomp of declaring that the agreement was made with the New Sweden Company "under the protection and patronage of the most illustrious and most mighty Princess and Virgin, Christina, (who was now all of eleven-years-old) elected Queen of the Swedes, Goths and Wends," there were likely glazed expressions on the faces of the sachems. Minuit then presented a generous array of gifts that got their full attention, relieving them from the legal tedium they had just endured. Though the European concept of ownership was alien to them, the Indians understood the purpose of the gifts, each putting their marks on a pre-prepared deed, rendered in Dutch due to the absence of a written native language. (The uncertainty of the sachems names by the Dutch interpreter provides a general air of fluidity).

They seemed further pleased, especially when everyone went ashore, erected a post with the Swedish Coat of Arms attached and made more noise with the cannons, as well as trumpets and drums. Minquas Kill was now formally changed to Elbe, after the river of the same name in Germany. Then, on second thought, it was changed to Christina Kill. The Dutch stubbornly refused to recognize the Swedish name though, and continued to refer to it as Minquas Kill for many more years, even on their maps. Nya Sverige was now a legal and binding entity.

The five Indian sachems signing the deed to the land that would become New Sweden.

✦ XIII ✦

History generally agrees that the area the Swedes had purchased (or assumed they had purchased) was roughly 67 miles of the western bank of the Delaware River, from Bombay Hook to the mouth of the Schuylkill River, and as far west as the sun set. To the Indians, it simply meant they would share the land with the oddly overdressed white men as long as the useful and exotic gifts kept coming.

Minuit set most of the men to the business of building a fort, planting crops and creating an environment suitable for long-term habitation. He then sailed the sloop north up the Delaware to do more exploring. In his previous years as an employee of the WIC, he had been partly responsible for the construction of Fort Nassau, the small trading post located some ten miles upstream on the opposite bank of the Delaware. He heard that it had been abandoned, and wanted to see if this was true. Since one of his main objectives would be trading for furs with the Indians, it could be an ideal setting if it was no longer in use by the Dutch. But it was.

On his trip upstream, Minuit passed by the outpost without being seen, but on his return was hailed by the Dutch officer in charge, demanding proof of passage. Minuit declined, claiming "his Queen" had as much right to the South River as they. A heated discussion ensued, threats were issued, and Minuit finally sailed off, convincing the Dutch that he had a larger force than they. Stymied for the time being, the Dutch commander sent word of the situation to New Amsterdam and Willem Kieft, Director-General of New Netherland–the same post previously held by Minuit.

A minor dispute between two major European powers now ensued over land neither had a legitimate claim to. Keift sent a threatening letter to Minuit explaining how the Dutch had long maintained possession of the South River, and if he continued with his plans to plant a colony and trade with the Indians, that "we shall maintain our jurisdiction in such manner as we shall deem most expedient."

Minuit ignored the letter. By the time he actually received it, construction of the Swedish fort was well under way, and an expedition was sent to develop trading relations with the Indians. The plan was to corner the market by offering more trade goods than the Dutch. It should not be too difficult—Minuit had chosen a portion of the Delaware that had only marginal use by the Dutch. It was also more convenient for the Indians. Fort Nassau was occupied just part of the year, and since Zwaandendael had failed, there were no other forts or holdings by the Dutch on the South River. Also, the two countries were friendly nations–any animosity would have to be handled diplomatically. To further solidify the position of the Swedes, the New Netherland colony was unstable since Kieft had taken the position, proving himself a poor administrator and creating a great deal of animosity toward the Indians.

Work continued on the New Sweden stronghold which Minuit called Fort Christina, now that the name would not be used at Ille de Sable. He had chosen a piece of land about two miles from the mouth of the Christina. With its stone landing and marshy surroundings, it was an easily defended position. It was also just out of reach of the Dutch, whom he wished to avoid until the colony was strong enough to stand on its own. It was here that the base of operations was placed–a typical European, bastioned, star-fort design of the times, except on a smaller scale, and constructed not of stone, but of earth and timber, the most abundant resources of the area. The Swedes and Finns would of course be quite familiar with wood working, but the lowland Dutch must have been astounded to see a land so covered in forest. Two log buildings were constructed inside palisaded walls, one as a barracks and the other as a storehouse. And this was where the imported bricks were used for fireplaces, chimneys and ovens.

Amid the fervor of construction, the two ships were sitting idle, which was

Fort Christina

"The Rocks" which Peter Minuit scouted as a prime location to situate his new colony in 1638 have been reduced over time to to widen the navigability of the Christina River. A park designed to commemorate the landing was built 300 years later and still encompasses what is left of the natural blue gneiss wharf. Archeological exploration has revealed no trace of the original fort.

detrimental since they were the most expensive components of the expedition. To have them unused at any point would be losing money, so it was decided to send the *Fogel Grip* on a trading mission since it required a smaller crew, leaving more workers at the fort. She sailed to the Jamestown colony to try and trade for tobacco, but Governor Berkeley refused them permission–he considered their colony a lawless intrusion on English territory. They returned empty-handed.

She was then sent on a double or nothing voyage to the Caribbean in an attempt to pay for the entire New Sweden expedition with one

Antoni Swart, or Black Anthony

daring maneuver. As an active privateer, she would try to capture a Spanish treasure ship. Again she failed. The only cargo she returned with was the first black man to set foot in the Delaware Valley. Called Antoni, he was acquired in the West Indies, but whether he was purchased as a slave or came of his own accord is not known. But he did live in New Sweden as a free man known as Antoni Swart, or Black Anthony, working for future governor Johan Printz as a farmer and a pilot of the governor's sloop

✦ ✦ ✦

It was now June, seven months after his departure from Gothenburg, and Minuit knew it was time to return to Sweden and report to the company officials. But with a remaining cargo of liquor and wine in the *Kalmar Nyckel,* he too set sail for the West Indies with the hopes of selling it and returning to Sweden with a cargo of tobacco. Måns Kling was placed in command of the fort and its contingent of twenty-four men, who would be responsible for keeping themselves alive and the fort running over the next winter. And of course continue trade with the Indians.

The expedition brought various types of seed and grain that included "two barrels of wheat and two barrels of barley for seed corn." Tobacco was also proposed, but apparently never made it onboard. Surprisingly, they found that the land was not a total wilderness, but was planted in areas with large fields of corn, the harvest of which the settlers were able to bargain for. They would eventually learn from the Indians how to cultivate it for themselves. The storehouse was stocked with large quantities of fish and game, and left in the charge of commissary Hendrick Huygen.

The *Kalmar Nyckel* and Peter Minuit departed the Delaware Valley and sailed to the island of Saint Kitts, (today also known as Saint Christopher) where the liquor supply was sold and a transaction for tobacco was made. After business had been conducted, Minuit was invited aboard a merchant ship from Rotterdam named the *Flying Deer* for a friendly visit with its captain, a Hollander he was undoubtedly acquainted with.

Without modern up-to-the-minute weather forecasts, seventeenth century seaman would have little advance warning of approaching storms. Which is what happened at Saint Kitts. A ferocious storm, possibly a hurricane, struck suddenly, forcing many ships to raise anchor and ride out the storm in open water, the *Flying Deer* among them. Peter Minuit never returned from his visit. Michel Symonssen, the first mate on the *Kalmar Nyckel*, waited for days for any sign of the *Flying Deer*. When at last it seemed futile to delay any longer, he sadly set sail for Gothenburg. The *Fogel Grip*, hampered by unfavorable winds, didn't return until the next year.

When the investors back in Sweden heard the news about Minuit, they were deeply saddened. They were saddened further when they tallied the cost of this first expedition against what was brought back, which consisted mostly of furs and tobacco. It was discovered that the New Sweden Company had taken a bit of a bath, spending more than it made. The Dutch officers were sorely disappointed–they expected the amount of furs to be on a par with that of the West India Company, of which it fell short. But despite their losses, the Swedes felt they were off to a promising start. Minuit had been right, furs and tobacco were better products than copper.

XIV

Back at Fort Christina, the inhabitants began to look almost immediately for the return of the next expedition, but they would have to wait a long time–nearly two years. There were, of course, complications. The Dutch investors refused to put up any more capital which put a burden on the Swedes, but Admiral Fleming clung tightly to the vision of New Sweden, even planning the next expedition before learning of Minuit's untimely death. He wanted families of settlers–farmers, craftsmen, carpenters, and the like to form a robust colony. The problem was that none of those types of people were willing to go, much like the same dilemma the Dutch had encountered. The Swedes were quite comfortable right where they were. Consequently, volunteers had to be coerced–a number of whom were army deserters, petty criminals, even adulterers, who were presented with the option of prison–or the New World. They were also given clothes, a pitiable amount of copper money, and a sentence of one or two years of servitude in New Sweden. It's not certain how many of these miscreants actually made the trip. For a subsequent voyage in 1643, the agents of the expedition where shocked to learn that a carpenter employed by the government actually volunteered his services to New Sweden. There was also the difficult problem of replacing Minuit, the man who knew more of the Delaware River Valley than any other, except for the Indians.

After returning to Sweden, the *Fogel Grip* foundered during a storm in August of 1639 and could not be salvaged. Since funds were not available for another ship, it was up to the *Kalmar Nyckel* to once again haul the next group of reluctant immigrants across the Atlantic. Setting sail in early September of 1639, the overburdened ship began leaking almost immediately. She put into north Holland for repairs, and sailed again. Then there were storms, then more repairs. Finally on February 7, 1640, she left Holland, bound for the Delaware Bay.

Onboard was a new skipper, Captain Poewel Jansen (needless to say a Dutchman), Joost van Langdonk as commissary, and Gregorius van Dyck as his assistant, who were also Dutchman. The new commander-director-governor was Lieutenant Peter Hollander Ridder. Unlike his predecessor Peter Minuit, or the yet to be introduced Johan Printz, we know precious little about Ridder, other than that his father was of Dutch ancestry and emigrated to Finland, and that his son served in the Swedish Navy. And once again, most of the sailors were Dutch. Other than the immigrants, there were only a few Swedish soldiers and a Lutheran minister, Reverend Reorus Torkillus, the first chaplain bound for New Sweden. The exact amount of colonists onboard is not known, possibly fifty at most, but it is almost a certainty that women and children were on this second voyage.

A few horses were brought as well, but there was still no milk or meat producing animals in the colony. By all accounts, it was a rough trip, not only because of miserable mid-winter weather, but discipline was lax, drunkenness ruled, and the Calvinist skipper and crew despised the Lutheran Torkillus, harassing him on a daily basis. Many were frequently sick, either from the rolling ship, or hangovers. Much to everyone's relief, they dropped anchor at Fort Christina on April 17, 1640.

Among the colonists was a young Swede named Peter Gunnerson who possessed an adventurous spirit and not much else. He would soon find himself in the backbreaking position of a field worker for which he received 10 guilders per month, a portion of which he would send home to his father in the Hisingen region of Sweden. Along with a new life, the 28-year-old laborer took a new name—he would now be Peter Gunnerson Rambo. To avoid the confusion of having to distinguish any of his future offspring from many others named "Peterson", he added the new surname "Ram" meaning raven and "bo" referring to "fortified dwelling", or "nest", all gleaned from Ramberget mountain near his native village. Although his position in a new and frightening land was humble and inauspicious, there would be far better days ahead for the young man.

✦ ✦ ✦

NOT ONLY WERE the new recruits to New Sweden happy to have survived the crossing, but those who had been left literally "holding the fort" were ecstatic to once again see the familiar profile of the *Kalmar Nyckel*. During the long absence the men had managed to not only survive, but kept up trade with the Indians. Måns Kling had taken the sloop upriver and acquired an impressive amount of beaver pelts from both the Lenape and Minquas, not an easy task since they had been at war with each other since before the Swedes arrived. Kling was able to dip into a generous inventory of trade goods, which helped quell the disagreements between the tribes, but also lured them away from the Dutch traders. Governor Kieft in New Amsterdam fumed about the competition in a letter to the directors of the WIC, claiming their fur trade was "entirely ruined by the Swedes." It was an exaggeration of course, but the Swedes were indeed stealing some of their business. But there was not much Kieft could do about it. He lacked a strong enough force on the South River to threaten Fort Christina, nor would his superiors have approved of any action—Sweden was far too powerful to lock horns with.

Ridder found that though Kling and company were successful at fur trading, they had not done as well in maintaining the fort, or creating a self-sustaining environment. They were completely inept as farmers, and had to rely on hunting, fishing and buying food from the Indians. The new colonists were not much better.

Along with their agricultural incompetence, their construction skills were lacking as well. The new governor complained that none of them could build the simplest of houses or even saw a piece of wood. He wrote back home asking for qualified workmen and expressing frustration over the men he did have that "it would be impossible to find more stupid people in all Sweden." This may have been a bit of administrative bluster, as Ridder was able to guide them in the construction of three more log houses, a new storehouse and a stable for the horses, and moving the two original cabins in the fort to different locations. He also requested barrels of tar, glass windows, hemp, salt, brandy, provisions for a year, and a lengthy list of grains to be used for seed. He also continued to maintain  Minuit's good relationship with the Indians, and through Huygen's bargaining skills, the Kalmar Nyckel was loaded with furs for her second return trip to Sweden.

Despite the improvements, Ridder's experience led him to believe that Fort Christina was too far from the South River to be effective militarily, but he lacked the authority and funds to build another fort in a more advantageous location–and then there was the scarcity of good construction workers. He decided instead to extend the territory of New Sweden. Coincidentally, the commissary Van Langdonk brought instructions from Sweden that more land was to be purchased. Ridder closed the deal himself. Using trade goods with which he was still well-stocked, he purchased land on the west bank of the South River, from the Schuylkill to Sankikan, which was the region of "the falles" at Trenton, "about 36 or 40 miles above Fort Nassau."

The Dutch commandant at Fort Nassau continued to send threats to the Swedish interlopers, especially after Ridder made a couple of inspection trips upriver in the sloop, still complaining that the entire river belonged to the WIC. But like his predecessor, Minuit, Ridder ignored the protests. His strict orders were to stay on peaceful terms with the Dutch, which he could best accomplish by doing nothing.

Outside the walls of Fort Christina, things were progressing, but on the inside, not so much. Ridder proved to be a poor disciplinarian, unable to quell the simplest dispute between colonists, and van Langdonk didn't get along with either the governor or the Swedes.

This tense relationship continued until the spring of 1641 when a mutual threat to both the Dutch and Swedes emerged. The English had decided to crash the party, which we'll delve into in Part IV.

✦ INTERMISSION ✦

It is now time to step back and try to sort this all out. The Dutch create the New Netherland colony on land claimed by the English. The English object but do nothing. The Swedes start their own colony within the territory now claimed by the Dutch. The Dutch object but do nothing. The Native People can only try and make sense of it all.

The map on the following page is intended to give some visual clarity to the colonial mash-up that was the 17th century North Atlantic seaboard.

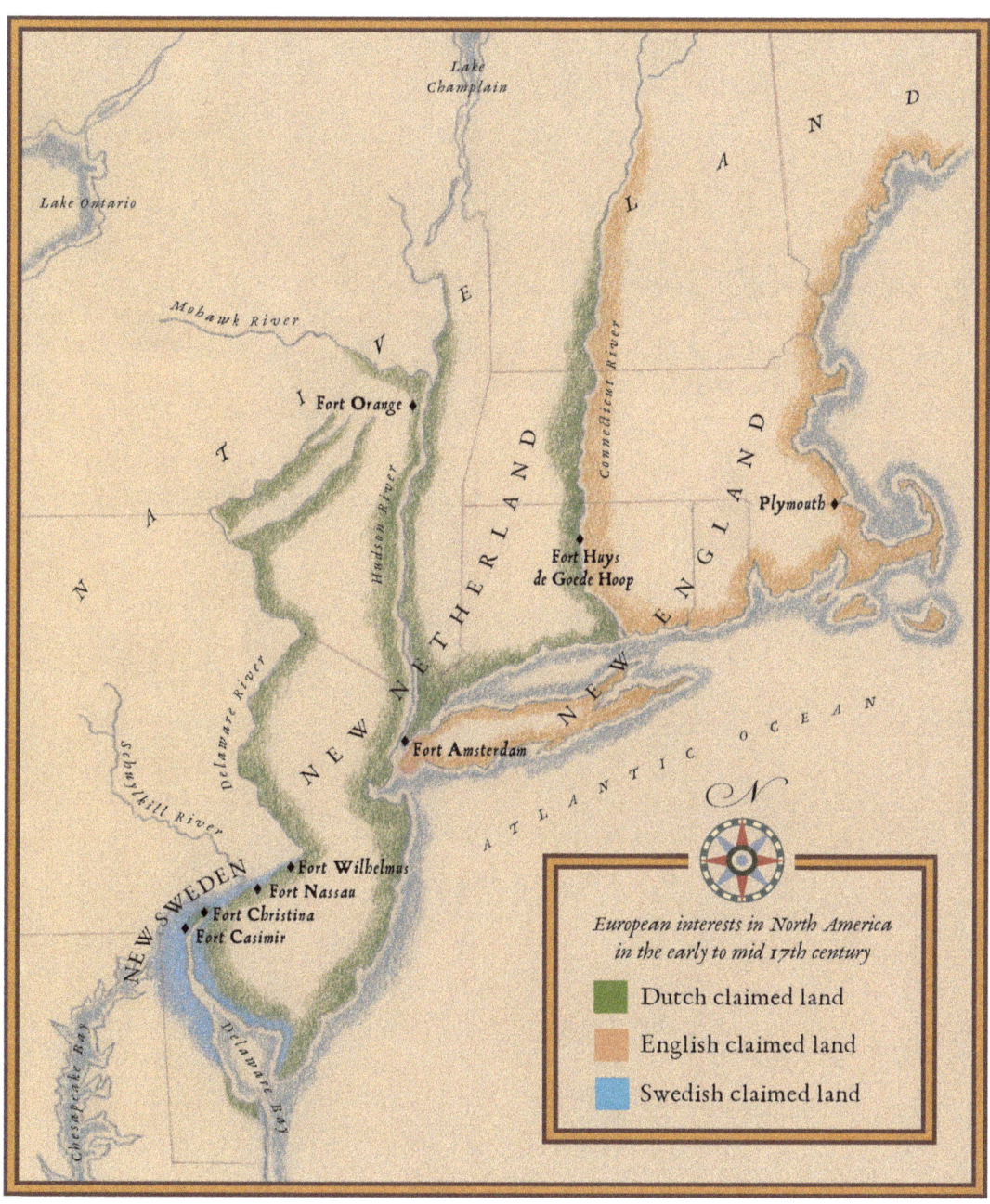

The boundaries shown here are approximate, because the claimants were not sure of the limits themselves. Also because they were almost constantly in flux, especially New Sweden and New Netherland. Note how the settlement of the colonies follow the courses of the rivers, and not modern state boundaries which are included for reference.

The Silver Ship

Back in the Netherlands, conditions were deteriorating for farmers, particularly in Utrecht. Harvests had been poor, but taxes were increasing. The prospect of free land and few taxes in New Netherland sounded very appealing. Though the West India Company had been recruiting prospective colonists, the conditions were not favorable in the late 1630s to finance their relocation, so the farmers turned instead to the Swedes. Surely they would be happy to have fresh faces on the Delaware. But the Swedes were wary of more Dutch involvement. However, some smooth talking and a persuasive presentation by one Joost van den Bogaert was able to convince the original trio of Blommaert, Spiring, and Oxenstierna to grant a charter for a Dutch colony. The colony would not meld with the Fort Christina community, but be placed about twenty miles above the fort, also on the west side of the Delaware, and there be given all the rights and privileges of their Swedish neighbors, provided the land they acquired would be improved within ten years.

The ship *Freedenburgh* was commissioned and departed Holland in late July or August of 1640, carrying about fifty passengers, and landed in New Sweden in November. And no sooner do the Hollanders arrive than their trail starts to go cold. It does appear that they built some dwellings, but whether it was at the intended location or elsewhere is not known. Within two years they had simply vanished. After 1642, nothing else was heard from them.

Dan Cashin, who spent 50 years working at the Philadelphia Navy Yard, and grew up on the Schuykill, recalls hearing tales from some old-timers about a Dutch ship that sank in the river near Bartram's Gardens. Nothing unusual about that, boats tend to sink from time to time but…supposedly this ship was loaded with silver. Dan speculates that the cargo may have been part of the Spanish silver fleet taken in 1628, and that a rogue crew might have siphoned off some of the treasure and spirited it away, looking for an appropriate place to hide the loot. These were privateers after all, just pirates once removed. Could it be they were trying to get to Fort Nassau, across the river from the mouth of the Schuylkill, or perhaps Burlington Island? Or maybe they were trying to find the Utrecht colony. And if they did, maybe that's what happened to the colony itself–nouveau riche Dutchmen heading back to the Netherlands to live like royalty, or perhaps quietly filtering north into the Catskills creating new personas as country gentleman. Maybe the silver-bearing ship was sunk intentionally, to be retrieved at some later date. The mind boggles.

It's not such a far-fetched tale as might be imagined: In 1643, the Dutch at "Manathans" captured several Spanish prizes. Inspired, Governor Printz ambitiously reasoned that perhaps New Sweden should have their own well-armed ship to prey on Spanish silver fleets as well.

✦ XV ✦

On November 7, 1641, the *Kalmar Nyckel* returned to The Rocks at Fort Christina after her third trip across the Atlantic. She was accompanied by the Charitas (Charity), a merchant ship with limited weaponry that was designed to carry large cargoes. Offloaded were horses, cows, sheep…and Finns.

The colony still needed, well…colonists, and now more than ever because by this time the Dutch could see little chance to recoup their investments. It was clear to the WIC that the Swedes were causing a decline in their business and convinced the Dutch New Sweden investors that their continued involvement was almost treasonous. They sold their interests to the Swedes. There would be no more Dutch involvement.

Although Finland had been part of the Swedish kingdom for hundreds of years, its people had far different ethnic roots than the Swedes. They were looked upon as mavericks–an independent people occasionally suspected of dealing in the black arts. Stories were told of how they could harness the wind: three knots were tied in a string–when one was untied, a strong breeze would blow–a second would bring a gale…and the third would unleash a hurricane.

To clear land for farming, these "Forest Finns", as they would become known, would burn down stands of forests using the slash-and-burn tactic still deployed in some countries today. The technique was originally encouraged by Swedish monarch Charles IX in order to establish homesteads in the sparsely populated interior regions of Finland, thus creating new tax revenue opportunities. The Finns were only too happy to oblige. But they managed to overdo it, destroying the fuel source used for neighboring mining and smelting industries. Restrictions were then placed on slash-and-burn, which required a lot of man power, creating an unemployed force of "stray Finns." Complaints arose over these out-of-work foresters who turned to poaching–living off land that was not their own and hunting elk for their hides, leaving the carcasses to rot. Many of the Finns also defected to remote parts of Sweden to escape conscription in the Swedish army and were now considered criminals. Since Swedes were still unwilling to immigrant to the New World, the Finns were considered excellent alternatives. They could burn all the forests they wanted to in America, and kill all the elk they desired. Many were rounded up and given the choice of immigration or confinement.

The New World seemed much like the Old World to the Finns. The heavily forested wilderness they were banished to even seemed to be home to the same types of fish and animals. They brought with them their reputations as fiercely independent outcasts as well, though many spoke Swedish and had lived in Sweden. Yielding to tribal instincts, they settled a bit to the north of the colony center at Fort Christina, creating their own community which became known, not surprisingly, as Finland. They were defined by neighboring northern Europeans more as a species than as an ethnic grouping, identified as: Askell the Finn, Karin "the Finnish woman", Anders the Finn, and in one case, a true criminal—that "miscreant, Iver the Fin."

A convicted offender, Iver—or Evert, or Ivert—Hindricksson, arrived on the third voyage of the *Kalmar Nyckel* along with his reputation as a "turbulent man." In just a short time after his arrival, the reputation was confirmed. While working as a farmhand, he was accused of violent assault with sticks, knives and an ax. He threatened to murder another immigrant, stoned a canoeist, committed bigamy, and was accused of having an illicit affair with the wife of another Finn. His behavior led to banishment from the community. He slowly made his way

Called a "granary", this log structure is typical of a type built by Finns, used to store grain and house animals.

back into the bosom of the colony, only to become involved later on in rebellious behavior against the administration of New Sweden.

Despite their crude method of forest clearing, the Finns were exceptionally talented wood-workers, especially adept in the construction of log houses. It has been said of them that "every Finn is a carpenter." Their reputation as log cabin builders spread though America over the years, their styles copied by many settlers. It became almost a status symbol for those who had achieved success (particularly politicians) to wax fondly over tales of a hardscrabble childhood spent in one of these humble dwellings.

With the arrival of these new settlers, the colony slowly began to gain modest footing. New homes were built, crops were planted and harvested, and the first windmill in the Delaware Valley was constructed for grinding grain into flour. And now, the colony was also about to experience something big—very big.

✦ ✦ ✦

THE ROCKS ON THE Christina River had seen familiar ships come and go in the past five years, but now on February 15, 1643, two new ones appeared. The *Fama* and *Svanen* (Swan) drifted close and crewmen jumped out to make them fast. A trumpet sounded, a drumroll began, and off of the Fama strode the largest white man yet seen in the Delaware River Valley. Lieutenant Colonel Johan Björnsson Printz had landed. He would be the next governor of New Sweden. Its first Swedish-born leader, the fifty-year-old Printz would rule over the colony for the next ten years.

It had taken three and a half months for Printz to actually make it to Fort Christina. The two ships left Gothenburg on the 1st of November, 1642, and finally arrived at the island of Antiqua in the Caribbean in late December. While the company recovered from the first leg of their journey, Printz and his administrative staff celebrated Christmas with the English governor of the island. They left the warm, inviting southern climes with oranges and lemons stuffed into every available corner of the ships, and sailed into the brutal January weather of the northeast Atlantic seaboard. Approaching the mouth of the South Bay, the two ships encountered a vicious, but typical nor'easter. The *Fama* ran ashore, lost her main mast, sprit sail, and three anchors, while the *Svanen* fared slightly better, suffering minor damage and the loss of precious supplies. After two weeks' worth of repairs, the ships finally sailed up-river and landed at "the Rocks."

First impressions are not to be taken lightly, and the initial view of Johan Printz left few with a loss of superlatives. David de Vries, the famed Dutch navigator described him as "a man of brave size, who weighed over four hundred pounds". The Indians, upon first sight of this man mountain, immediately dubbed him "Big Belly". Europeans referred to him as "Round John" behind his back. Along with his size, Printz brought with him a swagger that had not been seen before in the

PART III

colony. He also brought most of his family: wife, son, and five daughters.

Raised to be a clergyman like his father, and his father before him, Printz's early life took an unusual turn when he was pressed into the German army while in that country pursuing theological studies. Rather than reject his fate, he embraced it, becoming a career military man, first serving the Kaiser, then working for the Danish army, and finally enlisting back home in the Swedish army. His assignment would be with the West Gotha cavalry, whose horses must have been visibly shaken upon seeing him enter the stables.

During the Thirty Years War, Printz, as the commanding officer of the fortress and town of Chemnitz, Germany, was forced to surrender to a superior force. He returned to Sweden where he was promptly arrested—not for capitulating, but for leaving without permission. Court-martialed, stripped of his rank and privileges, Printz found himself outside the embrace of the military. Things appeared grim for the big man, especially when his wife, whom he had left behind in Germany, died in 1640.

Not one to succumb to adversity, he settled in Finland, working himself back into the good graces of the Swedish government as a recruiting agent for craftsmen and workers to be sent to America. As a reward, he was knighted and presented with the governorship of New Sweden. There has been speculation that the position may have been one of glorified exile in an effort to remove a troublesome individual to a remote location, where his overwhelming character might actually be put to good use. Further speculation is fed by evidence that he was given an exhaustive set of very specific instructions, signed off on by Queen Christina, which he carried to the New World, leaving very little room for error.

✦ ✦ ✦

RIDDER'S COMMAND was now at an end, coinciding with the termination of Dutch involvement. Printz took over immediately to administer his instructions, which would consist of growing tobacco, increasing domestic animal production, cultivating grapes, creating a salt works, searching for mining opportunities, cutting timber for export, establishing fisheries and the rather ambitious scheme of raising silk worms. He was also to maintain good relations with the Dutch, the small band of English on Varken's Kill (whom we will soon meet), and treat the Indians with kindness and respect…and to instruct them in the ways of Christianity. This may have been the most difficult of his assignments. It plagued him to no end that such a beautiful land "should not be settled by real Christians, but by these wild Indians." He needed to maintain a healthy relationship with the Indians if he was to keep the fur trade intact. But he often became exasperated at their unreliability, at one point threatening to kill all the elders, forcing the rest to bend to his wishes.

In addition to the citrus fruits picked up in the West Indies, the Printz expedition brought an extensive variety of supplies form Gothenburg: wine, malt, grain, nets, muskets, shoes and other clothing, and stationary. Horses, cattle, sheep and possibly chickens along with their feed, were loaded on as well. Building materials–bricks, mortar, and window glass, and heavy artillery, whose use would soon become clear, were stowed onboard. Immigrants were still difficult to recruit so a few more criminals were rounded up to work off their sentences on the Delaware. And since this was now a totally Swedish campaign, Dutch soldiers would be replaced with Swedes. Still, the manifest was disappointingly meager; less than one hundred men, women, and children.

Printz immediately drew up a request for more colonists to be sent back to Stockholm on the *Fama*. But Sweden had far bigger problems to consider than the little community across the Atlantic, chirping like baby birds demanding worms. A new war had broken out with Denmark, requiring immediate attention. The Swedish navy could spare no ships for transporting colonists–the Fama, along with the *Kalmar Nyckel*, were requisitioned for the latest campaign. A further and even more serious setback to New Sweden's existence occurred when its director, Admiral Clas Fleming, was killed by a Danish bullet. Chancellor Oxenstierna took over his position, but with the immense responsibility of ruling an empire, and directing a war, the care and feeding of New Sweden was moved to the bottom of the to-do list. There is speculation that the entire New Sweden project may have actually died along with Fleming.

Just south of today's Philadelphia International Airport lies Tinicum Island. It is an island no more, and never really one to begin with, having separation from the mainland by only a stream. It was originally called Matinicum, and this was where Governor Printz decided to relocate the capital of New Sweden. For a variety of reasons Fort Christina didn't suit his needs, probably because he wanted something more refined for his predominately female family. He called his new governor's home Printzhoff, or Printz Hall. A two-story affair, it was an unusually grand dwelling, especially for a colonial setting. It was extravagantly furnished with imported bricks and tiles, plank flooring and something else that was nearly unheard of–windows made of glass brought from Sweden. How they survived an Atlantic crossing, and all its hazards, is almost beyond belief. It was the finest house in the New World between Virginia and Manhattan Island.

But before pleasure came business. Printz, along with Ridder, some soldiers and an Indian guide toured the whole river from Cape Henlopen all the way to Sankikan taking note of what areas looked promising for farms–and the defense of Nya Sverige. Printz concurred with Ridder about Fort Christina being too far from the traffic of the Delaware and found what appeared to be an ideal location near the

Varken's Kill (Salem River). Even better, the Swedes already owned the land. From this vantage point, he could have complete control of the river.

Construction soon began on a triangular fortification of earth, wood and stone, armed at the three angles with four iron and four brass twelve-pounders and a mortar. It was named Fort Nya Alfsbörg, (New Alfsbörg) to commemorate the fortress that stood watch over the harbor of Gothenburg, Sweden. More commonly known as Fort Elfsborg, it was manned by thirteen soldiers under the command of Lieutenant Sven Skute, with Gregorius van Dyck as head guard. Situated on swampy ground at the river's edge, the inhabitants soon came to despise their station. The mosquito population was so vast that the men were tortured night and day by overwhelming hordes of bloodthirsty creatures. Swedish engineer Peter Lindeström wrote: "From the continued stinging and sucking of the mosquitos the people were so swollen, that they appeared as if they had been affected with some horrible disease." Understandably, the men re-named it "Fort Myggenborgh" (Fort Mosquito).

Printz used the presence of the fort not only as a defense mechanism, but as a symbol of his self-imposed mastery of the river. With it he would bully visiting trading vessels, in particular those of the Dutch. Northbound ships would be forced to strike their flags, pay a toll, and then send an official to get Printz's approval before being permitted to sail up-river. An English ship learned a hard lesson by ignoring Printz's authority. Trying to avoid the toll, the ship intended to keep on course until the fort fired a warning shot across their bows. Forced to submit, she grudgingly paid the tribute, to which Printz additionally attached the cost of the shot.

To further bolster the defenses of New Sweden, another fortification was built on Tinicum. This also paid tribute to Gothenburg–Fort New Gothenburg. Built of large hemlock logs laid horizontally, it was not quite as heavily armed as Elfsborg, using only four small copper cannons. Together with Printzhoff, this stronghold would now become the seat of government for New Sweden. And just south of Tinicum an additional defensive position was constructed, this one a blockhouse. The neighborhood was dubbed Upland by the few settlers given some land there, in remembrance of their home in Sweden.

Meanwhile, Fort Christina, the original outpost, had become somewhat decayed. It was given a makeover and assigned as the principal storehouse for the colony. It also housed the blacksmith and the barber-surgeon. Printz thought very little of the wind powered gristmill that Ridder had built, so a location was scouted north of New Gothenburg, on what is now known as Cobb's Creek, which the Swedes dubbed Mölndal. There, a water-powered mill was built and a blockhouse to protect it. It was the first of its kind in the colony.

Yet another blockhouse called Nya Vasa was constructed a little further south where an enclave of young "freemen" bachelors had settled, among them our young friend Peter Gunnerson Rambo. Known to the Indians as Kingsessing, it was close to the Minquas trail that led to the Conestoga and Susquehanna Rivers, from where the source of the beaver trade sprang. (Remarkably, parts of this trail still exist where it crosses Ridley Creek in Rose Valley, PA.)

And one more blockhouse called New Korsholm (Cross Island) was situated on a small island, located just west of the mouth of the Schuykill, surrounded by a palisade. This all may seem like defensive overkill, but to the colonists you just couldn't have enough protection to survive in this wild and lawless land.

With the safety of the colony reasonably secured, the business of self-sustainability came front and center. The sound of axes and adzes rang through the countryside as habitats were constructed, land was cleared, and crops were planted. And one of Printz's main goals was initiated—the continuation of business with the Indians. It would be an erratic relationship. When New Sweden was flush with trade goods, the Indians would happily exchange plenty of furs, but when the supplies ran low, they would turn to their old reliable customers–the Dutch and English. The Swedes would then have to wait, often for long periods of time, for fresh supplies to reestablish their relationships with the natives. This was clearly a task

Nicotiana Tabacum

Printz did not relish, but his orders were emphatic—stay on friendly terms with the natives. By following this simple plan, the Swedes managed to avoid the tragic consequences that occurred in New Netherland.

After successful attacks on the English and Dutch settlements in 1644, the normally peaceful local tribes began to feel empowered and grew arrogant. Printz, sensing trouble brewing locally, let it be known that ships would soon be arriving with many more settlers. When only one ship arrived with just a few Swedes, the Indians, feeling they had been deceived, killed five colonists. Printz then began retaliatory preparations, causing great alarm through the Indian villages. They approached the governor claiming the killings were beyond their knowledge, asking for a peace settlement. Peace was indeed granted but with the Printz stipulation "that if they after this would commit the least offense against our people, then we would not let a soul of them live."

Aside from this minor detour, Printz followed his orders. But he simply did not trust them, even recommending at one point that 200 soldiers should be sent from

Sweden with the sole purpose of exterminating all the natives in the territory. Despite Printz's scorched earth attitude, there were relatively few incidents of violence.

The growing of tobacco was another project that would continue for some time with the intention of turning it into a cash crop for export. Two main plantations were sowed and maintained. But it was indeed a project, and would never really become successful. In the meantime, it was purchased from the neighboring Europeans, and shipped back to Sweden for re-sale.

✦ ✦ ✦

THE SWEDES HAD COME with a variety of objectives intended to benefit the mother country, but the pursuit of precious metals was not high on the list. If they were aware of the legendary El Dorado, gold fever doesn't seem to have taken hold. However, there were incidents that could have spiked it.

Peter Lindeström, a Swedish military engineer whom we'll encounter later, told the tale of a mountain far up the South River that the Indians called Meckansio. He reported that the river banks were "covered with firestones. They are quite round, and when you strike them, you find kernels inside, like small peas, both large and small, of pure silver, and I have done this several hundred times."

On another occasion, a "savage" noticed Governor Printz's wife wearing a gold ring and remarked that it was sad that a woman of her position to be wearing such "trash." When asked why he considered the item to be of such low value, he remarked "We have a whole mountain of such metal at home." Intrigued, Printz offered the man red and blue cloth, lead, gunpowder, mirrors, sewing needles, and an awl if he would reveal the location of this fabulous mountain. He cleverly dodged the request, but returned some time later with a large chunk of gold bearing ore, the "size of two fists." Printz made good on the reward, but still wanted to know where the mountain was. This time the Indian said he didn't have time to show him, but that he would be back. The man returned to his tribe, displaying his treasures, and bragging of how he got them, which soon caught the attention of his chief. The man was promptly killed as a precaution, lest the location of the gold mountain be revealed. Which of course begs the question: if the Indians thought so little of gold, why would they murder one of their own to keep the horde a secret? Needless to say, the mountain of gold was never found. And that is where the incident ends, as mysteriously as it began.

✦ ✦ ✦

LIFE ALWAYS HAS ITS ups and downs, and so did Nya Sverige. One of the downs occurred shortly before the Christmas holidays of 1645 when Sven Vass, a gunner at New Gothenburg, was on guard duty and fell asleep. He left a candle burning which set the fort ablaze. Alarms were sounded, everyone ran to save what precious property they could, but the fire quickly roared out of control. The powder supply exploded, spreading the fire even more, and soon, Printzhoff was also engulfed in flames. By dawn of the next day, all that remained was a barn. The governor and his family had lost everything. Not surprisingly, Vass was sent back to Sweden and thrown into prison–for how long is not known.

The residents of Tinicum suffered through a cold, miserable winter, but with the coming of warmer weather, construction began and eventually everything was rebuilt. Despite such setbacks, the colony persevered. Printz detractors would have to admit he was an industrious, resourceful administrator. But they would also have reason to doubt his integrity. True enough, it was necessary to rebuild Printzhoff and the fort, but the work was done at the expense of the farmers who were disrupted from planting season, and other workers who had to postpone the thousand tasks that needed doing. And most of the work was done for free, in lieu of their taxes, owed the governor. Accusations were also leveled at Printz for possibly keeping profits from the beaver trade for himself. Through skillful financial manipulation, legal or otherwise, it seems Printz was able to profit handsomely from his Tinicum Island estate. It was a preview of things to come.

During this era of defensive enhancements and expansion, small farms and primitive homesteads slowly spread along the banks of the Delaware. Marriages took place, despite the scarcity of eligible females, and families begun. One of the unions was between Printz's daughter Armegot and Lieutenant Johan Papegoja, commandant of Fort Christina, who would eventually become Printz's successor. Young Mr. Rambo ended his bachelorhood as well, when he married Britta Mattsdotter from Vasa, Finland. It's thought she may have been a servant in Lt. Mans Kling's household.

Still, the colony was severely underpopulated. There were occasional visits from the Mother land, but by 1647 there were still only 183 persons in all of New Sweden. A number of the soldiers began grumbling about returning home, as well as their servants, the poachers and deserters who had served their time. Printz would continually send requests to Sweden for supplies, but most of all, more colonists.

The Dutch had even fewer people on the Delaware and continually howled over the Swedish incursions on their territory. But Governor Kieft settled down when he realized that Swedish enforcements could actually deter intrusions by the English, who were bearing down on New Netherland. All was calm for a time until Jan Jansen van Ilpendam, the commander of Fort Nassau, who was actually on civil terms with Printz, was removed. His replacement, Andreas Hudde, proved to be a far more aggressive adversary. Kieft ordered Hudde to buy land on the west side of the Delaware, north of the Schuykill in an area known as Passyunk, to once again put the Dutch in the top position to trade with the Minquas. This was the same land purchased by Arent Corssen in 1633. It was also the same land purchased by Peter Hollander Ridder in 1640. Printz retaliated, having his commissary tear down the newly erected marker claiming Dutch possession. Hudde then fired off a letter of protest to be personally delivered to the Printzhoff by an envoy consisting of one A. Boyer and two soldiers. Upon receipt of the letter, the hefty Swedish governor threw it to the ground and bellowed "There, take care of that", to a nearby underling, then continued speaking to an English visitor. When the envoy asked for a reply, Printz grabbed a nearby firearm and turned to shoot, at which point the Dutch contingent were quickly shown the door, luckily escaping intact.

XVI

Governor Kieft eventually proved himself ineffectual in recovering the once dominant Dutch fur trade on the Delaware. He was over his head in relationships with the Indians on Manhattan as well. A good deal of unnecessary blood was being spilled, and as a result, Kieft was recalled by the West India Company. He never made it back to his homeland, however. The ship he sailed on was wrecked, and Willem Kieft was drowned.

His replacement was a man cut from a similar cloth as Printz—Peter Stuyvesant—a career military man, raised in a deeply religious family, his father also a minister. His association with the WIC began ten years into his career as a supervisor for the Dutch holdings in Brazil. After later being promoted to Governor of Curaçao and the adjacent Leeward Islands, he was involved in a battle on St. Martin where he lost one of his legs in a race with a Spanish cannon ball. Forever after, people would be attuned to his presence by the sound of his silver-banded wooden leg. Although history gives us the distorted picture of a crotchety old pirate with a peg-leg, he was still a relatively young man of about thirty-six when he was appointed governor of New Netherland. Stuyvesant was as dedicated to his job as Printz was to his, but more highly principled. Printz allowed self-interests to corrupt his administration. But the two men had other similarities: both could be ill-tempered, blustery and unwilling to compromise.

Right from the start of his administration, Stuyvesant stepped into a colonial crossfire of bickering. It would soon came to a head. Hudde ordered a fortification built on the newly acquired land by the Schuykill. It would be called Fort Beversreede, (Beaver Road). A number of Dutch colonists from New Amsterdam were brought in to begin construction on homes nearby. Swedes arrived and pulled down the homes, burnt the timbers, and tore down part of the palisades of the fort. The Dutch rebuilt. The Swedes tore them down again. The Dutch rebuilt some more. Then the Swedes built a blockhouse directly in front of the Dutch fort, nearly touching it, and blocking the fort from the view of passing ships on the river. But remarkably, through all of this, no blood was spilled, not even when yet another delegation was sent to the Printzhoff to complain, and Printz kept them waiting outside in the rain. When finally Commissioner Hudde stated his case that the Dutch were the earliest settlers on the river, even before the Swedes arrived, the Governor shot back "the devil was the oldest proprietor of Hell, yet sometimes admitted a younger one."

By 1651, the New Sweden colony was spread out along the west bank of the Delaware from Fort Christina on the Minquas Kill, to Tinnecum, the seat of the governorship, to the fortifications on the Schuykill, with a few homesteads and plantations dotting the landscape in between. There was also Fort Elfsborg on the east bank, but the population of the entire colony had dwindled to between 80 and 90 settlers. Despite the sparsity of the Swedes, the Dutch tried repeatedly, but could maintain no more than a weak toehold on the South River.

Peter Stuyvesant had his hands full. Not only were the Swedes blatantly stealing from the Dutch & Indian trade on New Netherland's southern border, but the rapidly growing English colonies posed a constant threat of encroachment to its north. Something needed to be done. So he personally traveled to Hartford, in

The Swedish defenders had no answer for the mighty dutch flotilla sailing right past their noses.

the Connecticut colony, to negotiate a treaty with its governor, Edward Hopkins. Stuyvesant gave up Dutch claims along the full length of the Connecticut River in order to secure a boundary on Long Island. It made New Netherland even smaller, but now eased the pressure on Stuyvesant enough for him to turn his attention to the Swedish pests on the South River.

It was time for him to test the waters…literally. He sent a well-armed and well-manned Dutch ship up the Delaware to anchor several miles below Fort Christina, blocking the river in a menacing manner. Printz retaliated by sending his yacht filled with cannon, ammunition and thirty men to challenge the intrusion. The Dutch ship then weighed anchor and quietly left. Stuyvesant now knew he would have to make a serious statement to gain control of the Delaware. With over one hundred soldiers accompanying him, Stuyvesant himself marched overland from Manhattan, following an old Indian trail, while a flotilla of eleven Dutch ships made their way up the Delaware to rendezvous at Fort Nassau. They sailed past Fort Elfsborg with drums beating and colors flying in an impressive show of military might, the largest ever seen on the Delaware. The few frightened Swedes on guard did not dare to fire a shot. The ships continued north past the mouth of the Christina River, again encountering no resistance despite the presence of Fort Christina within earshot of the menacing Dutch fleet. It was obvious from this great show of intimidation that the Dutch could have put an end to the New Sweden colony right then and there, but it was Stuyvesant's intention to avoid an international incident. He had other plans. Once all the Dutch forces met at Fort Nassau, the installation was dismantled and all usable materials and weaponry were loaded onto the vessels. The same was done to Fort Beversreede.

XVII

About five miles below Fort Christina was a prominent point of land on the South River that earlier Dutch explorers had named Sant Hoeck (Sand Point). It had a deep harbor and access to the Indian trade routes that ran to the west. It was Stuyvesant's intention to build a citadel here and establish a major Dutch military and trading facility, along with a town to accommodate the fort. It was to this spot that the Dutch fleet sailed back downriver, once again making all the noise they could, creating a massive show of strength for the benefit of their Swedish adversaries and the Indians as well.

Work began on the new fortress, to be named Fort Casimir, referring to Ernst Casimir of Orange-Nassau, a boyhood hero from Stuyvesant's native province of Friesland. Using a labor force of about 200 men, the fort began to take shape. It would be much like Fort Christina, making use of the same available building materials. Approximately 160 square feet, it would be armed at the corners with twelve guns. Inside the walls would be a barracks and storehouses. Homes were to be built in the shadow of the fort for families transferred from Fort Nassau and others to arrive from New Amsterdam. Stuyvesant remained to supervise until the fort was completed, then returned to Manhattan, leaving Gerrit Bicker as commander, and Andreas Hudde as commissary. With one maneuver, he had effectively out-flanked the Swedes and taken complete control of the Delaware.

Johan Printz watched the Dutch invasion, but was powerless to respond, other than sending a feeble protest claiming ownership of the property. He would now have to do his best to keep his crumbling colony going and pray that people and supplies would somehow arrive. He gave up New Korsholm and the mill and the blockhouse on the Schuykill in order to consolidate his resources. Fort Elfsborg had to be abandoned as well. It was not only rendered useless by Fort Casimir, but also because the men were literally driven out by the mosquitoes.

Still, there was no support from home. He sent Sven Skute, Johan Papegoja, and even his son Gustaf back to Sweden to beg for assistance for the colony, but they returned empty-handed. Printz soon had other problems as well. The Swedish colonists voiced open discontent in the form of an eleven point grievance, signed by twenty-two of the settlers, including the by now experienced pioneer, Peter Rambo, and the aforementioned "miscreant, Iver the Fin." They accused Printz of forbidding trade with basically anyone, while he was free to engage in whatever commercial trade he wished, mostly fur and tobacco. Fishing rights, seed, the timber in the forests, planting—were all denied them. According to their petition, Printz had actually become such a tyrant that he claimed everything they owned was his property. Printz was angered far beyond his usual temperate capacity. As a result, Anders Jönsson (known to the opposition as "Anders, the Finn") was arrested as the inciter, charged with treason, and after a brief trial, was hanged.

Even though New Sweden could ill afford to lose a single man, Printz felt his hand was forced to maintain his stature and authority. There would be no more resistance to the governor's overbearing grip, but it was the beginning of the end of his rule. He had been overpowered and outdistanced by the Dutch, his own people were demoralized and resentful, and he was receiving next to no support from the mother country–not a single letter or message had been received in the past six years. Governor Printz was tired.

He called for a meeting with the Indian sachems at Printzhoff, distributed gifts, and promised his subjects that he would return within a year, or at least send a shipload of supplies. After ten years of only modest progress, frustration and constant bickering with Indians, Dutch and English, he turned command of the colony over to his son-in-law Johan Papegoja. In October of 1653, he left with his wife, four daughters and about twenty-five settlers on an overland trek to New Amsterdam where they boarded the first ship bound for Europe. Printz would never return to America.

While Printz and company were sailing east to Europe, two other ships were heading west. They were the *Örn* (Eagle) and the *Gyllene Haj* (Golden Shark) carrying Johan Rising, the next governor of New Sweden and over 300 fresh colonists heading for a new home. But before joining the *Örn* on the Delaware, the *Gyllene Haj* would sail to Puerto Rico to address the issue of the Swedish ship *Kattan*, carrying much needed colonists, which had been plundered by the Spanish in 1649. (More about this incident to come.)

Little did Printz know at the time of his decision to abandon his colony that there had been a resurgence of interest in it. Eric Oxenstierna, son of Axel, the chancellor, was named general director of a new branch of the Swedish government known as the Commercial College, organized to promote foreign trade.

The arrival of the Örn, and New Sweden's last governor, Johan Rising.

Rising (pronounced Ree-sing) was chosen to lead the expedition because of his training in economics and an extensive background in commerce, trade and agriculture. Once in New Sweden, he would serve under Johan Printz. But it was too late for that.

✦ ✦ ✦

ALMOST IMMEDIATELY upon completion, Fort Casimir fell into a state of neglect. Things were quiet on the river with Printz gone, and Stuyvesant found little need to keep up constant vigilance. He was also short on manpower to defend New Amsterdam against renewed threats from the English, despite the recent border agreement. By the time Rising and company arrived in the Delaware Bay in 1654, the condition of the fort had greatly deteriorated. The *Örn* anchored in the bay close by the deserted Fort Elfsborg, which was even more decrepit since its abandonment.

At Fort Casimir, Gerrit Bicker was shocked when he found a Swedish ship had arrived in the river. He sent Adriaen van Tienhoven and four other soldiers to board her and "ascertain whence she came." Rising received the men courteously, stated his business, and questioned the Hollanders in return. Learning that there was only a skeleton crew manning the fort, and that they were out of powder, Rising spotted an opportunity unfolding before him. Although he was under strict orders to avoid aggressive behavior, the vague instructions communicated to him in writing suggested that if he should find the Dutch in a compromised position, he should take advantage. Which he did.

The next morning he sailed across the bay just off Fort Casimir and fired a salute. According to procedure, the proper response from the Dutch garrison would have been to answer the salute. Nothing. Rising ordered another shot. Still nothing. A landing party was then sent to the fort with powder so the Dutch could respond properly. They finally fired the required return salute, and the garrison of only nine men were then ordered to surrender the fort, which they did, offering little resistance aside from some grumbling. The flag of the WIC was lowered, the Swedish flag hoisted and the uncontested seizure of Fort Casimir was complete. And since the day happened to fall on a religious holiday, the Swedes changed the name of the decrepit fortress to "Trefaldighet"– Trinity Sunday.

Onboard the *Örn* with Rising and the other colonists was a young Swedish engineer named Peter Lindeström. Possessed of brilliant skills of observation, he recorded eye-witness accounts of his experiences in New Sweden: the weather, agriculture, Indian religion and lifestyles, their trading habits, and the hostilities between the Dutch and Swedes. He made numerous drawings of various aspects of the region, including a map of the whole of the known Delaware with the help of Andreas Hudde, former commissary of Fort Casimir. He was then called upon to restore the newly named Fort Trefaldighet and its storehouses to their original condition, but it was in such a dilapidated state that he practically had to rebuild from the ground up, plus, an additional palisade was constructed in front of the fort. Sven Skute, the former lieutenant at Fort Elfsborg and now promoted to captain, would be its new commander. He was also placed in charge of the restoration and new construction. Nearby the fort were twenty-one Dutch families, occupying as many homes. They were offered complete immunity if they would swear an oath of allegiance to Sweden. There was little argument over the offer.

Almost overnight, the population of New Sweden swelled from just seventy-five persons to well over three hundred. Unfortunately, this was not necessarily a good thing. The voyage of the *Örn* had been a difficult affair, and many of the new arrivals were suffering from various diseases and barely in a condition to care for themselves. Infection spread through the neighboring Indian trading communities, cutting off supplies of meat, fish and maize that the colonists had come to depend on. Rising was forced to send a sloop to Hartford to buy supplies, and in time, the colony began to recover. Eventually, tracts of land were laid out along the river between Forts Trinity and Christina. And in the fields to the north of Fort Christina, a small town began to form. Still honoring the Swedish Queen, it was named Christinahamn.

Land was cleared, crops were planted, sown and harvested. But much more was expected–Rising was presented with a laundry list of assignments to be addressed: sow grain, hemp, linseed, cultivate grapes and fruit trees…basically, the same tasks that were demanded of Printz. And they still would not let the idea of raising silkworms go. Rising requested Eric Oxenstierna to send him a wife, with no other expectations other than she be able "to look after the garden and the cattle, to spin and to weave both the linen and the wool…to keep the nets and seines in order, to make malt, to brew the ale, to cook the food, to milk the cows, to make the cheese and butter."

Within a year of Rising's arrival, the New Sweden colony began to flourish. More so than it ever had in the last sixteen years. The Dutch rivalry was gone, and new love affairs with the Indians were established. Lands they had previously sold to the Dutch were presented as gifts. The Swedes now owned all the river.

But as surely as things go well, they just as surely go otherwise. Despite many in-roads, the colony was not totally self-sufficient. They still relied on fresh food and provisions from both the Indians and neighboring English colonists. The expected arrival of the *Gyllene Haj* with its abundant cargo of supplies was highly anticipated, but it failed to make an appearance.

As mentioned previously, despite being blessed with an ample coastline, the Swedes never proved themselves as top-rate mariners. After his initial stop at Puerto Rico, Hans Amundson Besk, the captain of the *Haj*, sailed north to reach the Delaware, but missed it by 200 miles. Sailing into the North River instead, the ship was seized, and all aboard, including the future commissary Hendrick van Elswyck, were placed in the New Amsterdam guard-house. The cargo was confiscated, the ship was re-named *Diemen*, and put into the service of the West India Company. It was a tremendous loss to the Swedes, but by now they were almost used to such set-backs. They would survive.

❖ ❖ ❖

ABOUT A WEEK after Johan Rising arrived, he wrote a letter addressed to Governor Stuyvesant informing him that the Swedes had "summoned" Fort Casimir and that the Dutch inhabitants had sworn allegiance to the Queen of Sweden. The missive was not intended as an insult, but merely to apprise him of the situation. It was, however, met with stark indignation. The news reached Amsterdam as quickly as Stuyvesant could get it there, where it was received by the incredulous Lords Directors of the WIC. Their outrage knew no bounds as they pondered the audacity of the Swedes! Communications were returned to Stuyvesant ordering him to drive them from the river. Drums were beaten as the call for volunteers sounded throughout Amsterdam. Two WIC ships, the *Groote Christoffel* (Great Christopher), and the *Swarte Arent* (Black Eagle) were prepared for battle and dispatched to Manhattan. Stuyvesant was authorized to obtain other vessels as well, and attack "before the Swedes were reinforced." Another ship, the *Waegh* (Scales), was also enlisted for reinforcement. Chartered from the city of Amsterdam, she was armed with 36 pieces of ordnance and two hundred soldiers. But this swift retaliation would have to wait…Stuyvesant was on vacation.

Although planned in greatest secrecy, Rising soon learned of the impending Dutch invasion. He called for a council of war where it was decided that Fort Trinity must not be lost. Weapons, powder, food, fourteen gallons of brandy and numerous barrels of beer were brought in. The fort would be defended right down to the last bottle of brandy—or the last barrel of beer…whichever survived longest.

When at last, the Dutch fleet arrived in the Delaware, it was recorded as having happened on two different dates: Rising gives August 30, 1655, while the Dutch version is September 9. The Dutch calendar at this time was ten days ahead of the Swedish. (Other measurements differed as well, such as the Dutch mile from the Swedish mile, etc.) The second Dutch flotilla in four years anchored off the deserted Fort Elfsborg where its forces were landed on shore to assemble for the coming action. Two days later, amidst the beating of drums and blowing of trumpets, they passed by Trefaldighet, whose guns were strangely silent. If Peter Lindeström and Lieutenant Gyllengren had their way, however, the guns would have come alive. But the cooler and more experienced Capt. Skute prevailed, although he would later be admonished for his decision.

Fifty troops were landed to the south of the Christina Kill to cut off communication between the two forts, but no hostile action was taken as yet. In an utmost attempt at civilized arbitration, negotiations began and continued for several days, often with a Dutch emissary returning after a session swaying under a brandied cloud.

On Sept. 11, when those involved had exhausted all avenues of compromise, Captain Skute finally surrendered the fort. The only concession he had been awarded was to allow his men to exit the fort with armed matchlocks and bullets in their mouths to show they had not been subdued.

And now in direct opposition to the events of Trinity Sunday a year ago, the Swedish flag came down, and the Dutch colors returned to wave in the river breezes. But as the lowly band of Swedes marched out of Trefaldighet, they were confronted by Stuyvesant who asked of Skute where he intended to go. The Captain replied they were going to Christina. "Nay, it is not so written," scolded Stuyvesant. "You shall stay here, where I want you!"

The demoralized Skute, along with Lindeström and the other officers, were placed under arrest, shamed and ridiculed, and then in an odd gesture of gentleman-

The Dutch fleet gathers at the abandoned Fort Elfsborg to prepare for the upcoming seige.

ly good will, were awarded the pleasure of dining with Governor Stuyvesant that very evening. The remaining garrison of soldiers were not treated nearly as well. Declared prisoners of war, they were loaded on the Dutch ship, ironically named *Love*, and taken to New Amsterdam. Later, Lindeström placed the blame for the surrender squarely on the hapless Skute. The soldiers held him in such contempt that he was "considered by every man as a shoe-rag." But in truth, Skute probably saved everyone's skin by holding his fire. Any shots directed at the Dutch fleet would have meant annihilation of all in the fort.

Rising sat watching and waiting at Fort Christina, and when he heard Dutch cannons firing in a celebratory manner, he knew Trefaldighet had fallen. Now he needed to know what Stuyvesant would do next. To find out, he sent the commissary van Elswyck to Stuyvesant to inquire of his intentions and to try and dissuade him from any further hostilities. Despite van Elswyck's pleadings and threats, Stuyvesant bluntly replied that he intended to reclaim the entire river. In a defiant retort, van Elswyck exclaimed, "Hodie mihi, cras tibi" (Today me, tomorrow you). Little did either man realize how prophetic these words were. On van Elswyck's return, Rising ordered the reinforcing of Fort Christina in an attempt to withstand the inevitable siege. Before long, the Dutch obliged, completely surrounding the fort with men, guns and ships. They also went on a rampage of looting, killing the settlers' livestock, plundering their houses throughout the colony, even threatening Printzhoff, and burning the tiny village of Christinahamn to the ground.

The Dutch flag was raised again over the former Fort Trafaldighet

The siege itself lasted nearly two weeks, during which rounds of negotiations took place on an almost daily basis. On the twelfth day, after conferring with his council, Rising surrendered everything. The defenders were marched out of the fort–only thirty men—the Dutch flag was hoisted, and the war was over without a drop of blood being spilled, except for that of a Swedish deserter at Trefaldighet who was shot in the leg by his own officer.

Included among the troops that accompanied Stuyvesant was the familiar name of Van Winkle. It belonged to an ancestor of the lovable character in Washington Ir-

The defeated Swedish officers were invited to dine with Governor Stuyvesant

ving's classic tale "Rip Van Winkle" according to the author, who wrote "In that same village, and in one of these very houses, there lived, many years since, while the country was yet a province of Great Britain, a simple, good-natured fellow, of the name of Rip Van Winkle. He was a descendant of the Van Winkles who figured so gallantly in the chivalrous days of Peter Stuyvesant, and accompanied him to the siege of Fort Christina. He inherited, however, but little of the martial character of his ancestors. I have observed that he was a simple, good-natured man; he was, moreover, a kind neighbor and an obedient, henpecked husband."

Peter Lindström recorded that "General Stijfvesandt" (Swedish spelling) "came tilting on his wooden leg to us", meaning the Swedish officers, to accept the surrender of the fort. The terms were extraordinarily lenient–because they had been drawn up by the Swedes themselves, who told Stuyvesant they "would accept no law unless Swedes had a hand in its making." There were not enough Dutch forces to defend both the North and South River holdings, so the only alternative was to leave the Swedes where they were. If they did wish to remain, they would have only to swear oaths of allegiance to New Netherland. They could retain all their property and continue following their own religion. If they wished to leave, they could do so at Dutch expense. The negotiating team of Olaf Stille, Peter Larsson Kock, Ake Helm and Peter Rambo would be appointed magistrates of the Upland Court, the newly-formed governing body of the remaining Swedish colonists.

The Dutch would hold on to Fort Casimir (returned to its former title) and Fort Christina, which Stuyvesant now re-named Fort Altena. Rising was suspicious, but he was unaware that Stuyvesant was being called back to Manhattan as quickly as possible. As soon as the Dutch fleet had left New Amsterdam, the Indians took advantage, killing a hundred colonists throughout the countryside, and capturing one hundred and fifty more. Three hundred family's homes and farmsteads had been destroyed, sending the settlers to New Amsterdam to find safety. Stuyvesant needed to get home.

Rising chose to leave also. On October 11, 1655, the Swedish governor, his officers and soldiers and a number of settlers, set sail for New Amsterdam where they would continue their journey across the Atlantic to Gothenburg. Nya Sverige was no more.

✦ ✦ ✦

UNFORTUNATELY, there was no way to get this news to the manifest of 110 Finns and Swedes onboard a ship named the *Mercurius*, making its way to the newly defunct colony. Because of the confiscation of the *Gyllene Haj*, a new expedition had been organized almost immediately. How ironic that for all those years previously, nothing was heard from the motherland, and now that the colony was lost, people couldn't immigrate fast enough. Johan Papegoja and Hendrick Huygen, the two leaders of the expedition, must have been shocked beyond belief when they learned of the new set of circumstances that confronted them when they arrived at Fort Casimir. The ship dropped anchor and they made their way ashore where they met with Jean Paul Jacquet, the Dutch Vice-Director and chief magistrate of the region, recently given "supreme command over all officers, soldiers and freemen" on the Delaware.

Jacquet was shocked as well; he was expecting Swedes to be departing, not arriving. He was now thrust into an extraordinary situation: since Stuyvesant had taken nearly every available fighting man back to New Amsterdam, he now found that with the arrival of these new immigrants the balance of population to be completely in the Swedes favor. They could have re-taken their former territory, but were apparently unable to process the situation at the time. Jacquet acted more quickly, arresting Huygen as an enemy of the state and ordering Papegoja to keep his passengers and cargo aboard their ship until he could receive instructions from his Director-General. Stuyvesant soon replied that the new immigrants must not be allowed to embark. He issued a pass for the Mercurius to sail to Manhattan for refitting and supplying for a return trip to Sweden or wherever else they wished…except the Delaware.

Weeks passed, but there was no sign of the ship in New Amsterdam. It was decided to send Dutch troops aboard the warship *Waegh* to investigate, and if necessary, address any problems. There was indeed a problem. The *Mercurius* had been boarded by existing Swedes, Finns, and friendly Indians, and taken to Tinicum, where the passengers finally embarked amid their own countrymen. As for the *Waegh*, it promptly ran aground upon entering the Delaware Bay and sat helpless until help arrived. She was then accompanied on her return trip by the now very contrite and very empty *Mercurius*. This ended the last official New Sweden expedition.

Director-General Stuyvesant was frustrated by the attempt to refuse entry to the last Swedes, but there was not really much he could do about it other than to let them be. Besides, they had dispersed in the region north of the Christina River, which had become more or less the geographical divide between the Dutch and Swedish colonies. Finding themselves without leadership, other than the indifferent command at Fort Casimir, the Swedes and Finns turned to those who had played significant roles under Printz and Rising. Under the guidance of men like Sven Skute, now recovered from former disgrace, Gregorius van Dyck, Lieutenant Elias Gyllengren, Anders Dalbo, Jacob Swenson, Peter Rambo, Peter Cock and others, they set about forming the Upland Court, which would be the governing body of the "Swedish Nation on the Delaware." It would be a separate entity from the Dutch administrators down the river.

The Dutch displayed little objection because they were now greatly outnumbered since the arrival of the last colonists. They feared a takeover by the Swedes more now than before the capitulation of New Sweden. In the words of author Christopher Ward, "If one wanted to make a South River Dutchman jump, it could be done by saying 'Swede!' suddenly behind him." The Swedes were actually more successful now under Dutch rule than they had ever been before. But the Dutch fears were completely unfounded. There never was any plotting of rebellion or resistance–only complete submission to their situation.

They were hard working peasant stock, perfectly suited to crafting homesteads out of wilderness. Working their farms six days a week and spending the seventh in prayerful duty was their idea of contentment. To Penn they were "a plain strong industrious people…proper and strong of body, so that they have fine children and almost every house full…I see few young men more sober and industrious."

But one young man was not so sober—at least on one particular evening in 1685. John Rambo, the youngest son of Peter, displayed great interest in Brigitta, the daughter of neighbor Peter Cock. After hitting the cider jug a little too exuberantly, young John made his way to her family's home to pay a friendly but clandestine visit. Removing a plank from the wall of Brigitta's bedroom, he snuck in to find her sharing a bed with two of her younger sisters. Somehow, during the course of the night, it was John sharing the bed with Brigitta, and not the sisters. When dawn came, young Romeo left by the same passage through which he had arrived.

Within a short period of time, Brigitta announced that she was with child, which in itself was scandalous enough, but John, who was assumed to be the father, refused to do the right thing. Because of the colonial legal system, the young lovers were indicted and brought to trial. Both were found guilty, fined £10 each, and ordered to marry before the birth of the child. But John still would not make her an honest woman. He argued that because he had paid his fine, he was free to pursue other interests, mainly, a young Dutch girl named Anneka van Sluys. John wanted to marry her instead of Brigitta. But Gloria Dei Church would not post the wedding unless Brigitta gave her consent. Brigitta refused, and continued to refuse until she and John were finally joined. They established a 300-acre farm in present day Gloucester County–far enough away from gossip, but close enough to still visit their families in Pennsylvania.

Left to their own devises, the Finns and Swedes gradually and steadily extended their holdings ever northward along the original highway–the Delaware. From the core area around Fort Christina they continued to populate Upland (now Chester), Passayunk, Kingsessing, and as far as Wicaco, which would eventually become Philadelphia. Some headed to the Sassafras River in Maryland, and some along the Schuylkill Valley, all the while following the banks of the rivers and their tributaries—the colonial transportation system. Others crossed the Delaware to New Jersey and settled along Raccoon Creek (Swedesboro), Penn's Neck, Finn's Point, and some of them built that little cabin in Gibbstown. Still others ventured as far as the Maurice River on the Delaware Bayshore, and further still to Egg Harbor near present day Atlantic City.

An example of what a Swedish/Finnish farm may have looked like along the Delaware River in the mid-seventeenth century.

The Kattan Disaster

The eighth expedition to New Sweden arrived via the *Swan* in 1648 with trade goods and supplies, but few colonists. The population slowly dwindled as deserters snuck away to the Maryland and Virginia colonies, and miscreants whose sentences were expired returned to their homeland. Although most farmers were content with their occupation, the remaining soldiers and servants were not, including Governor Printz. His original contract required his services for three years, but he was now asked to remain. He had to have more settlers or the colony would not survive against the advance of the Dutch and English. Five times in two and one-half years he had written home begging for more people, but he heard nothing.

Finally, in 1649, his demands were addressed. For reasons that are not fully understood, about 300 Finns petitioned Queen Christina for immigration to America. She expressed surprise that they would want to leave when there was so much land to develop at home. The petition came to naught, but it did stir up renewed interest in immigration. Along with some Finns accused of illegal moose hunting, about seventy Swedish colonists consisting of men, women and children huddled together at Gothenburg to board a ship named the *Kattan*. A cargo of badly needed supplies for New Sweden, as well as for the voyage itself, was loaded, and the ship set sail on July 3. She made it to the Caribbean without mishap, and in August, after taking on fresh water and supplies, began the long final leg of her journey that would take her up the coast of North America to the Delaware. But the captain soon found himself in unfamiliar waters. The *Kattan* struck a reef two times and was able to work free. But a third time found her stuck fast. The lifeboats were deployed and all the passengers and crew rowed themselves to a small uninhabited island. Then their troubles began in earnest.

Two Spanish ships arrived, which picked up the stranded immigrants and took them to Puerto Rico, but not before stopping to loot the now abandoned Kattan. The shipwreck survivors were treated as prisoners of war and paraded through the streets amid great fanfare. A bonfire was kindled by Spanish priests who took great delight in burning the victims "heretical" Swedish books. Many of the prisoners were tortured; some until they renounced their religion, others to reveal any alleged treasures they had brought with them.

Despite the horrible dilemma the immigrants found themselves in, some were amused the site of fellow passenger Reverend Matthias Nertunius. He hid money in his stockings under his trousers, and pulled out his long shirt and let it fall loosely, deceiving the Spaniards into thinking he had no pants on. The deception became even more humorous when the Spanish commandant took pity on finding he was a man of the cloth, and gave him some clothes.

The Swedes were now stranded on Puerto Rico, at the mercy of their Spanish hosts, but they were allowed to send letters to Stockholm to request a vessel to be sent to their aid. While they waited, a Dutch slave ship named the *Prophet Daniel* arrived which the Swedes hoped would be their salvation, but the Spanish governor seized the ship, took the Dutch captain's money, and made ready to send the ship to Spain as a gift to the king. Still, the desperate Swedes begged to be allowed to travel on the ship back to Spain, anything to be free from Puerto Rico. Just before departure, however, the governor became ill, suspending orders for the Swedish immigrants to depart. But strangely, this excluded their commander, Hans Amundsson, who sailed off, leaving the others behind in despair.

Not until April of 1650 were the rest of the Swedes able to leave when two of their party somehow managed to purchase a small boat. There were now just twenty-four refugees remaining as they sailed toward the island of St. Christopher, in hopes of meeting Hollanders, or basically anyone who could provide transport, either back to their homes or New Sweden.

However, fortune refused to smile upon the hapless group. Off the island of St. Cruz they were overtaken by a French bark. Their passes were confiscated and the unfortunate Swedes were removed to the island. The French descended on them "like wild dogs", stripping them of their clothing and what remained of their belongings. But they were soon treated far worse. Many were subjected to even more brutal torture than they had suffered at the hands of the Spanish, in an attempt to make them reveal a supposedly buried cache of money and jewelry. One of the women was raped by the governor, who then had her put to death. Still others were sold into slavery.

The skipper of a Dutch bark who was trading in the vicinity heard of the Swedes misery and set out to try and help. When he arrived at St. Cruz, the only immigrants left alive were Johan Jonsson Rudders, two women and two children. One by one they died as well, leaving only Rudders who gradually made his way back to Sweden. And it is from him that we have come to hear this tale.

There are those who believe this unfortunate saga may have had some basis for Shakespeare's play "The Tempest." There are still more who believe that a good deal of the story was highly exaggerated. Other versions claim as many as nineteen survivors returning to Stockholm. Be that as it may, the whole expedition was a disaster, not only for the passengers and crew of the Kattan, but for the New Sweden colony as well. The people and supplies it so desperately needed were lost, including essential goods needed for continuing the fur trade.

◆ PART IV ◆

The English Return

✦ XVIII ✦

In the northern portion of New Netherland, near the Connecticut River, an English colony was trying to establish itself the same year that Peter Minuit and company landed on the Minquas Kill. It would become known as the New Haven colony. And like New Sweden, it was a doomed venture. The founders of the colony failed to procure a royal charter—a legal right to exist, which led to its eventual takeover by the larger Connecticut colony. But in the interim, they managed to insert themselves into the already complicated mix of business and colonization on the Delaware River.

The New Haven settlers were led by a group of Puritan businessmen from London that included Minister John Davenport and wealthy merchant Theophilus Eaton. They were later joined by a number of disgruntled members of the Massachusetts Bay Colony. No farmers among them, and the land poor for that purpose anyway, they hoped to sustain themselves by engaging in the fur trade. But beaver furs were even at this early date nearly depleted along the Connecticut River. They were inclined to "settle themselves elsewhere more commodious for their subsistence." They turned their attention to the south, where beaver was still plentiful.

They formed a "Delaware Company", and in the spring of 1641, Nathaniel Turner and George Lamberton, two of the Bay Colony Puritans, along with a dozen of their countrymen, sailed up the Delaware in a sloop dubbed *The Cock* to do some exploring. They met with the local tribesmen to barter for furs, and also managed to purchase land from Lenape chiefs Usquata and Wehenset on the east side of the Delaware along the tributary called Varken's Kill (Hogs Creek, known today as the Salem River). They were unaware at the time that the land they just bought was the intended epicenter of a tract that was granted by Charles I to Sir Edmund Plowden, who we'll meet soon enough.

Word spread quickly among the Swedes and Dutch that there was new competition for the beaver trade. Before the ink was dry on their deeds, the English trespassers had a visitor in the person of Peter Hollander Ridder, governor of New Sweden. He and Goverer Kieft of New Netherland put aside their differences for the time being to unite against a common threat. Ridder found himself protesting this intrusion by the English, just as the Dutch had protested his own incursion earlier. And just as he had done to the Dutch, the English ignored him. However, Ridder would be unable to force the issue as England and Sweden were two of the very few nations of Europe who were not at war with each other. It would be unwise not to keep it that way. So he tried another tactic: meeting with another Lenape sachem Wickusi, whose grounds were also on the east side of the Delaware, he negotiated the purchase of a long stretch of river front real estate—from Narriticons Creek (at the foot of today's Commodore Barry Bridge) all the way south to Cape May. This now extended New Sweden to both sides of the Delaware, including the property that Lamberton and Turner had purchased. Which is exactly what Ridder intended, insisting the transaction was made three days before the English acquisition.

The English ignored the counter-claims, left a handful of men and sailed back to New Haven. They returned the following year to reinforce their meager settlement and to buy more property on the Delaware. This they purchased from Mattahorn, the Lenape sachem who had sold much of the same land to Minuit several years earlier. But this property was situated on the west side of the river, near the Schuylkill's convergence with the Delaware, which put them in closer contact with the Indian fur trappers than either the Dutch or Swedes. A block house was constructed along with several dwellings to serve as a base of trading operations. By offering better deals, it was now the English who stole the fur trade from the

Swedes…who had stolen it from the Dutch.

This was too much for Kieft. Protesting obviously did nothing. He sent orders to Jan Jansen van Ilpendam, the commandant at Fort Nassau, to remove the English from their new settlement by stern but peaceful means. Two armed sloops were also sent from New Amsterdam for support. Jansen gave the English two hours to pack their belongings, then set fire to their buildings, burning them to the ground. Finding themselves at an obvious disadvantage, the English were removed without a fight and taken to New Amsterdam. They were then shipped back to New Haven. And that was the end of the English foothold on the Schuylkill, ironically, their first settlement in what forty years later would become the English Quaker colony of Pennsylvania.

As for the Englishmen on the Varken's Kill, of which there were now about twenty families, Ridder left alone. Not because he was fond of them or wanted more neighbors, but because they were not infringing on the fur business—and they were beginning to cultivate tobacco, something Ridder had been trying to coax his own people into doing. There was still an enormous market for the stuff in Europe, and if the Swedish venture failed, then he might have a supplier right across the river. The Dutch let them be as well—as long as they stayed out of the fur trade.

✦ ✦ ✦

BEFORE JOHAN PRINTZ arrived as the new governor of the Swedish colony in 1643, he was already aware of the English settlers. He was not as tolerant as Ridder, however, referring to them as "evil neighbors", fearing that they might try to expand their tiny colony. Much of this was typical Printz bluster as he did find them useful as business associates, consigning the tobacco they grew along with his own farmers' and shipping it to Sweden. But this was only after a personal visit, forcing them to swear allegiance to Queen Christina. After that he referred to them "our English at Farckens Kill."

Later that same year, George Lamberton returned from New Haven with associates John Thickpenny and interpreter John Woolen to the scene of the earlier English humiliation. Apparently, he had not had enough. Anchoring his trusty pinnace, the Cock, about three miles upriver from Fort Christina, he opened up trade with the Minquas. Possibly as a reprisal for past indignities, he offered bribes to the Indians if they would murder all the Swedes and Hollanders and destroy their settlements. At least this is what was told to Governor Printz one Sunday morning as he was leaving prayer services. After careful thought, he wrote a letter to Lamberton claiming that an Indian had stolen a fictitious gold watch and chain belonging to his wife, and asked for assistance in having it returned. He then sent the two individuals who had apprised him of the plot, barber-surgeon Timon Stidden and servant Gottfried Harmer to deliver the letter, and using discretion, determine if the rumor was true or not. They were invited onboard the pinnace, and after awkward introductions, were informed that many Indian trappers would be arriving the next day for a trading session. The two Swedes requested permission to stay overnight on the chance that they might be able to identify the thief among them (it was reported that the alleged culprit had a strange mark on his face). After finding nothing incriminating, the two returned to report to Printz. But the governor was not satisfied and sent another letter requesting Lamberton's presence at Fort Christina on a matter of great importance. When Lamberton complied, he and his crew were immediately placed under arrest. Interrogation ensued, although once more, nothing was learned. John Woolen, the English interpreter, was then singled out for more intense grilling. In an attempt to loosen his tongue, he was plied with wine and beer. But he had nothing to offer. Then Printz joined in, matching drink for drink and professing his love for him as if he were his own son, and offering him gifts of property and gold and silver if he would please confess. But still Woolen would not admit to any wrongdoing. With his generosity and friendship rejected, Printz then threw a fit befitting his size, stomping his mighty feet and personally clapping Woolen in irons. For three more days, Woolen remained in a drunken stupor, constantly refreshed with beer and sherry,

and still no confession was made. Printz eventually released the prisoners, but made Lamberton promise to return for legal proceedings.

Printz then decided to exert all the authority he could muster, which was quite a lot. A court of inquiry was convened to hear evidence, render a decision and impose sentencing. The main objective would be to rid New Sweden of any future English encroachment—and Lamberton would be the scapegoat. On July 10, 1643, the first legal trial to take place in the Delaware Valley commenced. And possibly the strangest.

A tribunal was assembled with Captain Christiaen Boij as presiding member. Nine others, comprised of Swedes and Dutchmen, would act as both judges and jurors. Printz would be the prosecuting attorney. Three indictments would be brought forth: first, that the English had no right to the land along Varken's Kill; second, that Lamberton traded illegally with the Minquas, and third; that he had bribed the Indians to massacre the Swedish and Dutch colonials.

Lamberton claimed he had been coerced into buying land by Jan Jansen Ilpendam in answer to the first count; pleaded ignorance on the second count—he was unaware he couldn't trade on the river—and flat out denied the third charge. He asked that John Woolen be called to reinforce his denial, but Printz refused the request, asserting that Mr. Woolen had already been examined. And then in a strange and complicated twist, the governor-prosecutor-witness Printz withdrew the third count citing that the defendant was a foreigner and "would not confess to the charge," therefore dismissing the case—even though the court found the prisoner guilty as charged. As to the other charges, however, it was found that the English possessed no land "at, in or around this river," that Lamberton had no right to be there, his ship and cargo were to be confiscated, and he would have to pay double duty on whatever furs he had acquired. He would then be discharged, never to return to the region again.

In the aftermath, Lamberton returned to New Haven complaining bitterly about the treatment received at the hands of the Swedes. Massachusetts Governor Winthrop wrote a multi-page letter to Printz in which he took umbrage at the cruel interrogation inflicted upon poor Woolen and the oppression of Lamberton, and claimed the whole continent for England, on which the Swedes were the trespassers... and on, and on. To ease the situation, Printz then called for a second trial in which he would be defendant, chief justice and prosecuting attorney. A number of the English from Varken's Kill were called back, including Woolen, who swore that he not been coerced into giving false testimony, only the truth. Printz, the prosecutor, refused to press charges against Printz, the plaintiff, and Printz, the chief justice... dismissed himself.

✦ ✦ ✦

BECAUSE OF THE DEBACLE on the Delaware, the New Haven colony was nearly depleted of capital. To this point, they had used the Massachusetts Bay Company to ship their goods to England, but now arranged to have their own merchant ship built. And this is where Mr. Lamberton re-enters the story—as master of the vessel. In the winter of 1646, the ship, imaginatively named the *Great Shippe*, set out from the icy Long Island Sound with a cargo of peas, wheat, hides and other typical New World products, bound for England. Also aboard were a number of the more prominent members of the New Haven colony. Months went by with no word of the ship or passengers or crew. Then in June of 1647, a Flying Dutchman-like apparition appeared over New Haven harbor during heavy thunderstorms. Those who saw the vision claimed that as they watched, the masts and rigging collapsed, and they could make out people on the bow as the ship rolled on its side and disappeared into the mists of the storm. Many believed it was a sign from the heavens to provide closure for the bereaved. So engrained did this tale become in New England lore that poet Henry Wadsworth Longfellow memorialized it in his poem "The Phantom Ship" more than 200 years later.

It would seem that the New Haven colony at Varken's Kill slowly dissolved, many of the settlers having been taken down by dysentery, the survivors making their way back to Connecticut. Yet a number of persistent but unsubstantiated sources put English colonists on the Cape May peninsula in the early 1640s. Cape May County's first documentation of European settlement doesn't begin until 1685. Still, these earliest records repeat some of the same names involved in the Varken's Kill colony such as Osborne, Mason, Badcock and Godfrey. It has also long been rumored that whalers from Long Island and New England settled long-forgotten Portsmouth Town near today's Town Bank, north of Cape May Point. These early pioneers might have shared common lineages with the New Haven colonists, but any hard evidence has been washed away over the centuries by tidal action and storms.

✦ XIX ✦

Far from the Cape de Mey, ingredients were being prepared for the foundation of a very complicated colonization stew. In London, the recently titled Sir George Calvert came down with New World fever. The desire to create a colony or two in America became an obsession. He invested money in both the Virginia and New England companies and purchased a tract of land on the coast of Newfoundland. Calvert, an alumni of Trinity College, worked indirectly for King James I as the secretary to the King's advisor, Sir Robert Cecil. He was rewarded for his distinguished service with a Knighthood in 1617 and appointed Secretary of State to James I two years later. He quickly rose through the political ranks, achieving a number of positions including a seat on the House of Commons. It was during this time that James I called on Calvert to assist in creating an alliance with the Habsburgs of Spain. This created a great stir in Parliament whose members feared that far too much Catholic influence would be imposed on the state.

The proposed alliance failed miserably, and as a result, the members of the House cast a suspicious eye on Calvert over the close ties he had formed with the Spanish court. In fact, humoring the Spanish ambassador became his lone duty. But his relationship with James I was still on a high level. Because of his loyalty the king retained him on the Privy Council and granted him another title: First Baron of Baltimore, in County Longford, Ireland. In 1625, Calvert resigned his positions, and in a move that surprised some but was expected by others, joined the Church of Rome.

His original passion for colonization was based purely on commerce, but since changing faiths, he became more interested in establishing a refuge for English Catholics. Since he already owned property on a lonely peninsula in Newfoundland, it seemed the perfect setting for his colony. He named it Avalon after the place where Christianity was first introduced in Britain. Calvert intended to become personally involved in the guidance of the settlement which was precluded by a short visit in 1627. He departed for Newfoundland again the next year with his wife, children and some 40 settlers. Unfortunately, the Canadian winter did not cooperate with Lord Baltimore's well-intentioned plans. After nine months of one of the worst winters in Canadian memory, he and the survivors of Avalon limped back to England, a sickly, half-starved band of pilgrims.

Undaunted, Lord Baltimore continued in his quest for a haven somewhere in

Modern society would be aghast at the translation of the Calvert motto:
DEEDS ARE MASCULINE, WORDS FEMININE

the New World, preferably one that was a bit warmer. Virginia seemed a friendlier place with a climate conducive to growing tobacco. He requested a charter, and while awaiting word on its progress, sailed to Jamestown, arriving in the fall of 1629. But the established colonists, suspecting Lord Baltimore had designs on their territory, gave him a cool reception. The fact that he wanted to establish a Catholic colony did not sit well either. He left for England after only two weeks to check on the status of his charter. The granting of the charter took far longer than Calvert ever imagined. He spent the last two years of his life in persistent lobbying as his fortune dwindled, his health declined and plague infected his household. Finally, in 1632, the king finally granted the long-awaited charter. After negotiating a location, it was drawn to the north of the Potomac River, on both sides of the Chesapeake Bay. One of its boundaries was a part of the Delaware Bay "which lieth under the 40th degree of north latitude."

Sir George Calvert, Baron of Baltimore, died just five weeks before the charter received the Royal Seal. The title of Lord Baltimore was passed on to Calvert's son Cecil as well as the land grant which came to be known as Maryland. It is officially named for Queen Henrietta Maria, the wife of King Charles I, although many Catholics tended to believe the name was bestowed by Sir George Calvert himself to honor the Virgin Mary. But larger and more enduring disputes concerning Lord Baltimore's charter would arise.

PART IV

✦ XX ✦

Upon the dissolution of New Sweden, the Dutch West India Company now found itself in control of more real estate than it had bargained for. The Dutch holdings on the South River had gone from just a couple of lowly trading posts to two disparate colonies, each anchored by a fort: the former Christina on the Minquas Kill, occupied mostly by the vanquished and compliant Swedes and Finns, and Casimir to its south, with its meager supporting core of Dutch, interspersed with yet more Swedes and Finns. Stuyvesant's re-conquest had been expensive, and with the additional burden of colonies in South America and the Guinea coast of Africa, the WIC was stretched dangerously thin.

To relieve its debts, Casimir was transferred to the commercial powerhouse that was the City of Amsterdam. As of 1657, it became the property of the Burgomasters who named it New Amstel, after a suburb of Amsterdam. The WIC, or "The Company", would retain its holdings to the north.

✦ ✦ ✦

BEFORE STUYVESANT returned to Manhattan, he left temporary Commander Jean Paul Jacquet with orders to lay out a town to the immediate south of the recaptured Fort Casimir, which at this point was occupied by only twelve or thirteen families. It was to consist of lots "40 to 50 feet in width and one hundred feet in length, the street to be at least 4 to 5 rods wide." Little has changed of that scheme to this day.

Other orders were imposed regarding civilized treatment of the Swedes, of whom the Dutch were still quite wary, and the Indians, prohibiting them from entering the fort at night, or from "running about in the country", or drinking and swearing on the Sabbath. Taxes were introduced to provide support for what was now expected to become a viable community.

Jacob Alrichs soon arrived as the permanent director along with a hundred and twenty-five immigrants. On his heels followed Captain Martin Krygier and Lieutenant Alexander d'Hinoyossa with forty soldiers to man Fort Casimir and even more colonists, including the first schoolmaster on the Delaware and the first Dutch clergyman, bringing the total newcomers to about 200. Remembering their difficult earlier attempts at luring willing participants, the States Generals made this later process much easier: free transportation, free land for their habitation, a company store where clothing and supplies could be purchased for cost, police protection, and administrators. They would also be free of taxes for ten years, and be given the right to hunt and fish and harvest timber. Any minerals and precious stones would become the property of the finder. In the words of Christopher Ward, it was the "land of free everything." Progress began in earnest—by the end of 1657, there were one hundred buildings including a brickyard, bake house, guardhouse and a forge. It was a watershed year for New Amstel.

It did not take long for a tavern to appear, owned and operated by a man with possibly the most colorful name in all the colonies: Foppe Jansen Outhout. His is also one of the most consistent names to appear throughout the early history of the Delaware River settlements. Born in The Netherlands in 1631, he is first recorded as the quartermaster for Stuyvesant's expedition to recapture Fort Casimir. He then became a permanent resident of New Amstel and built his establishment on what is now the Read property. He was probably the first Dutch brewer on the river. It was said to be a popular meeting place for male villagers and soldiers from Fort Casimir.

Outhout later became a court justice after the English took control of New Netherland in 1664. In 1680, he moved across the river to Penn's Neck to a farm on land he had purchased from the Indians. There he spent the rest of his days until his final one in 1693. Historian-translator Charles Gehring had a pet flying squirrel named Foppe Outhout which enjoyed sitting on a shelf in a coat closet, and launching himself at people when they walked by.

PART IV

Tavern owner was a respectable enough position, but Foppe rose to even higher status, his name showing up in court records as a court justice after the final English subjugation of the Dutch holdings. In 1665, he become the owner of a farm across the river on land purchased from local tribesmen Machierick, Hictock, Taspeemick, Wenamink, and Keckquenner. Ever at the forefront, this made Foppe the first permanent resident of European stock along that stretch of the river. It would eventually be part of Salem County, named by Major John Fenwick, who purchased adjacent property on Varkenskill. And on the deed to that acquisition, prominently displayed, is the name of Meneer Outhout.

On paper, everything looked exciting and promising. But in reality, there were no farmers, artisans, or craftsmen. The commissioners in Holland sent clerks and tradesmen; and women, children, and servants. The fledgling colony soon had to turn to Manhattan for basic necessities. They also sought help from the neighboring Swedes and Finns, who were prospering along the Christina. The promising beginnings of New Amstel quickly deteriorated. And Alrichs poured gasoline on the flames by imposing strict trade laws with the Indians and hampering basic activities, causing a great deal of grousing and resistance. Famine, disease, and worst of all, discouragement, began to seep through the colony. A rumor surfaced that Lord Baltimore was planning a conquest of the South River, causing panic among those who had the strength to flee. Governor Stuyvesant, during an inspection tour of the WIC colonies in 1658, stopped at New Amstel to interview Alrichs. His report to the company stated that "Many things there were not as they ought to be." Shortly after, some fifty settlers left to find refuge among the Virginia and Maryland colonies. By September of 1659, there were scarcely thirty families left in New Amstel.

Colonel Utie and his henchmen

The rumor of an impending invasion by the English into Dutch territory was not without some foundation. Governor Fendall of Maryland wrote to Alrichs explaining that neither his position nor an independent Dutch colony was recognized and expected them to clear out. Then into this town of despair there strode a lackey of Governor Fendall—Colonel Nathaniel Utie, with four other soldiers and a servant. They swaggered into Foppe Outhout's tavern, like the Dalton Gang. Not bothering to introduce themselves or present their credentials, they spent the next three days skulking through the village, noting the decayed condition of the fort, and menacing the townsfolk, insinuating that they should think about migrating to Maryland. When at last a meeting did take place with Governor Alrichs, Utie reiterated the same threat he had been intimidating the townspeople with–that the people of New Amstel should declare themselves English citizens, or depart immediately under the threat of bloodshed. Badly shaken, Governor Alrichs begged time to think it over. Utie gave him three weeks, at the end of which time he would return with 500 soldiers. With that, Utie and company returned to from whence they came, not to be seen again. Lord Baltimore was ready to capitalize on the age-old English claim to North America.

In answer to this seditious demand, Stuyvesant sent the diplomatic team of Augustine Herrman and Resolved Waldron to Maryland to meet with Governor Fendall. Fendall argued on behalf of Lord Baltimore that Charles I had granted him the exact territory that included New Netherland. He even dug up the old Cabot claim of 1497. The envoys argued heartily against it, claiming Dutch rights all the way back to the finds of Columbus by way of the King of Spain, and that the murdered colonists at Zwaanendael had paid for the land with their blood.

The argument was not over, but what brought it to mutual indecision were two words in the charter issued by Charles I that stated the disputed land as *hactenus inculta*— not yet cultivated, whereas the Dutch had proof of just such cultivation at Zwaanendael which predated Lord Baltimore's claim… by just one year.

✦ XXI ✦

The Adventures of Lord Plowden

When Sir Edmund Plowden heard about George Calvert's royal charter for creating a colony in the New World, well, he just had to have one too. It would not be too difficult as King Charles I was fond of granting charters. Not because the recipients had done glorious deeds and were deserving of rewards—but because The King was broke. Royal charters could be had for a price, which is how Sir Edmund Plowden came into the possession of what would become: half of Delaware and Maryland, the southern half of eastern Pennsylvania, and two thirds of New Jersey. Basically, a rectangle that ran from Sandy Hook to Cape May, and extending inland about as far. It would also include "the Isle of Plowden, or Long Isle." The English grasp of American geography was not well advanced, so one might think that it didn't actually mean the Long Island, since it was out of the realm of the neatly parceled area. But apparently, it was indeed included in the grant. And, "all and singular islands and isles, floating or to float, and being in the sea within ten leagues of the shore of said region." Plowden seemed to expect big things especially from "Long Isle", which would also be a selling point– timber for pitch, tar, and masts; iron, gold, and copper ore; better fishing even than at Newfoundland; a long growing season; a lucrative trade in furs; and really stretching the limits of reality: "a race of buffaloes which will be ridden and brought to drawn to plough and be milked."

This grant was not merely a charter, but a County Palatine, or a kingdom within a kingdom, and Plowden would henceforth carry the 800 pound, gilded, bejeweled, resplendent title…"the Right Honorable and Mighty Lord Edmund, by Divine Providence Lord Proprietor, Earl Palatine, Governor and Captain-Generall of the Province of New Albion."

Born in 1590, Plowden came from good Catholic stock based in Oxford. He married a woman of equally good standing named Mabel Marriner, who as well as being a wealthy heiress, brought considerable income from landed property to the table. She also brought a personality that was in sharp contrast to her husband's. Practically the whole of their married lives would be subject to violent arguments. Plowden was not well liked. Possessed of a great deal of raw energy and ambition, he was also a bully who was so enamored with litigation that between 1620 and his death in 1659, he was involved in seventy lawsuits in England, and forty-two in Virginia. He also held official positions in Ireland, and may have had legal actions there as well, but many of the court records in Dublin were destroyed by a fire in 1921.

It was in Ireland where Plowden first petitioned the King. He had been issued a compulsory knighthood, which was necessary before applying for a charter. It's not clear why he wanted to start such a colony, but the King was more than willing to help fulfill his wish, for it would provide resistance to the Dutch incursion, and the acquisition of a great deal of natural resources which were becoming more apparent with each voyage to the New World. It would also result in the forfeiture of Plowden's fortune to the crown in the event of his death.

The charter was granted. The King was pleased, Lord Plowden was pleased, but there was a problem. Lord Baltimore's charter must have slipped the King's mind, although it had been assured just a month before, resulting in the two grants overlapping each other. And not by just a few acres, but by a large chunk of real estate. To the monarchies of Europe, especially England, the vast wilderness of the New World had become a convenient monetary substitute for paying down debts. Determining who owned what property were matters to be sorted out in the courts where barristers clutched "parchments crackling like musketry-fire as they shook them in the faces of each other, a battle of words and windy phrases, with no apparent prospect of a decision." For the meantime, the discrepancy would simply be ignored, but it was far from the last time that the Maryland charter would be brought under dispute.

With his new position as a palatine, Plowden took advantage of this great power to fabricate an entire kingdom at his disposal. There was even a background story to provide a foundation for its very existence—"The Albion Knights for the Conversion of the Twenty-three Kings." Plowden was under the impression that within his new palatine were twenty-three

Indian tribes, each with its own King, none of them Christian. They must be converted, which is where the "Knights of Conversion" enter the story. In a recruitment drive reminiscent of the Crusades, Plowden searched for unemployed gentlemen to come to New Albion and become a Knight in the worthy cause of introducing the Indian Kings to Christianity, or the sword. He even had a medal designed to commemorate such service which featured an open book, a hand grasping a dagger and twenty-three Indian heads, vividly illustrating the expected campaign.

At the seat of it would be his own manor which he named Watcessit, located near the present site of Salem, encompassing some three hundred thousand acres of choice land. The nobility would naturally be his family, of which there was a lot. His favorite daughter would become Lady Barbara, Baroness of Richneck; Francis Lord Plowden, Governor and Baron of Mount Royal; Thomas Lord Plowden, High Admiral and Baron of Royalmount; Winifred, Baroness of Uvedale, and on and on through seventeen children, lords of a realm that was not real–nor ever would be.

Aside from the sale of the charter, Charles also stood to make money from New Albion if it was successful, but more importantly, it was intended to help make Britain an independently commercial empire, and to act as a trade and military buffer against the Dutch. But "if" became the operative word.

It was fully eight years from the granting of the charter before Lord Plowden was finally ready to embark for the New World in 1642. He had been far too busy with lawsuits against tenants, creditors, debtors…and his wife. He so desperately wanted her to accompany him to his empire in the New World that he threatened her with bodily harm. That was enough for the Archbishop of Canterbury to grant a separation and alimony. But Sir Edmund refused the situation and was thrown in jail. He was released only after he paid a £1,500 bond and agreed to support his wife. He then promptly sued the warden for false imprisonment.

But before he could set sail, Lord Plowden was informed of "the entry and intrusions of certain aliens" on New Albion. This was of course the Swedes, Dutch, and New Englanders who had "unlawfully entered, builded, and settled them[selves] within Delaware Bay or Charles River." He petitioned Charles for help in evicting them, for which Charles complied, in the form of an open letter to all the squatters informing them that they would be removed and "declared as [public] enemies."

Finally underway with this missive and additional orders, Plowden took his family and a small band of indentured servants not to the wondrous and mystical kingdom of New Albion…but to Virginia. Governor William Berkeley was presented with Plowden's official grievances and instructed to give assistance. The governor acted in accordance, firing off a letter of protest to Governor Printz, reminding him of England's original claim to the Delaware and that he must recognize Lord Plowden's title and submit to his authority. Not surprisingly, Printz ignored it.

Within a short period after settling in Virginia, things started to unravel for Sir Edmund. He ran short of money and resorted to his usual obsession with lawsuits. Then his servants went to court to be relieved of service to him, as their terms of indenture were for New Albion only. He was ordered to either launch New Albion, or release his servants. As a result of the decision, he resolved to finally begin the settlement of his empire. But first he would have to remove the New Haven intruders from his manor.

What happens next has two versions. Not surprisingly, historical documentation gets frayed around the edges, fades, and is even distorted by biased reporting.

Version One (and probably the most credible), goes like this:

IN MAY OF 1643, Lord Plowden set out with sixteen of his people on a voyage to Watcessit. Unfortunately, he didn't get very far. His "people" just happened to be the disgruntled servants, who along with the captain of the vessel, mutinied, and following a pirate custom of the time, marooned Sir Edmund and two young pages on Smith's Island off Cape Charles in the Chesapeake Bay. The scornful servants then continued to the Delaware Bay hoping to find an English vessel to spirit them away. Arriving at Fort Elfsborg, who should they encounter but Governor Printz himself, who was supervising work on the still unfinished fortification. The mutineers inquired about any ships that might be sailing to England, which aroused suspicion in the hefty governor. When they could produce no passes that satisfied Printz, he had them arrested.

Plowden and his young companions were rescued after a four day ordeal in which the Earl was described as being "half dead and as black as the ground." Several months later, the same sloop used for the rescue mission set out along the coast to search for the criminals, eventually learning they were being held at Fort Christina. Printz turned over the prisoners to the commander, and true to form, presented a bill for their incarceration.

And Version Two:

SIR EDMUND ACTUALLY sailed up the Delaware to Varken's Kill to confront the New Haven renegades, squatting on his very manor! He then forced them to swear obedience to him as their governor and sailed off again for Virginia where the story of his stranding and rescue is the same as version one. This may be Plowden's account as it is doubtful the English would swear allegiance to New Albion, and then a short time later to Governor Printz and New Sweden as well.

After his rescue, Lord Edmund returned to Virginia to nurse his health and wounded pride, and resume his favorite pastime of litigation. His unfortunate adventure had been the only attempt to physically settle New Albion. After serving their terms of service, all his servants gradually made their way back to England. And so did Lord Plowden. In 1648, he left Virginia for the long journey home, but not before stopping briefly at New Amsterdam and Boston to make new enemies. New Albion never became more than a fantasy, neither did the manor of Watcessit, and no Indian Kings were ever converted.

Lawsuits continued right up to the time of his death in 1659. The charter for New Albion would pop up from time to time, particularly in regard to Lord Baltimore's claim of Delaware. Finally, in 1773, the charter was revived one final time by the great-great-grandson of Sir Edmund - Francis Plowden, who sold a partial interest in the claim to English attorney Charles Varlo, made him governor of the extinct colony and sent him to America. Varlo was there not to try and reclaim the alleged land of New Albion… but to sue for back rents from the unsuspecting tenants. Sir Edmund would have been proud.

✦ XXII ✦

It may have been the experience of being cast upon an unknown land, it may have been the weather, or the water, but it seems many colonists exhibited exceptional qualities, while nothing but contemptuousness seeped out of others, much like Wellington's Law of Command: The cream rises to the top. So does the scum. A prime example of the latter was Lieutenant Alexander d'Hinoyossa.

His career had brought him from military service in Brazil to a position as vice-director of New Netherland. Before assignment to New Amstel, he re-occupied High Island after it had been abandoned by Minuit and the Walloon settlers, reportedly outfitting it with pleasure gardens, a farm, and a residence befitting one of his position.

Director of New Amstel Jacob Alrichs had been ill for a long time, and on December 30, 1659, sensing the end was near, called his military commander d'Hinoyossa, as well as Gerrit van Sweeringen, and Cornelius van Gezel to his bedside. He appointed the lieutenant to be his successor and the other two as his councillors, at least until the Powers that Be in Holland named replacements. D'Hinoyossa grasped the dying man's hand, praised him for his years of service and swore that he would defend the honor and position of his Director. Alrichs passed away believing that the future of New Amstel was in good hands.

Alrichs was an ineffectual director, that was clear. He had not stood up to Fendall, let alone Utie, who it turns out had no 500 men with which to invade New Amstel, and had done very little to improve the fortunes of the village, although hampered by illness. His successor was much more forceful, but extremely lacking in scruples.

Before the deceased director's body was cold, d'Hinoyossa began rifling through the old man's papers and books looking for any incriminating evidence with which to discredit him, declared him guilty of misconduct, malfeasance, and disobedience, and confiscated all of his property for the City's use. He then asked for approval from the councillors in his actions. Alrich's nephew and heir Commissary van Gezel did not approve, whereupon d'Hinoyossa had him confined to his house, threatening to send him back to Holland. Frightened out of his wits, van Gezel escaped to Fort Altena, begging to be protected from "d'Hinoyossa's violence." The new director then declared him a fugitive from justice. Van Gezel's wife also fled, but had to leave her four-month-old child behind to escape detection.

D'Hinoyossa arrested the child and held it prisoner for three days. This was an early but typical episode in the abusive administration of Alexander d'Hinoyossa, a narcissistic tyrant who would later be dubbed "the Little Prince."

The new director quickly dismissed Alrich's officials and replaced them with a network of cronies who would do his bidding, legally or otherwise. Injustice and humiliation was heaped upon the settlers, as their possessions were stolen outright. Company property was confiscated for personal gain while guns and liquor were traded to the Indians; powder and musket balls from Fort Casimir were traded for tobacco. One would almost think author and supreme cynic Ambrose Bierce had d'Hinoyossa in mind when he wrote: "everything that is not nailed down is mine, and anything I can pry loose is not nailed down"–as in tearing out sections of the palisades from the fort to use as fuel for his private brewery.

His desire for wealth and power was surpassed only by his arrogance, defying orders from New Amsterdam, and declaring himself above their jurisdiction. When objections arose, he threatened the same type of revenge that Peter Minuit had used against the WIC, only he would invite the English, or Portuguese, or whomever, to take over New Amstel. Stuyvesant fumed, but he could only request the Amsterdam City's Commissioners make this new despot behave, but it was a tedious and ineffective process. They thwarted him in every instance.

While all these accusations are quite valid, d'Hinoyossa did manage to maintain power for four and a half years. In 1663, he sailed to Holland to meet with the Directors of the Colony and unveil a plan he had actually propositioned some years previously: If they would just take over the South River colony, recruit a thousand farmers and invest 100,000 guilders to back them, then the whole project would be a resounding success. For all his lack of warmth and good will in New Amstel, d'Hinoyossa gave a charmingly persuasive presentation to the City Commissioners of how prosperous the Swedes and Finns had become, how fertile the land was, the profits to be made trading with the English and thousands of pelts to be had from the Indians.

The Little Prince must have been very proud believing that it was his sales pitch, and his alone that decided the City of Amsterdam to actually take over what was left of the West India Company's holdings: "the said Southriver from the sea upwards to as far as the river reaches…" But in reality, the States General had for some time been weighing the possibility of relieving the WIC from its debts incurred on the Delaware, and placing it in a better position to keep the English out of Manhattan. They fancied the South River and its potential to replace products grown in France or around the Baltic. And to d'Hinoyossa's delight (and Stuyvesant's dismay) he was made director of the entire colony. Stuyvesant was ordered to adopt a hands-off policy, except to keep the English away from the South River colonies.

Fresh from his triumph in Amsterdam, D'Hinoyossa returned to New Amstel not with the promised 1,000 settlers—it was more like 150, from widely divergent backgrounds. They filled the nearly empty village, but their prospects soon dimmed when the Director unveiled his new strategy of moving the capital to a site on Appoquinimink Creek (today's Odessa, DE), claiming it would provide easier access for trade with the Indians and Maryland colonists. His loyalties resided only within his own private boundaries. He had already established a secret trade route along with Augustine Hermann that became known as the "Smuggler's Path" that ran from New Bohemia in Maryland to Appoquinimink. In exchange for tax-free tobacco grown in the Maryland colony, the Dutch would in turn funnel African slaves and strong beer. So confident was d'Hinoyossa in the Appoquinimink deal, that he took out a patent on nearby real estate and began draining the land for agricultural use. An air of gloom descended on the already beleaguered land owners in New Amstel and Altena.

But there was more to come. He heaped on additional abuse by depriving any private parties of dealing in tobacco and furs. All business was to be conducted through agents of the Burgomasters. A further and completely disheartening edict prohibited the brewing of beer or distilling of brandy, either for sale or private use. So much for a depressed people having at least one bright spot in their lives.

✦ ✦ ✦

IN THE SUMMER OF 1663, a ship named the *St. Jacob* touched the shore at Hoerenkil (there's that name again!) where 24 families, the first new colonists on the South Bay in thirty-two years, embarked. They were led by one Peter Cornelius Plockhoy who had the intention of creating a utopian society in the New World.

Although the original plan as described by the City of Amsterdam was to recruit 1,000 colonists, they didn't expect them to immigrate overnight. But it was hoped to reach that number in just a few years. Refugees from Germany, Norway, and France were pouring into Holland, so there were indeed people enough. Which is how the Peter Plockhoy party came to be on the South Bay. They were Mennonites, a religious movement similar to the Quakers, but with a twist: calling themselves "Collegiates"; members were encouraged to discuss religion in open forums. Plockhoy had originally gone to England to try and obtain financing for his planned community, but he arrived a bit late. Cromwell was unseated, and he had to return to Holland without any hoped-for backing.

However, they were precisely what the Amsterdam Burgomasters were looking for. Enticement was presented in the form of a 100 guilder start-up fund for each family. Free land would be provided, free transportation, and exemption from taxes for twenty years. Fashioning the society as a commune of farmers, they would eventually divide the land into individual properties after a period of five years. Their approach to aggressive behavior was also like that of the Quakers, but with an unusual contradiction—those who found it necessary to fight for the protection of the community were free to do so, while those who wished to remain pacifists were equally free.

Religious tolerance was naturally inherent in this progressive community. Everyone was free to pursue whatever sectarian course they wished…with a few exceptions: "all intractable people, such as those in communion with the Roman see, usurious Jews, English stiff-necked Quakers, foolhardy believers in the millennium and obstinate pretenders to revelation." And one other restriction—no clergymen.

Aside from the tyrant who now ruled all of the South River territory, things were peaceful and on the upswing. Even relations with the Maryland colony, which had been touchy since the incursion by Utie, had calmed and were actually cordial to some extent. But the winds of change, which start as slight breezes, were slowly picking up force.

PART IV

✦ XXIII ✦

In the spring of 1664, English warships were sighted in American waters. They were an expedition sent by James, Duke of York, brother of King Charles II.

The English colonies of Virginia and Maryland to the south, and New England in the north, had not experienced the financial and administrative woes of the beleaguered Delaware enclaves. The Dutch had ensconced themselves in a buffer zone, and it was only a matter of time before the two English territories would meet. The real estate was not only vast and attractive, but the Dutch had infringed on Britain's world trade for years.

Politics and economics aside, another factor was that James Stuart, the future James II, did not care for the Dutch. He had been in exile along with his brother in Holland during the British Civil Wars, and his experience there had apparently not been to his liking. And so it was that the Duke of York decided that the time was now ripe to simply seize New Netherland and tell Holland about it later. Charles then granted his brother one of the most generous and extraordinary gifts in history: an enormous tract of land that stretched from the St. Croix River to the East Bank of the Delaware, ..."Together with all the Lands, Islands, Soils, Rivers, Harbors, Mines, Minerals, Quarries, Woods, Marshes, Waters, Lakes, Fishings, Hawking, Hunting and Fowling, and all other Royalties, Profits, Commodities and Hereditaments to the said several Islands, Lands and Premises."

James' grant did not actually extend to the Dutch holdings on the west side of the Delaware, but it would be seized anyway—just for safe keeping. Though he had encroached on Lord Baltimore's claim to the lower counties, the Duke would make good on the confiscated property in due time (due time taking more than 100 years.) This would effectively give Britain control of the eastern seaboard of North America from Maine to Florida.

✦ ✦ ✦

THE NEWS OF THE ENGLISH fleet sent Director-General Stuyvesant and his Council into a panic. Measures were hastily taken to fortify New Amsterdam against impending invasion. But it was a false alarm. The ships were headed to New England instead. But three weeks later, the false alarm was replaced with a very real one. Four heavily armed English Men-O-War under the command of Colonel Richard Nicolls, a faithful supporter of James during his exile, sailed into New Amsterdam's harbor. Nicolls parked his fleet and called for the city's surrender.

But Stuyvesant refused, and did so for ten days. Despite resumed preparations, it was hopeless for Manhattan to resist. Their defenses consisted of but twenty guns, very little powder and only fifty trained soldiers. They would be facing a hundred and twenty guns and nearly a thousand men. But stubbornness ran through the one-legged governor like a streak of ferrous oxide. It was not until September 8, when two clergymen begged him not to be responsible for the shedding of blood, that he finally submitted, bitterly grumbling, "Well, let it be so, though I had rather be carried to my grave." New Amsterdam became New York on October 1, 1664, re-named by Colonel Nicolls, who now became Deputy Governor Nicolls.

On September 3, Sir Robert Carr led two of the fleet's ships out of the harbor at New Amsterdam, bound for the South River and Fort Casimir. They were the *Guinea,* armed with thirty-six guns, and the *William & Nicholas,* with ten pieces, and enough soldiers to handle its surrender–or reduction–if necessary. It was a long and arduous voyage that took nearly a month, despite the relatively short distance, due to the pilots being unfamiliar with the area, and the "sholeness of the water." Arriving at New Amstel on September 30, they sailed past it and continued north to meet not with Dutch authorities, but the Swedes.

Carr's instructions were to establish amicable relations with the Swedes and Finns, offering them recognition of their properties, freedom to practice their religion, freedom of trade, and the ability to govern themselves if they would submit peacefully to English rule. The Swedes, having been through this several times already with little harm done, seemed agreeable, and after three days of discussions, "were soone our friends," reported Carr.

He now turned his attention to New Amstel. An ultimatum was sent informing the residents that in return for peaceful capitulation they would fairly and generously be allowed to continue to maintain their farms, houses, goods and

possessions, "only that they change their masters." Troops were landed and found Fort Casimir–Trefaldighet–Casimir in its usual condition of neglect, manned by a handful of men with just a few cannon. But the heroic d'Hinoyossa, strutting proudly, decided valor was the better part of destruction and foolishly refused to submit. Nicolls, the consummate gentleman, had been extremely patient with Stuyvesant and let things play out at their own pace. But Carr was wound a good bit tighter.

He unleashed two broadsides from the ships and then launched an assault. In mere moments, it was over.

After the smoke cleared, three Dutchmen were killed, ten wounded, and d'Hinoyossa literally lost his house, farm and property, including slaves, taken over by Carr himself. He also lost all control of his self-styled kingdom. The town was looted and everything of value that could be was removed as property of the King. Blood had finally been spilled on the Delaware, after years of nothing more than a shoving match between the rival colonies.

Carr left the town in the care of his brother, Captain John Carr, and swept downriver to Horenkill and continued the rampage against Plockhoy's colony. Perhaps because of Plockhoy's near association with Cromwell, he was particularly harsh with the settlers and their properties, destroying nearly every building "to a very Naile." The colony barely survived before it became caught in the middle of the never-ending dispute over Lord Baltimore's land, and was destroyed again in 1673 by troops from Maryland. The survivors gradually disbanded, some drifting to Maryland, some remaining, and a few eventually heading to a new colony near

Philadelphia known as Germantown. Just as New Sweden had been erased from the Delaware, so now were the Dutch holdings. New Amstel became New Castle, also re-named by Colonel Nicolls after he arrived to relieve Robert Carr following his overzealous sacking of the Delaware River Dutch.

As for d'Hinoyossa, he meekly offered his services to the English after his thrashing at Casimir, but was rejected. He later moved his family and what was left of his possessions to London, where he again proposed working for the English, but was refused a final time. He then rejoined the Dutch army and was given the assignment of defending the city of Wesel from a French invasion. But this time, in reverse of his experience at New Amstel, he surrendered too quickly. It resulted in charges of treason, mutiny and cowardice, ending with his execution.

✦ ✦ ✦

AT LAST, IN FEBRUARY of 1665, after New Netherland had surrendered, war was formally declared. It should have been made with trepidation, since the navy of the Netherlands was at least equal to that of England's, making the two the most powerful forces on the seas. Aside from England experiencing its first invasion since the Norman Conquest and throwing London into a tizzy, nearly all the rest of the conflict was conducted on the water. It came to a halt with the Treaty of Breda, signed and sealed in 1667. The Dutch were awarded the sugar plantations of Suriname, and the Duke kept what he had wanted all along—New Netherland.

Thus concluded the second Anglo-Dutch War—which proved to be an interlude, as a reprise would soon be played. On the surface, England and the United Provinces of The Netherlands became allied against Louis XIV, who had recently invaded the newly vacated Spanish Netherlands. But below, a secret treaty was forged in which Louis would reward Charles with a beautiful young Frenchwoman and an extremely handsome yearly allowance to join with France against the Dutch. It was not long before the usual hostilities resumed, the outcome this time occurring in reverse.

On August 9, 1673, the Dutch flag once again flew over New York harbor, which now acquired yet another name: New Orange. New Castle was restored to New Amstel and allegiances were sworn once more. But in February of 1674, peace broke out—this time in accordance with The Treaty of Westminster, and the Dutch cities in the New World regained their English names for the final time.

In the space of fifty years, New Castle had been under the auspices of the Dutch West India Company, New Sweden, the DWIC again, the Swedes again, back to the WIC, the City of Amsterdam, England, Amsterdam—AGAIN!, and finally Britain, until of course, the American Revolution.

The Long Finn

Despite New Castle becoming an English town, it was that in name only. The Dutch remained with a smattering of English, Germans and Scots, pledging loyalty to a new boss, and the Swedes and Finns did the same. They did not see themselves as the vanquished, nor were they treated as such. In many respects, they thrived. But there was an underlying tone of resentment and frustration with some of the Norse population. A bad taste was left in the mouths of certain members of the Swedish military, who felt they had not been given enough of a chance to defend their positions when Stuyvesant's forces arrived. Opinions were held that their officers had behaved incompetently, including Sven Skute who, though he was returned to the good graces of some of his compatriots, was still held in contempt by others. Understandably, one of the malcontents was artilleryman Johan Stalcop (meaning "steel jacket" in Swedish, or translated still further to mean "armor") who had been forced to stand by fuming like the match he was holding to light the fuse of a cannon as the Dutch sailed past Fort Trafaldighet, unharmed.

It was into this air of discontent that a stranger arrived in the summer of 1669. He would spark an insurrection of such insignificant proportions that many later questioned whether it had even occurred at all. Over the years, it has become uncertain if the stranger was a Finn or a Swede, or even some other nationality, giving rise to the incident being called "Revolt of the Long Finn (or Swede), The Long Finn Rebellion, Uproar Among the Swedes, and other names that are longer than the actual occurrence itself.

The Long Finn (or Swede) in question referred to himself as descending from the German Swedish noble family of Königsmark, which produced two brothers who had both served in the Swedish army: Count Hans Christoff, and Otto Whilhelm. The latter was deployed as a diplomat accompanying the Swedish ambassador to France in 1665 to lobby for Sweden's claims against the Netherlands—including the restoration of New Sweden. It came to nothing, but the Long Finn may have picked up the gist of the endeavor, hoping to capitalize on it in some way. Having changed hands so many times, it was conceivable that New Castle would not, in all likelihood, remain in English hands. This territory was still up for grabs, and a return to Swedish control was not out of the question.

The term "long", or "lång", in Swedish, refers to the physical stature of the man. He also came to be known by several other names, but the most commonly agreed upon is Marcus Jacobson. He was evidently not one of the original settlers; nothing is known of him before 1668. He may have been one of the re-enforcing immigrants who arrived on the Mercurious, yet other evidence points to him arriving via the Maryland colony where he had been an indentured servant, sent to the colonies after committing some crime in England. After showing up in New Castle, he traveled between local farms working as an itinerant laborer, possibly sniffing an air of restlessness among the owners, as it seems it was during this time that he began to formulate his plan of insurrection.

Jacobson soon began to appear in various neighborhoods along the river arranging dinner parties to which he would invite heads of households, as well as young, able-bodied men. There would be an abundance of food supplied, as well as generous amounts of strong drink. As the evening progressed and the guests became more open to suggestion, Jacobson would take the floor, urging them to "throw off the yoke, reminding them how they had suffered from the English, and how they, partly by treachery, partly by force, took from them one big piece of land after another." He would end the festivities by posing the question "if they held with the King of Sweden, or the King of England?" The desired result was inevitably Sweden's King. He would then incite further frenzy by encouraging them to take up arms and make ready for the arrival of a Swedish fleet which always seemed to be poised just over the horizon.

There may have been something more to this New Sweden Restoration conspiracy than just rowdy dinner parties. There were hints that stronger influences were at work, including shadowy inferences to Armegot Printz. She stayed behind to occupy the Printzfoff, when her father and the rest of her family returned to Sweden. It has been suggested that her fierce loyalty to her father's position led to some mysterious background role in the affair, perhaps even recruiting Jacobson as an unwitting catalyst.

However, if the clandestine dinner gatherings actually grew into a full-fledged conspiracy, it did not last long. Rumors of an impending insurrection made their way to the ears of then New York Governor Francis Lovelace, who sent his secretary Matthias Nicolls to apprehend the Long Finn and put him on trial. In August of 1669, during one of the "Riotous, Routous & Vnlawfull Assemblyes", possibly at Stalcop's house, some of the more stalwart members of the Swedish community, who were totally opposed to Jacobson's behavior, broke in on the festivities. Peter Cock tried to confine the Finn in the house by holding the door shut and calling for help. Jacobson pushed back. Cock pulled a knife and slashed the Finn's hand through a crack in the door. The struggle continued, but Jacobson managed to slip away into the night.

Jacobson was allied with another Finn, Henry Colman (or Kolman), a farmer living in Kingsessing, who took Jacobson quite seriously, giving up his livestock and crops to follow him. Colman helped the Long Finn escape from the authorities and hide among the Indians, who Colman knew fairly well. The Lenape collaborators seemed to have taken a liking to the Finn, as after his capture, they threatened grave retributions on New Castle saying "they would kill man woman and Childe and burn the how'll plase." This seemed somewhat plausible, as the Indians were still resentful of the Dutch conquest of their favored trading partners, the Swedes.

Like a scene from an old western, a posse was formed, this one rather diverse, consisting of English, Dutch, a couple of Swedes, and members of the constabulary: Sheriff William Tom and his Deputy Michael Barron. They eventually tracked down the fugitives and took them to New Castle, clapped in irons to await trial. The co-conspirators, which may have included our old acquaintance Ivert the Finn, were rounded up as well, but most were released on bail. Johan Stalcop was not as fortunate, sharing the same treatment as Colman and Jacobson.

Of the actual trial, we know next to nothing as the records seem to have vanished. All that remains of the incident is a copy of the commission for the trial, the terms for how it was to be carried out, and the actual punishment. All of the Finn's fervent followers were fined to varying degrees, according to their involvement, which left only the Long Finn to face the most serious retribution. He was sentenced to be "publicly & severely whipt & stigmatiz'd or Branded in the fface with the Letter (R) with an Inscription written in great Letters & putt upon his Breast." Then he was to be sold as a slave and shipped to "Barbados or some other of those remoter Plantations." He was indeed taken to the Caribbean in January of 1670, and that was the last anyone ever saw of the Long Finn.

XXIV

When Charles gifted the Dutch grant to his brother James, he in turn presented a portion of it to two of the staunchest supporters of the Stuarts during their time of exile. The land bordered on the north by the Hudson River, and the south by the Delaware was gifted to Sir George Carteret and John, Lord Berkeley. Carteret was the Bailiff of the Isle of Jersey, and it was for him that the province was named—Nova Caesarea, or New Jersey. Berkeley had been a true soldier in the field and close personal friend of both Charles and James. Each were members of the Privy Council.

The tract was weirdly carved into diagonal portions, with Carteret as proprietor of the east and Berkeley in possession of the west. They were also presented with the responsibility of governing the domain. The frame of it proved to be surprisingly liberal, guaranteeing religious freedom, a condition unheard of in England. New settlers began to migrate to northern East Jersey from New England and Long Island, establishing towns and villages. West Jersey, however, remained relatively uncultivated, inhabited by the Lenape and just a few white settlers, mostly Finnish and Swedish farming families who had migrated across the Delaware.

✦ ✦ ✦

DURING THIS TIME, a great religious upheaval was taking place on the other side of the Atlantic. A number of dissenting Christian denominations began to emerge which included The Society of Friends, founded by George Fox. Known as the Quakers (it was said they should "quake" before God), they promoted belief in a direct spiritual relationship with God without the use of clergy or ritual. As with any new ideological movement which is misunderstood, they were of course persecuted, severely, by the established Church of England. In 1662, the Quaker Act was passed, making it a crime to be one. Understandably, the practitioners began to look for safer situations in which to observe their faith, mostly the new colonies in New England and Maryland.

Fox himself ventured to the New World in 1671 and made his way to Maryland by way of Barbados and Jamaica. He visited New Castle, crossed the Delaware and tramped through West Jersey accompanied by Indian guides. He paused for an evening at an abandoned tavern owned by one Pierre Jegou, where the City of Burlington now stands. The next day, he reported swimming to Metedeconck Island, site of the Walloon settlement of nearly fifty years earlier. He continued north through

East Jersey, New York, and on into New England, taking stock the whole while of a rich, bountiful land. He then reversed course, heading south again through the Jerseys into what would become Pennsylvania, back through New Castle, and into Virginia and Carolina before departing once again from Maryland for England, a journey of nearly three years.

Upon his return, Fox found himself in familiar surroundings–prison, where he had already spent much of his adult life as punishment for his dissenting beliefs. But this time his release was secured by a very influential follower—William Penn. It was also during this time when Fox related the tales of his travels to the New World and the wonderful sites he had witnessed, that undoubtedly influenced Penn to formulate a plan that would result in thousands of Quakers crossing the Atlantic to their very own colony in what he would call his "Holy Experiment."

And almost as if by divine intervention, Lord Berkeley picked just this precipitous moment to sell his half of the Jerseys. Since it was largely uninhabited (except for the native population), it proved unprofitable. He found a buyer in his friend Edward Byllynge, a former officer in Cromwell's army–turned brewer–turned Quaker. He was among a growing group of entrepreneurs who had become followers of George Fox's teachings. Unfortunately, Byllynge was in deep financial straits. Fiscal punishment was levied against him for his involvement with the Quakers, forcing him to the brink of bankruptcy. But fellow officer Major John Fenwick, also a recent convert to the Society of Friends, was recruited to act as an agent and hold the property in trust for the asking price of £1,000. He also invested a sum of his own money in return for a portion of the land. In March of 1674, the transaction was completed and the territory of West Jersey was divided into 100 parts. However, the Duke of York refused to recognize it—Fenwick had been in charge of protecting the scaffolding when the Duke's father, Charles I was executed.

From this point the purchase becomes as obtuse as Shakespeare to a sheep. Byllynge and Fenwick had a major falling out over how much property each was entitled to. Following Quaker procedure, an arbitrator was called in to settle the dispute. In this case, it was the ubiquitous William Penn who humbly wrote to Fenwick, "I am an impartial man."

Both Byllynge and Fenwick proved to be stubborn participants, making the negotiation a long, drawn out affair. But in May of 1675, Fenwick finally accepted a tenth interest in the West Jersey transaction along with £400 in cash. The next month, Byllynge also turned to Penn for help in untangling his messy financial affairs. Along with Penn, Gawen Lawrie and Nicholas Lucas joined together to form the Byllynge Trustees, to determine the usage of the West Jersey territory. An opportunity now presented itself—it could become a refuge for the much persecuted Friends. It took the group nearly three years of planning, including the absolution of the Duke of York's objections and negotiating a boundary with the Carteret interests, to build the basis for a religious sanctuary. But in the interim, Fenwick became impatient. He was intent on founding an independent colony.

Acting without the aid or consent of Byllynge, Penn, or other Quakers, Fenwick advertised for skilled artisans and trades people to accompany him in creating a colony in his portion of the New World on the Delaware. In the fall of 1675, the Fenwick expedition crossed the Atlantic on the *Griffin* and landed at old Fort Elfsborg, near Varken's Kill, the site of the failed New Haven colony. Fenwick would call the new community Salem, a corruption of the Hebrew Shalom. He gathered the leaders of the local Lenape tribe and provided in trade what they agreed would be fair compensation for rights to what would encompass today's Salem and Cumberland Counties. It would became the first permanent English-speaking settlement on the Delaware.

One year later, the Fenwick Quakers held their first organized meeting in the home of Samuel Nicholson, proclaimed "the wealthiest man in Salem Towne." Which was like saying he had a dime and everyone else had ten cents. There were not many settlers, rich or poor that inhabited Salem at that date. He had been allotted sixteen acres of prime real estate on which stood The Salem Oak, which survives to this day. The Quakers continued to hold their meetings, rotating between members' homes, including the house of Andrew Thompson, who built one of the first brick dwellings on the Delaware. Located near the mouth of Varken's Kill, renamed Salem Creek, it became known as The Emigrant House, where those arriving from a trans-Atlantic crossing could first set foot in the New World.

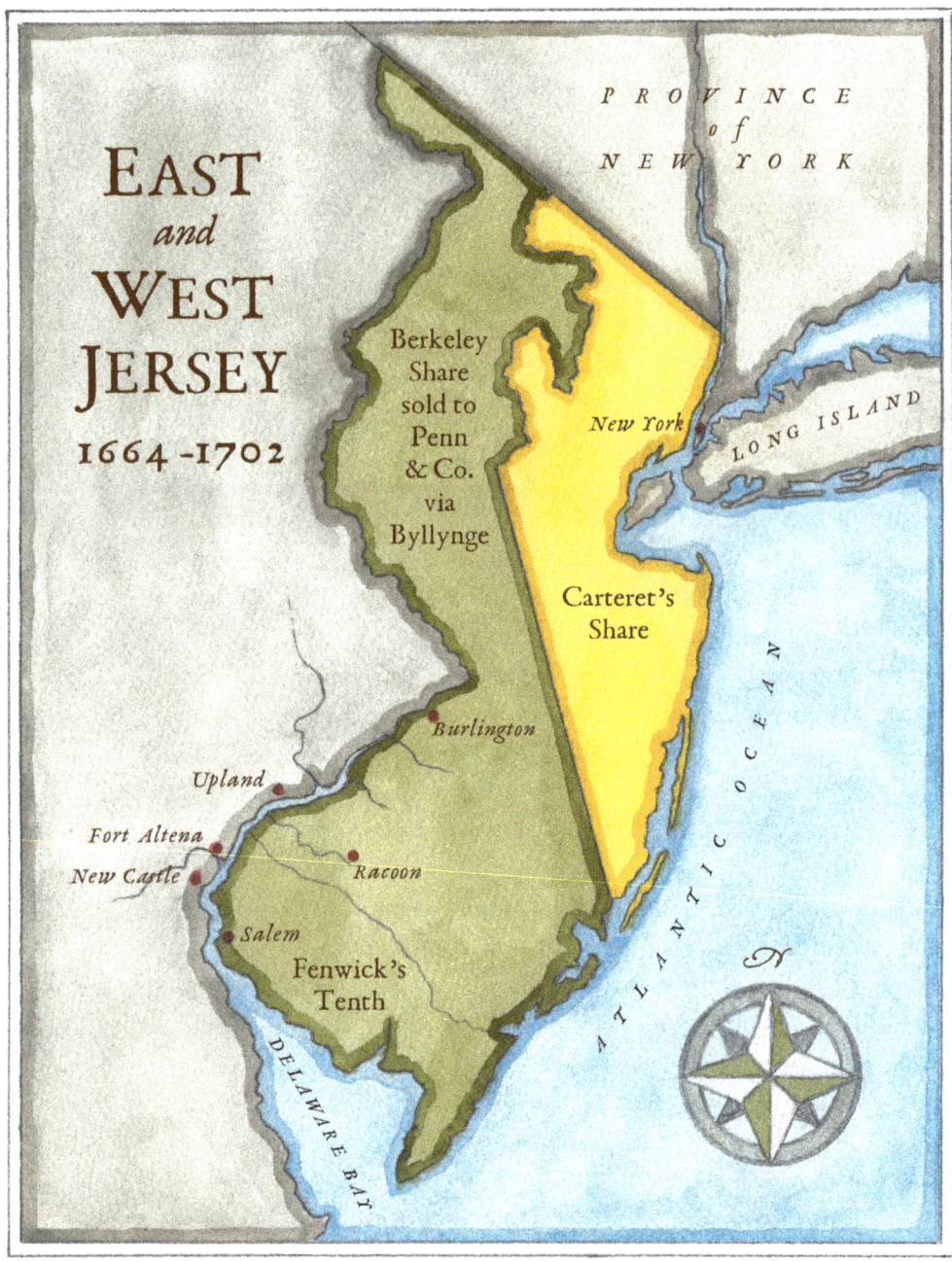

After Nova Cesaeria was divided between John Lord Berkeley and Sir George Carteret, the portions were never actually surveyed until much later, resulting in many years of drawn and re-drawn demarcation lines and often violent disputes. This illustration (liberally interpreted) shows just one version defined by the Quintipartite Deed of 1676 in which Berkeley sold his portion to John Fenwick on behalf of Edward Byllynge and his trustees, William Penn, Gawen Lawrie, and Nicholas Lucas. For his trouble, Fenwick was presented with one tenth of the total territory of East Jersey, which was eventually whittled down to just Salem County.

PART IV

✦ ✦ ✦

ON JULY 1, 1676, the Byllynge Trustees drew up the Quintipartite Deed, which established a firm division between the two Jerseys and divided West Jersey into one hundred shares or "proprieties" to be advertised and heartily recommended to prospective Quaker colonists. A constitution accompanied the deed–"Concessions and Agreements of the Proprietors, Freeholders, and Inhabitants of the Province of West New-Jersey in America." For its time, it was extremely progressive, guaranteeing freedom of worship, right to a trial by jury, and the banning of illegal arrest and imprisonment for debt. In it can be seen the genus that would eventually coalesce into the U.S. Constitution over one hundred years later. It also served as a prototype for Penn, setting the stage for his greatest achievement across the Delaware.

In the fall of 1677, the first group of Byllynge colonists set sail from England onboard the *Kent*, Godfrey Marlow, master. As they passed the royal barge on their trip down the Thames, the King gave them the most casual wave he could muster, his indifference one of the major causes for them to be leaving in the first place. Crammed with livestock, basic living necessities, and 230 Quakers from Yorkshire and London, they finally landed at the Swedish settlement of Raccoon Creek.

After careful preliminary scouting, negotiations were made with the local tribesman to secure land along the river south of "the falls", across from High Island/Metedeconck, where George Fox had visited on his North American pilgrimage. The spot they chose was also an island, "Chygoe's Island", though like Tinicum, was separated from the mainland by only a stream. Laying out the town was entrusted to one Richard Noble, surveyor to the Duke of York who had come to shores of the Delaware two years previously with Fenwick. A main thoroughfare named High Street was run south from the river which would be the dividing line between the Yorkshire and London companies. The street still exists in its original configuration—one of the oldest in the Delaware Valley.

A name was needed for their brand new town, and after haggling for a bit, New Beverly was decided upon. But after sleeping on it for a while, it was changed to Bridlington. Still not satisfied, it took on the final title of Burlington, after an old village in Yorkshire. Later in the fall, the *Willing Mind* arrived in the lower Delaware with a few dozen more Quaker hopefuls, some of whom settled at Salem, the rest at Burlington. It was soon followed by over one hundred more incoming colonists. There were now over 300 Quaker pioneers in and around the new settlement, nearly all seeking shelter from the oncoming winter. Crude dwellings, even caves were hastily thrown together. They also relied heavily on the local Indians who generously shared wigwams and traded for corn and venison.

Nearly a year later, the *Shield of Stockton* arrived after a sixteen week Atlantic crossing that saw the loss of two passengers, who were replaced by the birth of two new ones. The story is told that the night of the arrival at Burlington, a rapid cold front moved through the area, freezing the river itself. In the morning, the immigrants disembarked by walking across the ice to the shoreline.

It did not take long before the initial pilgrims were joined by scores of others. By 1681, more than 1,400 Quakers were to be counted in West Jersey, including Irish Quakers who left Dublin to found the Irish Tenth in present Gloucester County. This stretch of riverfront communities would become the prototype for Penn's grand design across the river.

Poor Major Fenwick did not fare as well. Not long after the establishment of "Fenwick's Colony", he ran afoul of then New York governor Edmund Andros, who in an ugly affair, had him arrested and dragged in chains to New York for illegally assuming a governorship. To add to his misfortune, he had left his financial and personal affairs in England in a rather messy state. They had to be untangled by the Byllynge trustees which resulted in Fenwick's holdings being reduced to the neighborhood of his colony, and his remaining shares passing into the hands of William Penn. His imprisonment by Andros was not the only time Fenwick found himself behind bars. His name appears frequently in the court records of Delaware and Pennsylvania, as well as New York.

It was not long before the estate of the recently deceased Sir George Carteret was found to be lacking as well. To settle his debts, Carteret's share of the Duke of York's grant now also came into the possession of Penn, along with twenty-three other proprietaries. William Penn was now one of the largest non-monarchial land owners in the western world. But his holdings would soon be even larger.

A number of negative political and social events in England made prospects in the New World more and more appealing to Penn. He began to prepare for an exodus of the mass oppressed of Europe to what he intended to be a utopia of tolerance.

PART IV

XXV

William Penn's father was Admiral Sir William Penn, a loyal friend to the Stuarts over the years. He became Sir William for his part in retrieving Charles from exile in Holland to be restored to the throne, and Admiral for his appointment as Commissioner of the Royal Navy. He was equally recognized by Charles' brother James (who just happened to be Lord High Admiral), commanding his flagship during the Second Anglo-Dutch War.

ADMIRAL PENN

When he passed away in 1670, Sir William was owed considerable back pay. But in truth, the King was flat broke. Titles and appointments are lovely sentiments, but not as useful as cash. Charles' clandestine allowance from Louis XIV had expired, and his credit score was in a minus state. As had been the case in the past, whenever the monarchy (both Charles I and his son) had debts to settle, they did so by presenting their creditors with land grants. And the New World seemed to them an endless commodity–a get-out-of-debt-free card with no expiration date.

The younger Penn was well aware of this, and now the opportunity to capitalize clearly presented itself. In lieu of the £16,000 owed, Penn petitioned for a vast chunk of real estate directly across the river from his New Jersey holdings. It was to be located between the 39th and 42nd degrees north latitude, and from the start of the Delaware River continuing 5 degrees longitude. Although the western boundary was as yet undefined, the tract would total some 45,000 acres. Penn named it "New Wales", then changed his mind and called it "Sylvania". It was the king who would add "Penn", in honor of his worthy admiral. But Penn argued that adding his family name to the property would be far too narcissistic for Quaker sensibilities. However, the king would not be swayed, which led Penn to try changing the name by a different method: in a letter to his friend Robert Turner, Penn admitted "though I much opposed it, and went to the king to have its struck out and altered, he said 'twas past…nor could twenty guineas move the under secretary to vary the name." Charles actually believed he had gotten the better of the deal. He had paid off a large, outstanding debt, and as a bonus, relieved his country of the annoying Quakers.

The charter was signed and sealed on March 4, 1681. It consisted of twenty-three articles, one of which made Penn the Lord Proprietary, who in homage to the King, was required to pay two beaver skins every January 1st. Aside from the beaver skins, the generous gift was free from any other stipulations. But there was still one very tedious detail: the exhausting dispute over the contested Maryland territory. Though put on hold back in 1659, it resurfaced once it was revealed that Penn's charter would include the original Dutch and Swedish settlements, now ceded to the Duke of York. Charles Calvert, the third Lord Baltimore, did not object to Penn's charter as long as it remained above the 40th parallel, retaining access to the Delaware as indicated in the original land of 1632. He would also recognize the Duke's acquisition of New Castle.

Penn knew the vast region he was requesting—lands to the west of the river, and north of Maryland—but the 40th parallel boundary of Lord Baltimore's colony was rather uncertain. It had been crudely surveyed a number of times, with no firm conclusion established. To resolve the question, the Duke's secretary Sir John Werden proposed setting the southern limit of Penn's claim thirty miles above New Castle, to which Penn quickly objected, fearing that he would be left without navigable access to the Delaware. Werden acquiesced, and reduced the limit to twelve miles, resulting in the creation of a twelve-mile "circle", centered from the middle of New Castle.

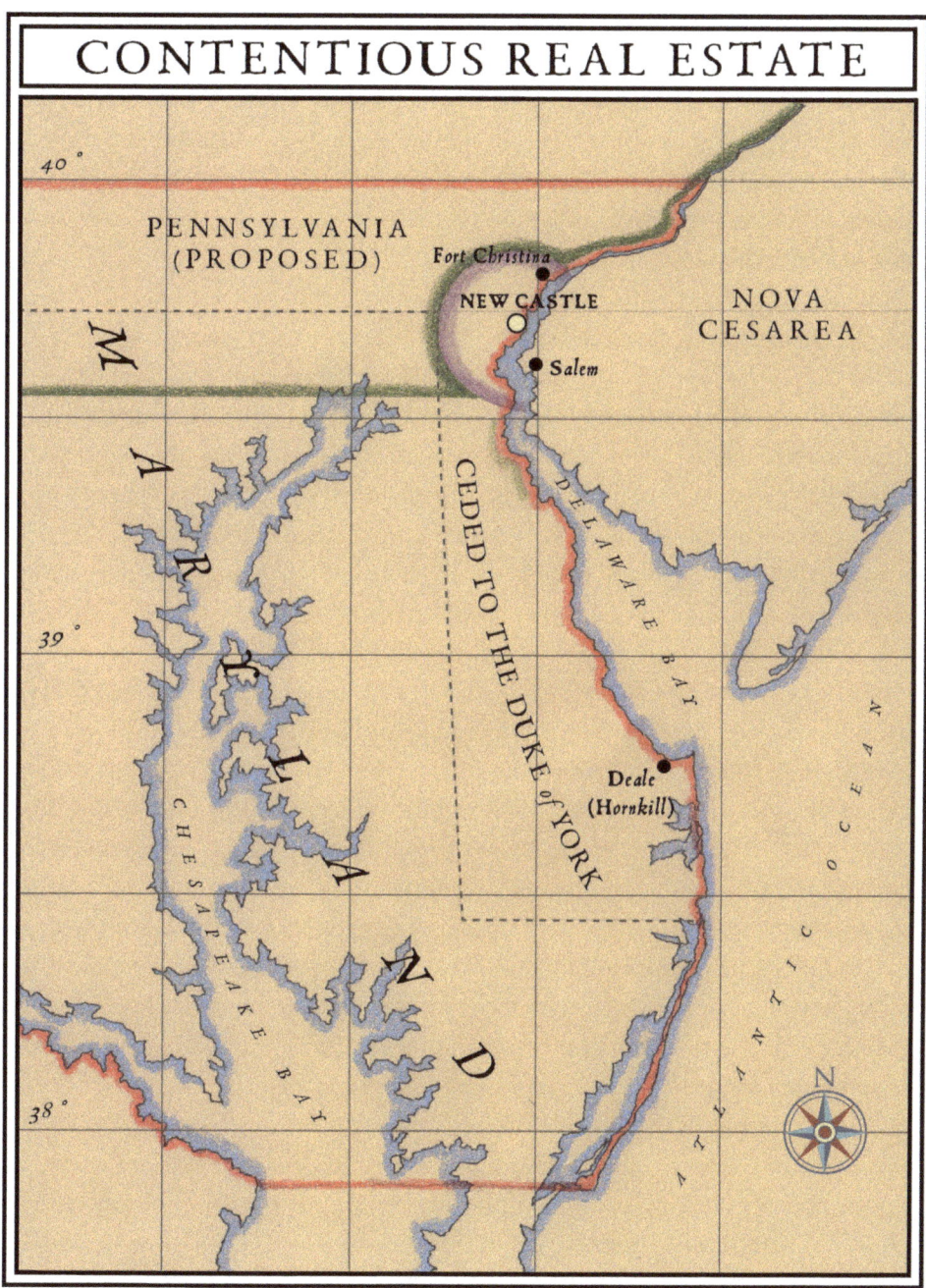

- 🟥 Original boundary of the Maryland Colony - 1632
- 🟩 Penn's proposed boundary of Pennsylvania, providing access to both the Delaware and Chesapeake Bays
- 🟪 The Duke of York's twelve mile circle encompassing his possession of New Castle
- --- Modern state borders

But Penn still was not content. He wanted control of the entire Delaware valley, including some access to the waters of the Chesapeake. He wrote two letters to the Duke making clear his request, explaining the urgent need for a navigable waterway to meet the needs of the large proportions of his proposed colonial project. After an interval in monarchial time, the Duke agreed to Penn's request, granting him the "Lower Counties", which would eventually become the State of Delaware. It was good to have friends in high places.

Once again, Lord Baltimore found his grant compromised. Although Plowden's charter never came to fruition, the new Penn charter proved a very frustrating affair to the Calverts, English Parliament, and Penn himself. The argument dragged on for over eighty-five years until it was finally settled by the surveying team of Charles Mason and Jeremiah Dixon, long after the patriarchs of the two proprietary families were gone. It would plague Penn for the rest of life, and prevent him from spending quality time in his Delaware River colony. Even as recently as 1934, the boundary dispute was still being argued in the U.S. Supreme Court, which declared the Duke of York's title to the Lower Counties "inured by estoppel" to Penn.

A month after the charter was signed, Penn published a prospectus through Benjamin Clark of London as a guide for the anticipated mass migration of dissidents, in which he extolled the many virtues of this new and exciting land. Though he had as yet not been there, he had poured over fastidiously prepared reports from many sources, confident in his interpretation of the bounties of the Delaware River valley: In the Pennsylvania colony one could expect to find opportunities for commerce based on the navigational aspects of the Delaware and its tributaries, abundance of wild game, excellent farmland, proximity to Virginia for trade, as well as to the Indians for furs, and most importantly of all–religious freedom. But, "they must be willing to be two or three years without some of the conveniences they enjoy at home," He wished them happiness, that he was not some businessman who intended to get rich from their labors, and that they would be free to govern themselves. He would join them in a few months.

Until then, Penn's cousin, William Markham, was put in charge of the operation as deputy governor. He sailed alone, first landing at New York to confer with Governor Andros and then up the Delaware to the Swedish village of Upland. A number of local dignitaries were on hand to greet him, including Charles Calvert. Penn had presented Markham with the painfully delicate task of personally trying to settle the boundary dispute with his new neighbor. The disagreement was addressed immediately, and just as quickly dropped when the two charters were compared and did not agree.

Penn had also arranged for three commissioners to meet with Markham and select a site for the proposed city and lay it out. In addition, a letter he had composed was sent along to be delivered to the Indians, advising them of his good intentions and that they would be treated fairly and respectfully. Although it was suggested to the commissioners that Upland should be considered as the site, much of the waterfront property was already occupied by Swedes, Dutch and English colonists who were well established and had no plans to sell. Instead, Wicaco was selected.

During the same time, three ships, each with a cargo of settlers eager to place their claims, sailed up the Delaware. Finding no ready-made habitations of any sort, they took advantage of the steep river bank and proceeded to dig caves while more suitable accommodations could be constructed in the city that was yet to be laid out. It was in these crude dwellings that they spent the winter of 1681.

Finally, Penn and approximately 100 passengers set sail on the *Welcome* from Deal, Kent on August 30, 1682, and arrived at New Castle on October 27. It was the first in a fleet of twenty-three ships that would bring more than 2,000 colonists to Pennsylvania over the next year. The voyage would have been uneventful, were it not for the shipboard smallpox epidemic that swept through the vessel, taking the lives of thirty individuals. The skyline of New Castle must have appeared majestic to the survivors after so long at sea, even though the town was anything but a thriving metropolis with its rustic Dutch cottages and windmill. But there were hordes of people on shore: European settlers eagerly awaiting the first glimpse of

PENN LANDS *at* NEW CASTLE · 1682

their new governor, mingling with the Indians, who were always on hand to witness a ship's arrival.

The next morning, Penn disembarked and was greeted by Markham, surveyor Thomas Holme, and representatives for His Royal Highness, John Moll and Ephraim Harman. They turned over possession of the town of New Castle "with twelve miles circle or compass of the said town", and Penn repeated the ancient livery of seisin ritual in the crumbling remains of old Fort Casimir that had been conducted a hundred years previously by Sir Humphrey Gilbert on the rocky shores of Newfoundland. The town fathers also presented a document proclaiming themselves loyal subjects of their new Governor. The Swedes, represented by our friend

Peter Gunnerson Rambo, who was now a magistrate, offered a special welcoming statement that "they would love, serve, and obey him with all they had; that it was the best day they ever had." Though opportunities for advancement were scarce in such an uncertain environment, Rambo had been able to work his way up the ranks through three different colonial power exchanges. The deliverance of the grant was now complete.

Despite the disappointment of the rest of the passengers of not being able to set foot on land yet, Penn returned to the ship the same day to sail upriver to the attractive little village of Upland, where he and his company gratefully made their way to Essex House, owned by fellow Quaker Robert Wade. Despite every nuance of this country he had studied in letters and reports beforehand, nothing prepared him for the actual experience of being there. His praise was limitless.

At some point shortly after his arrival, Penn changed the name of the little village to Chester, at the request of a man named Pearson, who wanted a remembrance of his home in England. And then it was off to see firsthand the site of the city for which he joined two Greek words philos and adelphos, creating a name worthy of his vision of a peaceable kingdom. As his boat slowly advanced upstream, Penn could see a place where the banks of the river were high above the waterline, and a tributary called Dock Creek flowed into a natural harbor with a sandy landing place.

There were already ten houses along the creek, in addition to the caves and shanties that the early arriving settlers had thrown together for protection. There was also the Blue Anchor Tavern, the first building constructed on the Philadelphia site. Built of brick and used as a post office, ferry house, taproom and inn for trappers and traders, it was already close to ten years old when Penn arrived.

William Penn and his associates disembarked and strode along the high banks marking where the streets and parks were to be placed, and speculating on the houses and gardens that would soon be sprouting in this "greene country towne." He must have felt enormous pride and gratification at finally setting foot on the place where a vision was about to become reality.

As Penn settled in to his new endeavor, he rented a home originally built for fellow Quaker Samuel Carpenter which was dubbed "The Slate Roof House" for obvious reasons. He only lived in it for two years before returning to England. The house served a variety of purposes before falling into disrepair and was eventually demolished in 1867. Today the site is memorialized as Welcome Park, an open air museum that honors the colony's founder.

✦ EPILOGUE ✦

Although Penn was a resident of his "Holy Experiment", for only four years, the tone he set would echo for years to come. By the time the Continental Congress met, nearly sixty years after his passing, local residents still carried his legacy, causing Clergyman Jacob Duché to remark: "The poorest laborer upon the shore of the Delaware thinks himself entitled to deliver his sentiments in matters of religion and politics with as much freedom as the gentleman or the scholar.... For every man expects one day or another to be upon a footing with his wealthiest neighbor."

✦ ✦ ✦

OF DUTCH INFLUENCE on the Delaware, nothing remains in a physical sense, only a smattering of words that have become part of everyday lexicon: blunderbuss, scow, sleigh, cookie, waffle, cole slaw, nitwit, Santa Claus (from Sinter Klass, a familiarization of St. Nicholas), Yankee–from Janke, similar to the English Johnny, or Jan Kees, "John Cheese", intended as an insult, and thus its use by the British in referring to the American rebels.

There is far more Dutch remembrance in New York, particularly in rural areas of the Hudson Valley where Dutch was spoken well into the 1940s. Famed abolitionist Sojourner Truth was raised as a slave in a Dutch family and spoke only their language until she became an adult.

✦ ✦ ✦

THE NEW SWEDEN COLONY only lasted about one generation officially. It's not even known exactly how many settlers were involved at its height, but its people made up the fabric of America just as much as any other immigrants. As so succinctly described by author Adrian C. Leiby:

> Overwhelmed by numbers of English, German and Scotch Irish neighbors, it would be hard to trace to the Swedes of New Jersey any distinct contributions to the ways of America. It would be hard too, to find a trace of any branch of the Delaware in the main stream, yet no thoughtful person will doubt that it is there.

EPILOGUE

Within their communities, the Swedes and Finns enjoyed a symbiotic relationship, but to outsiders, Finns were just another type of Swede. However, their people did make marked, if not widely recognized contributions: Eric Pålsson Mullica, who arrived in New Sweden with the Rising expedition in 1654, was of Finnish ancestry and has the distinction of having his name attached to the Mullica River, Mullica Township, and the town of Mullica Hill, rare remainders of Nordic influence.

On that same voyage was the great grandfather of John Morton. Morton, a member of the First and Second Continental Congress, was a signer of the Declaration of Independence and chairman of the committee that authored the Articles of Confederation.

✦ ✦ ✦

JOHAN PRINTZ RETURNED to Sweden with his wife and daughters in the spring of 1654, after sailing to Amsterdam and selling his personal supplies of furs and tobacco. He resumed his military career as a commandant and then county commissioner, while residing at Gunillaberg Manor, an opulent and spacious estate. He died in 1663, leaving a small fortune to his remaining family and a hat to the local vicar, Mr. Anders.

His fifth daughter Armegot remained at Printzhoff, while her husband Johan Papegoja followed his in-laws back to Sweden. One of the more colorful people to have ever been chronicled on the river, she inherited many of the traits of her literally larger-than-life father, which probably contributed to her husband wishing to be as far from her as possible. And it seems the feeling was mutual as she reverted to using her maiden name. After the river came back in control of the Dutch, she petitioned Governor Stuyvesant to let Tinicum remain in the possession of the Printz family, which he granted. And there she lived for the next twenty-three years, embroiled in litigation, contentious relations with her neighbors, and general tyranny.

She sold Tinicum in 1662 to a Frenchman named De la Grange and returned to Sweden. He died, however, before the final payment could be made. Returning to the Delaware, she then sued his wife for the remainder. But Madame De la Grange acquired a suitor; one M. la Motte who now offered to buy the land, perhaps to improve his position with the widow. But Madame Printz doubted his financial stability and took the matter to the New York Court of Assizes. She won handily, retaining possession of Tinicum.

The staff who served Ms. Printz gradually diminished, not surprisingly, as none of them showed "any inclination to live with her," leaving just one male servant. She did manage to have the land worked using outside help and acquired a license from Governor Lovelace to operate a still, from which she produced either corn liquor, or schnapps, depending upon who tells the story.

In 1676, Armegot sold Tinicum again, this time to Otto Cock for three hundred guilders, and once again returned to Sweden, this time for good. She left one last slight to her neighbors: in selling off the island, she sold the church and its bell that had been sent from Sweden. Though the new owner allowed them to use the church, they had to buy back the bell. Armegot Printz died in 1695.

✦ ✦ ✦

LIKE FORT NASSAU, no physical remains endure of the other fortifications and blockhouses along the Delaware and Schuykill; neither Dutch, Swedish, nor English.

✦ ✦ ✦

WASHINGTON IRVING, beloved American author who wrote almost exclusively of the Dutch settlers in and around New York, offered in the persona of Diedrich Knickerbocker, this creative evaluation of Fort Casimir's role in precipitating the American Revolution:

> "By the treacherous surprisal of Fort Casimir [by Rising] then, did the crafty Swedes enjoy a transient triumph, but drew upon their heads the vengeance of Peter Stuyvesant, who wrested all New Sweden from their hands. By the conquest of New Sweden, Peter Stuyvesant aroused the claims of Lord Baltimore, who appealed to the Cabinet of Great Britain, who subdued the whole province of New Netherlands. By this great achievement, the whole extent of North America from Nova Scotia to the Floridas was rendered one entire dependency upon the British crown. But mark the consequences: the hitherto scattered colonies, being thus consolidated and having no rival colonies to check or keep them in awe, waxed great and powerful, and, finally, becoming too strong for the mother-country, were enabled to shake off its bonds, and by a glorious revolution became an independent empire. But the chain of efforts stopped not there; the successful revolution in America produced the sanguinary revolution in France, which produced the puissant Buonaparte, who produced the French despotism, which has thrown the whole world into confusion!—Thus have these great powers been successively punished for their ill-starred conquests—and thus, as I asserted, have all the present convulsions, revolutions, and disasters that overwhelm mankind, originated in the capture of the little Fort Casimir, as recorded in this eventful history."

✦ NOTES ✦

PROLOGUE

Turner, Jack. *Spice*. (New York: Vintage Books, 2005), 5,7; Bryson, Bill. *At Home*. (New York: Doubleday, 2010), 175; Turner, 31-36; Rink, *Emergence of Empires: Netherlands, Encyclopedia of the North American Colonies*, 98.; Quinn, *The Age of Reconnaissance, Encyclopedia of the North American Colonies*, 54.

CHAPTER ONE

http://news.nationalgeographic.com/2016/03/160331-viking-discovery-north-america-canada-archaeology/; Bryson, Bill. *Made in America: An Informal History of the English Language in the United States*. (New York: HarperCollins, 1996), 10; Maine Museum, "The Goddard Norse Coin", www.state.me.us/anthropology/norsecoinpage.html; Morison, Samuel Eliot. *The European Discovery of America, The Northern Voyages A.D. 500-1600*. (London: Oxford University Press, 1971), 33-34; Horwitz, Tony. *A Voyage Long and Strange*. (New York: Picador, 2008), chp. 1; Encyclopedia of the North American Colonies, pg. 84; Lester, Toby. *The Fourth Part of the World*. (New York: Free Press, 2009), 209; Kurlansky, Mark. *Cod*. (New York: Penguin Books, 1997), various references throughout; Morison, 189; Lester, 283; Lester, preface; Morison, 163; Kraft, Herbert C. *The Lenape*. (Newark, NJ: New Jersey Historical Society, 1986), 195; Fernández-Arresto, Felipe. *Pathfinders: A Global History of Exploration*. (New York, W.W. Norton & Co., 2006), 160; Shorto, Russell. *The Island at the Center of the World*. (New York: Vintage Books 2005), 19.

CHAPTER TWO

Richard Hakluyt, University of Adelaide, ebook, Humphrey Gilbert Discourse; Lester, chp. 1; Dictionary of Canadian Biography, David B. Quinn; http://www.biographi.ca/en/bio.php?id_nbr=247; http://www.verrazzano.com; Morison, chp. 9; Horowitz, 294-295; Wright, Louis B. *The Atlantic Frontier, Colonial American Civilization (1607-1763)*. (New York: Alfred A. Knopf, 1951), chp. 1; Horowitz, 296-297; Fordham U., Modern History Sourcebook, Gilbert's voyage to Newfoundland, 1583, fordham.edu; National Park Service, Fort Raleigh, Sir Humphrey Gilbert, www.nps.gov

CHAPTER THREE

Morison, 669-679; Horwitz, 299-300; Tobacco: Its History and Associations. F.W. Fairholt, F.S.A. Chapman and Hall, 193, Piccadilly, London. 1859, on-line: https://archive.org/stream/tobaccoitshistor00fair#page/n7/mode/2up; Miller, Lee. *Roanoke.* (New York: MJF Books, 2000), various references throughout the book; Weslager, C.A. *The English on the Delaware, 1610-1682.* (Rutgers University Press. 1967), chp. 1; Wright, Louis B. *The Atlantic Frontier, Colonial American Civilization (1607-1763).* (New York: Alfred A. Knopf, 1951), chp. 1; https://en.wikipedia.org/wiki/John_Smith_(explorer)

CHAPTER FOUR

Wooley, Benjamin. *Savage Kingdom.* (New York: HarperCollins, 2007), chp. 13; Wright, chp. 2; Encyclopedia of the North American Colonies. Volume I. Various Editors (New York: Charles Scribner's Sons,1993), chp. 13, 16; Weslager, English, chp. 1, 2, 4; http://www.nyc99.org/1600/velasco.html; Bryson (America), 100.

CHAPTER FIVE

Ward, Christopher, *The Dutch & Swedes on the Delaware, 1609-64.* (University of Pennsylvania Press 1930). 10-23; http://www.lenapelifeways.org/lenape2.htm#shelters ; Heston, Alfred M. *South Jersey, A History 1664-1924.* (New York & Chicago: Lewis Historical Publishing Company, Inc., 1924), 20; Bryson, America, 158, 23; Ward, 14; Weslager, Delaware, 34, 35; Kraft, 156; http:/www.penntreatymuseum.org/americans.php ; http://www.tobaccoseed.ca/ ; Kraft, 165; https://static1.squarespace.com/static/50a02efce4b046b42952af27/t/50a8722de4b0ea694c52fffe/1353216557007/Rasieres.pdf

CHAPTER SIX

Shorto, chps. 1-2; Weslager, Dutch settlers, 27; Mancall, Peter C. *Fatal Journey, The Final Expedition of Henry Hudson.* (New York: MJF Books, 2009), 2, 22, 23, 69, 71; Shorto, 33, 36; Dersin, Denise. *What Life Was Like in Europe's Golden Age.* (Richmond, VA: Time-Life Books, 1999), 105

CHAPTER SEVEN

http://en.wikipedia.org/wiki/Nonsuch_House#cite_note-1; Taylor, Alan. American Colonies. (New York: Viking Penguin 2001), chp. 12; http://cwh.ucsc.edu/feinstein/A%20brief%20history%20of%20the%20beaver%20trade.html; http://www.newnetherlandinstitute.org/history-and-heritage/digital-exhibitions/a-tour-of-new-netherland/hudson-river/fur-trade/; Meek, Phil. http://meek-williams-familytree.blogspot.com/2010/08/cornelius-hendrickson-navigatorexplorer.html;

Weslager, Dutch settlers, 112; http://www.princeton.edu/~achaney/tmve/wiki100k/docs/Dutch_West_India_Company.html; Ward, 32; Shorto, chp. 3; http://www.princeton.edu/~achaney/tmve/wiki100k/docs/Dutch_West_India_Company.html; Ward, chp. 3; http://www.lenapelifeways.org/lenape2.htm#shelters; Shorto, chp. 3, Weslager, Dutch, chp. 3; Veit, Richard and Orr, David. *Historical Archaeology of the Delaware Valley, 1600-1850.* (Knoxville, TN The University of Tennessee Press, 2014), chp. 2); https://en.wikipedia.org/wiki/Portal:Hudson_Valley ; https://en.wikipedia.org/wiki/Battle_in_the_Bay_of_Matanzas

Chapter Eight

Weslager Dutch, chp 3; Shorto, chp. 5; Weslager Dutch, chp 5; Calm, 206; Fernow, B. *Documents Relating to the History of the Dutch and Swedish Settlements on the Delaware River.* (Albany, The Argus Company, 1877), 47
http://explorepahistory.com/hmarker.php?markerId=1-A-209

Chapter Nine

Narratives of Early Pennsylvania, West New Jersey and Delaware 1630–1707. Edited by Albert Cook Myers, Online: http://books.google.com/books?id=FDR-AAAAIAAJ&dq=Narratives+of+Early+Pennsylvania,+West+New+Jersey+and+Delaware+1630%E2%80%931707&printsec=frontcover&source=bl&ots=faFlWOM4GD&sig=2_mbQLX8dW0_Tg0jHFBBCWN2Bc&hl=en&ei=zoGuSrrrDYLGlAeahP3ZBg&sa=X&oi=book_resu#v=onepage&q&f=false;
Weslager, Dutch, chp. 4; ^William [Willem] Kieft (n.d. [1639], "Patent Granted to Cornelis Melyn for Staten-Island, Excepting as Much of It as Had Been Granted to David Pietersen de Vries for a Bouwery", in B. Fernow, Documents Relating to the History and Settlements of the Towns along the Hudson and Mohawk Rivers (with the Exception of Albany), from 1630 to 168, https://books.google.com/books?id=VggMAAAAYAAJ&pg=PA7#v=onepage&q&f=false, Documents Relative to the Colonial History of the State of New-York XIII (Repr., New York: AMS Press, Inc., 1969. ed.), Albany, NY: Weed, Parsons & Co., p. 6, retrieved 26 May 2013; Narratives of Early Pennsylvania, West New Jersey and Delaware 1630–1707. Edited by Albert Cook Myers., 7-29; Eckman, Jeannette. *New Castle on the Delaware, Dutch Tercentenary Edition.* (New Castle, DE: New Castle Historical Society, 1950), 33; Weslager Dutch, chp 3; Stockton, Frank R. *Stories of New Jersey.* (New Brunswick, NJ: Rutgers University Press, 1961), 22, 23; Rootsweb PA-OLD-CHESTER, Peter Plockhoy and the Hoornkill settlers 1663-1690s; http://archiver.rootsweb.ancestry.com/th/read/PA-OLD-CHESTER/2006-12/1166025870 ; Stockton, 22, 23; https://www.captaincooksociety.com/home/detail/fluyts-and-katts

CHAPTER TEN
Myers, 37-44; Ward, 57-58.

CHAPTER ELEVEN
http://www.lonelyplanet.com/sweden/history; http://en.wikipedia.org/wiki/Gustavus_Adolphus_of_Sweden; Ward, 70; http://en.wikipedia.org/wiki/Swedish_Empire; Ward pg. 69; Ruhnbro, Rune. *New Sweden in the New World 1638-1655*. (Sweden: Förlags AB Wiken, 1988), 30; Munroe, 14; Johnson, Amandus. The Swedish Settlements on the Delaware. (University of Pennsylvania, 1911), chp. VIII

CHAPTER TWELVE
Weslager, C.A. *New Sweden on The Delaware: 1638-1655*. (Wilmington, DE: Middle Atlantic Press, 1988), various points throughout; Ward, 70; Shorto, 75; http://www.kalmarnyckel.org/download/knf_guidebook.pdf; Munroe, 16; Weslager, 28; Ruhnbro, 56; Myers, 61; Weslager, 39; Ward, 88; http://www.newnetherlandinstitute.org/files/8813/5067/3657/2.2.pdf

CHAPTER THIRTEEN
Weslager, 49, 52-55; http://www.kalmarnyckel.org/docs/knf_guidebook.pdf

CHAPTER FOURTEEN
Weslager, 56-59; Rambo, Herbert R. *Peter Gunnerson Rambo of New Sweden* (Self-published); Ward, 96, 97; Johnson, 142,144, 322; Ward, 97-8.

CHAPTER FIFTEEN
Wedin, Maud. *The Forest Finns of Scandinavia*. (Finland: Finnbygdens Förlag in co-operation with FINNSAM, 2011), 3-6; Weslager, 68-69; Munroe, 25; Ward, 108; Ruhnbro, 60, 61, 63; Ward, 110, 111, 153; Weslager, 91, 96; http://www.stalcopfamily.com/familyhistory.two.html; Weslager, 80, 92, 97; Johnson, 147, 240, 303, 305, 329, 349-50, 376-79, 414; Bailyn, 302; Rydén, Josef. *Johan Printz of New Sweden; New Sweden in the New World 1638-1655*. (Sweden: Förlags AB Wiken, 1988), 59-63; Beijbom, Ulf. *Sweden's First Voyagers to America. New Sweden in the New World 1638-1655*. (Sweden: Förlags AB Wiken, 1988)., 79; Herb Rambo; Swahn, 120, 121; Tantillo, 80.

CHAPTER SIXTEEN
Weslager, 11-118; Ward, 128-135; Ward, 140-141; https://en.wikipedia.org/wiki/Treaty_of_Hartford; Johnson, 271; Lindquvist, Herman. "The Ship that Never Arrived," Sweden&America, January, 2015, 4-5.

CHAPTER SEVENTEEN
Rydén, 65-66; Gehring, Charles T., Forward from: Tantillo, L.F. *The Edge of New Netherland.* (Nassau, New York: Self-Published, 2011), 6, 7; Eckman, 24, 25; Ward, 155; Weslager, New Sweden, 127; Ward, 158; Gehring, 8; Weslager, 129; Tantillo, L.F., 70; https://www.libraries.psu.edu/content/dam/psul/up/digital/pahistory/liz_pdfs/geographia.pdf ; Ward, 180, 181, 186; Weslager, New Sweden, 165; Eckman, 27; Ward, 192-194, 196, 199; http://www.gutenberg.org/files/19721/19721-h/19721-h.htm#RIP_VAN_WINKLE; Ward, 200-202, 236-245; Rambo; Norman, Hans. "A Swedish Colony in North America", from New Sweden in the New World, 1638-1655, 20-22.

CHAPTER EIGHTEEN
Johnson, Chp. XXXVI, pg. 380; Weslager, C.A. *The English on the Delaware, 1610-1682.* (Rutgers University Press. 1967) 92-93; http://en.wikipedia.org/wiki/New_Haven_Colony; Weslager, C.A., New Sweden, 64, 65; Ward, 99, 100; Weslager, 66; Leiby, 33; Weslager, 113-122; Ward, 118-122; http://www.foundmyroots.com/2013/10/29/george-lamberton-the-phantom-ship/; Dorwart. 4-6.

CHAPTER NINETEEN
Weslager, C.A. The English...,(Rutgers University Press. 1967), xii; http://en.wikipedia.org/wiki/George_Calvert,_1st_Baron_Baltimore

CHAPTER TWENTY
Eckman, 28, 113; Monroe, 47; Ward, 232-33, 246, 248-249; Eckman, 29; http://www.delawarebeerhistory.com/early-ales/the-dutch/; http://archiver.rootsweb.ancestry.com/th/read/Dutch-Colonies/2005-07/1120286926; Ward, 272-273; Ward, chp. 49, chp. 53; Munroe, 47.

CHAPTER TWENTY-ONE
Carter, Edward C. & Lewis III, Clifford. *Sir Edmund Plowden and the New Albion Charter, 1632-1785.* (The Pennsylvania Magazine of History and Biography, Vol 83, No. 2 (Apr., 1959); Ward, 60, 65; http://www.delawareroots.org/index.php/history-of-delaware-j-thomas-scharf/40-history-of-delaware-scharf/114-chapter-6-sir-edmund-plowden-and-new-albion; Johnson, 381-82.

CHAPTER TWENTY-TWO
Landis, James G. *Tomahawks to Peace.* (Guys Mills, PA, Conquest Publishing, 2009), 19; Veit/Orr, 52; Monroe, 53, 54, 55; Eckman, 29; Ward, 312, Eckman, 30-31. Craig Lukezic, archeologist, Delaware Division of Historical and Cultural Af-

fairs, Alexander d'Hinoyossa" One of the most influential men in Colonial Delaware. June 20th, 2014, Blogging Delaware History, https://history.blogs.delaware.gov/2014/06/20/alexander-dhinoyossa-one-of-the-most-influential-men-in-colonial-delaware/ ; Ward, 328, 29, 333; http://archiver.rootsweb.ancestry.com/th/read/PA-OLD-CHESTER/2006-12/1166025870

CHAPTER TWENTY-THREE
Shorto, 294; Eckman, 33, 34; Ward, 351-352. 359-363; Ward, chp. 64; McCormick, Richard P. *New Jersey from Colony to State 1609-1789*. (Newark, NJ: New Jersey Historical Society 1981), 17; Munroe, chp. 3; http://archiver.rootsweb.ancestry.com/th/read/PA-OLD-CHESTER/2006-12/1166025870; http:/www.americanswedish.orgThe%20Delaware%20Finns%20of%20Colonial%20America.pdf

CHAPTER TWENTY-FOUR
Griscom, Lloyd E. *The Historic County of Burlington*. (The Burlington County Cultural and Heritage Commission 1973), 3; http://www.ushistory.org/penn/fox.htm; http://www.san.beck.org/GPJ14-Quakers.html; http://www.adamsonancestry.com/pioneering_spirit/#_Toc302021218; https://books.google.com/books?id=m5MmV8XwDLQC&pg=PA668&lpg=PA668&dq=major+john+fenwick&source=bl&ots=Cducg_IrJs&sig=BvHjnBx5RT9vvFpxfTkcXC9sJMA&hl=en&sa=X&ved=0ahUKEwjcqpqan7bKAhWIth4KHYIAAaE4ChDoAQg7MAY#v=onepage&q=major%20john%20fenwick&f=false; http://www.ushistory.org/penn/pennnj.htm; https://journals.psu.edu/pmhb/article/viewFile/30807/30562; http://westjersey.org/sjh/sjh_chap_2.htm; https://journals.psu.edu/pmhb/article/viewFile/30807/30562; McCormick, 40-41; http://www.ushistory.org/penn/scharf.htm; http://www.monroehistorical.org/articles/files/030809_penn.html; http://www.ushistory.org/penn/scharf.htm; http://www.phmc.state.pa.us/portal/communities/documents/1681-1776/pennsylvania-charter.html; Abbott, Elizabeth W. *History of Early Quaker Meeting Houses in the Salem Area of New Jersey*. (South Jersey Magazine. (Spring 1990); Schermerhorn.

CHAPTER TWENTY-FIVE
Munroe, 81, 82; Burt, 1 Peare, Catherine Owens. William Penn. (Philadelphia, PA: J.B. Lippincott Company 1957), 246-250; UShistory.org/welcomepark

EPILOGUE
Meacham, John. *Thomas Jefferson. The Art of Power*. (New York: Random House, 2013), 86; https://en.wikipedia.org/wiki/John_Morton_(politician); Rydén, WW66-68; Burt, 31; Eckman, 111.

✦ BIBLIOGRAPY ✦

Abbott, Elizabeth W. *History of Early Quaker Meeting Houses in the Salem Area of New Jersey.* (South Jersey Magazine. (Spring 1990).

Bailyn, Bernard. *The Barbarous Years. The Peopling of British North America: The Conflict of Civilizations, 1600-1675.* (New York: Random House, Inc., 2013) ebook

Beijbom, Ulf. *Sweden's First Voyagers to America. New Sweden in the New World 1638-1655.* (Sweden: Förlags AB Wiken, 1988).

Brazil, Robert Sean, *1609 Chronology,* blog: http://1609chronology.blogspot.com/2009/05/captain-argall-sets-sail-for-virginia.html

Bryson, Bill. *At Home.* (New York: Doubleday, 2010).

Bryson, Bill. *Made in America: An Informal History of the English Language in the United States.* (New York: HarperCollins, 1996).

Burt, Struthers. *Philadelphia. Holy Experiment.* (Garden City, NY: Doubleday, Doran & Co. Inc., 1945).

Carter, Edward C. & Lewis III, Clifford. *Sir Edmund Plowden and the New Albion Charter, 1632-1785.* (The Pennsylvania Magazine of History and Biography, Vol 83, No. 2 (Apr., 1959).

Dersin, Denise. *What Life Was Like in Europe's Golden Age.* (Richmond, VA: Time-Life Books, 1999).

Dictionary of Canadian Biography, David B. Quinn; http://www.biographi.ca/en/bio.php?id_nbr=247

Dorwart, Jeffrey M. *Cape May County, New Jersey. The Making of an American Resort Community.* (New Brunswick, NJ: Rutgers University Press, 1992).

Eckman, Jeannette. *New Castle on the Delaware, Dutch Tercentenary Edition.* (New Castle, DE: New Castle Historical Society, 1950).

Encyclopedia of the North American Colonies. Volume I. Various Editors (New York: Charles Scribner's Sons,1993).

Fausz, J. Frederick, *Dictionary of Virginia Biography,* online source: http://www.encyclopediavirginia.org/Argall_Samuel_bap_1580-1626

Fernow, B. *Documents Relating to the History of the Dutch and Swedish Settlements on the Delaware River.* (Albany, The Argus Company, 1877).

Fernández-Arresto, Felipe. *Pathfinders: A Global History of Exploration.* (New

York, W.W. Norton & Co., 2006).

Fordham U., Modern History Sourcebook, *Gilbert's voyage to Newfoundland, 1583,* fordham.edu

Griscom, Lloyd E. *The Historic County of Burlington.* (The Burlington County Cultural and Heritage Commission 1973).

Haefeli, Evan. *The Revolt of the Long Swede: Transatlantic Hopes and Fears on the Delaware, 1669.* The Pennsylvania Magazine of History and Biography Vol. 130, No. 2 (Apr., 2006, pp. 137-180) The Historical Society of Pennsylvania: University of Pennsylvania Press. http://www.jstor.org/stable20093851.

Hakluyt, Richard. *University of Adelaide, ebook, Humphrey Gilbert Discourse.*

Haley, K.H.D. *The Dutch in the Seventeenth Century.* (London: Thames and Hudson, Ltd., 1972).

Hartig, Otto. *John & Sebastian Cabot.* Published online by New Advent. http://www.newadvent.org/cathen/03126d.htm

Heston, Alfred M. *South Jersey, A History 1664-1924.* (New York & Chicago: Lewis Historical Publishing Company, Inc., 1924).

Hine, C.G. *The Old Mine Road.* (New Brunswick, NJ: Rutgers University Press, 1909, 1963).

Craig Lukezic, archaeologist, Delaware Division of Historical and Cultural Affairs; *Alexander d'Hinoyossa: One of the most influential men in Colonial Delaware.* June 20, 2014 http://history.blogs.delaware.gov/2014/06/20/alexander-dhinoyossa-one-of-the-most-influential-men-in-colonial-delaware/

Horwitz, Tony. *A Voyage Long and Strange.* (New York: Picador, 2008).

Johnson, Amandus. *The Swedish Settlements on the Delaware.* (University of Pennsylvania, 1911).

Kelso, William M. *Jamestown: The Buried Truth.* (Charlottesville, VA: University of Virginia Press, 2006).

Koedel, R. Craig. *South Jersey Heritage: A Social, Economic and Cultural History.* (Washington, D.C.: University Press of America, 1979). HTML version

Kraft, Herbert C. *The Lenape.* (Newark, NJ: New Jersey Historical Society, 1986).

Kurlansky, Mark. *Cod.* (New York: Penguin Books, 1997).

Landis, James G. *Tomahawks to Peace.* (Guys Mills, PA, Conquest Publishing, 2009).

Leiby, Adrian C. *The Early Dutch and Swedish Settlers of New Jersey.* (Princeton, NJ: D. Van Nostrand Company. 1964).

Lester, Toby. *The Fourth Part of the World.* (New York: Free Press, 2009).

Lindquvist, Herman. "The Ship that Never Arrived," Sweden & America, January, 2015, 4-5.

Mancall, Peter C. *Fatal Journey, The Final Expedition of Henry Hudson.* (New York:

MJF Books, 2009).

McCormick, Richard P. *New Jersey from Colony to State 1609-1789*. (Newark, NJ: New Jersey Historical Society 1981).

Meacham, John. *Thomas Jefferson. The Art of Power*. (New York: Random House, 2013).

Meek, Phil. http://meek-williamsfamilytree.blogspot.com/2010/08/cornelius-hendrickson-navigatorexplorer.html

Miller, Lee. *Roanoke*. (New York: MJF Books, 2000).

Morison, Samuel Eliot. *The European Discovery of America, The Northern Voyages A.D. 500-1600*. (London: Oxford University Press, 1971).

Morris, Jr., Roy. *Ambrose Bierce, Alone in Bad Company*. (New York, Crown Publishers. 1995).

Munroe, John A. *Colonial Delaware: A History*. (Millwood, NY: KTO Press, 1978).

Narratives of Early Pennsylvania, West New Jersey and Delaware 1630–1707. Edited by Albert Cook Myers. http://books.google.com/books?id=FDR-AAAAIAAJ&dq=Narratives+of+Early+Pennsylvania,+West+New+Jersey+and+Delaware+1630%E2%80%931707&printsec=frontcover&source=bl&ots=faFlWOM4GD&sig=2_mbQLX8dW0_T-g0jHFBBCWN2Bc&hl=en&ei=zoGuSrrrDYLGlAeahP3ZBg&sa=X&oi=book_resu#v=onepage&q&f=false

Native American Netroots, http://nativeamericannetroots.net/diary/961, Posted on May 14, 2011 by Ojibwa

Pieter Cornelis Plockhoy — *First Anabaptists in the New World*
http://thecommonlife.com.au/c/pieter-cornelis-plockhoy-first-anabaptists-in-the-new-world

Peare, Catherine Owens. *William Penn*. (Philadelphia, PA: J.B. Lippincott Company 1957).

Rambo, Herbert R. *Peter Gunnerson Rambo of New Sweden*.(Self-published)
Rootsweb PA-OLD-CHESTER, *Peter Plockhoy and the Hoornkill settlers 1663-1690s*, http://archiver.rootsweb.ancestry.com/th/read/PA-OLD-CHESTER/2006-12/1166025870

Ruhnbro, Rune. *New Sweden in the New World 1638-1655*. (Sweden: Förlags AB Wiken, 1988).

Ruddock, Alwyn. *John Cabot and the Discovery of America*. Wiley Online Library, May 2008, http://onlinelibrary.wiley.com/doi/10.1111/j.1468-2281.2007.00422.x/full

Rydén, Josef. *Johan Printz of New Sweden; New Sweden in the New World 1638-1655*. (Sweden: Förlags AB Wiken, 1988).

Schermerhorn, William E. *The History of Burlington*. (Burlington NJ: Enterprise Publishing 1927).

Shorto, Russell. *The Island at the Center of the World*. (New York: Vintage Books 2005).

Stalcop family history: http://www.stalcopfamily.com/familyhistory.two.html

Stewart, Frank H. *Indians of Southern New Jersey*. (Woodbury, NJ, Gloucester County Historical Society, 1932).

Stockton, Frank R. *Stories of New Jersey*. (New Brunswick, NJ: Rutgers University Press, 1961).

Swahn, Jan-Öjvind. *A World of Riches and Monsters. New Sweden in the New World 1638-1655*. (Sweden: Förlags AB Wiken, 1988).

Tantillo, L.F. *The Edge of New Netherland*. (Nassau, New York: Self-Published, 2011).

Taylor, Alan. *American Colonies*. (New York: Viking Penguin 2001).

Tobacco: Its History and Associations. F.W. Fairholt, F.S.A. Chapman and Hall, 193, Piccadilly, London. 1859. On-line: https://archive.org/stream/tobaccoitshistor00fair#page/n7/mode/2up

Turner, Jack. *Spice*. (New York: Vintage Books, 2005).

Veit, Richard. *Digging New Jersey's Past*. (New Brunswick, NJ: Rutgers University Press, 2002).

Veit, Richard and Orr, David. *Historical Archaeology of the Delaware Valley, 1600-1850*. (Knoxville, TN The University of Tennessee Press, 2014).

Ward, Christopher, *The Dutch & Swedes on the Delaware, 1609-64*. (Philadelphia, PA: University of Pennsylvania Press, 1930).

Wedin, Maud. *The Forest Finns of Scandinavia*. (Finland: Finnbygdens Förlag in co-operation with FINNSAM, 2011).

Weslager, C.A. *The Delaware Indians*.(New Brunswick, NJ: Rutgers University Press, 1972).

Weslager, C.A. *Dutch Explorers, Traders and Settlers in the Delaware Valley*. (Philadelphia, PA: University of Pennsylvania Press,1961).

Weslager, C.A. *New Sweden on The Delaware: 1638-1655*. (Wilmington, DE: Middle Atlantic Press, 1988).

Weslager, C.A. *The English on the Delaware, 1610-1682*. (Rutgers University Press. 1967).

Wooley, Benjamin. *Savage Kingdom*. (New York: HarperCollins, 2007).

Wright, Louis B. *The Atlantic Frontier, Colonial American Civilization (1607-1763)*. (New York: Alfred A. Knopf, 1951).

INDEX

Abbott, Charles Conrad, 51
adelphos, 171
Africa, pro., 137
    West, 48
"aji", pro.
Albany, 42, 49, 57
Algonquian(s), 12, 24, 55
Alrichs, Jacob, 137, 147
Amadas, Phillip, 12
America(n), 70, 113, 141, ep.
    Revolution, 154, ep.
Amerike, Richard, 6
Amsterdam, 36, 38, 42, 45, 52, 57, 117
    Chamber, 57
    City, 137, 148, 154
    Exchange, 38
    Fort, 49, 52
Anders, the Finn, 113
Andastakas, 28
Andros, Governor Edmund, 63, 164
Anglo-Dutch War, 154
Second, 154, 165
Antiqua, 98
Antwerp, 45
Appalachians, 66
Appoquinimink Creek, 149
Archbishop of Canterbury, 144
Argall, Samuel, 19-22
Armenverius, 65
Arms of Amsterdam, 53
Articles of Confederation (ep.
Asia, 7
    Southeast, 38
Assunpinks, 28
Atlantic, 20, 42, 80, 89, 96, 101, 159
Atlantic City, 123
Australia, 75
Avalon, 134

Baffin Island, 10
Baltic, 74, 149
region, 74
sea, 74
Baltimore, 134
    Baron of, 136
    First Baron, 134
    Lord, 134, 136, 139, 140, 153, 166, 168, ep.
Barbados, 158, 159
Barbary Coast, 18
Barende-gat, 46
Barndegat, 46
Barnegat, 46
Barentsz Sea, 38
Barentsz, Willem, 38
Barlowe, Arthur, 12
Barron, Deputy Michael, 157
Basque, 3
Batavia, 38
Bay Colony Puritans, 128
beaver, intro, 44-45
Beekman, William, 64
Berkeley, John Lord, 159
Berkeley, Governor William, 144
beschonken, 56
Besk, Hans Amundson, 116
Belgium, 48
Bergen County, 63
Bicker, Gerrit, 115
Big Timber Creek, 29, 54, 62
Blijde Boodschap, 47
Block, Adriaen, 45
Blommaert, Samuel, 57, 77-78,
Blue Anchor Tavern, intro., 25
bog ore, 30
Boij, Captain Christiaen, 131
Bombay Hook, 85

· 185 ·

Bristol, 4
Britain, 14, 45, 134, 151
    Great, ep.
    British, ep.
    Civil Wars, 151
Brandywine Creek, 29
Brown, Alexander, 22
Brazil, 37, 48, 109, 147
Bridlington, 163
Bryson, Bill, 3
Buonaparte, ep.
Burgh, Albert Conraets, 58
Burgomasters, 137, 149
Burlington, City of 159
Burlington Island, 50
Byllynge, Edward, 160-163
Byllynge Trustees, 163

Cabot, John, intro, 6, 22, 140
Cabot, Sebastian, 7
Caboto, Giovanni, 4
Calcutta Pepper, pro.
Calvert, Sir George, 134, 141
Calvert, Cecil, 136
Calvert, Charles, 166, 168
Canada, 74
Canadian, 8, 134
Canary Islands, pro., 12
Cape Cod, intro.
Cape Charles, 145
Cape Hatteras, 6, 40
Cape Henlopen (Hindlopen), 21, 57, 101
Cape Horn, 63
Cape May, 47, 58, 129, 141
Cape May-Lewes Ferry, intro.
Cape La Warre, 21
Cape of Good Hope, pro., 37
Cape Verde Islands, pro.
Carr, Sir Robert, 152-153
Carr, Captain John, 153
Carolina(s), 12, 49, 161
Caribbean, 37, 87, 98, 158
Carteret, Sir George, 159, 161, 162
Cartier, Jaques, 8
Cashin, Dan, 94
Casimir, Ernst of Orange-Nassau, 112

castor canadensis, 44
Cathay, 8, 33
Catskill, 40
caucus, 28
cawcawwassoughes, 28
Central America, pro.
Chancellor, Richard, 33
Charitas, (Charity), 96
Charles I (King), 24, 65, 136, 140, 141, 161, 165
Charles II (King), 165-166
Charles IX, 74, 96
Charles River, 65,
Charter of Freedoms and Exemptions, 57
Cecil, Sir Robert, 134
Chesapeake, 6, 14,
    Bay, 6, 14, 136, 145, 167-168
Chester, 170
chili, pro.
China, 7
Chiton (12
Christiaensen, Hendrick, 45
Christina, 77, 83
    Fort, 86, 89, 90, 97, 103, 110, 112, 119, 121, 137
    Island, 81
    Kill, 84, 118
    Queen, 83, 15, 18
    River, 47, 62, 80, (20
Christinahamn, 116, 119
Christianity, 100, 134
Church of England, 159
Church of Rome, 134
Chygoe's Island, 163
cinnamon, pro.
Cipango, 4
Clark, Benjamin, 168
cloves, pro.
Cobb's Creek, 103
Cock, The, 128
Cock, Brigitta, 122-123
Cock, Peter, 122, 157
Cock, Otto, ep.
cod, 4
Colman, Henry, 157

Colman, John, 40
Collegiates, 150
Columbus, intro., 20
Commercial College, 113
Commodore Barry Bridge, 129
Connecticut, 42, 111, 128
    River, 45, 49, 128
conestoga, 28
Constantinople, pro.
Continental Congress, ep.
    First and Second, ep.
Cooper, James Fenimore, 55
Corssen, Arent, 65, 107
coucorouse, 28
County Longford, 134
County Palatine, 141
Cristoff, Count Hans, 155
Croatoan, 14
Cromwell, 150, 153
Cross Island, 103
Crusades, 143
Cumberland County 161
Curaçao, 37, 109

d'Ayllon, Lucas Vasquez, 22
Dafoe, Daniel, 44
da Gama, Vasco, pro.
Dalbo, Anders, 122
Dare, Ananias, 14
Dare, Eleanor, 14
Dartmouth, 42
Davenport, John, 128
Davis, John, 10, 33
Davis Strait, 10
Deal (England), pro., 25
Deale, 63
de Champlain Samuel, 8
de Verenigde Ostindische Compagnie, pro., 38
de Vries, David Pietersen, 58-62, 67
De la Grange, ep.
    Madame, ep.
Delaware
    Bay (Bayshore), intro., 22, 26, 33, 45-46, 57, 65, 89, 115, 136, 145,
    Company, 128
    River, pro., 26, 27, 45, 54-55, 65, 74, 79, 85, 94, 111, 112, 128, 152, 154, 159, 166, ep.
    South River, 47, 50, 54, 65, 78, 85, 91, 110, 120, 137, 139, 149, 152
    South Bay, 47, 65, 81
    State of, 63, 141, 168
    Valley, intro, pro., 26, 62, 98, 131, 163, 89, 168
    Water Gap, 66
Denmark, 74, 101
Dermer, Thomas, 22
de Magalhães, Fernão, pro.
de Velasco, Don Alonso, 22
d'Hinoyossa, Lieutenant Alexander, 51, 64, 137, 147, 153
Discovery, 15, 20
Dixon, Jeremiah, 168
Dock Creek, 171
Drake, Sir Francis 12, 33
Dublin, 142, 164
duffel(s), 45, 56, 61
Duke of York, 151, 161, 166
    James, 151, 159, 165
    James II, 151
    Stuart, James, 151
Dutch, 24, 33, 43, 52, 66, 74, 77, 80, 83, 85, 89, 92, 94, 100, 103, 106-123, 128-129, 137, 144, 151, ep.
    Dutchmen 46, 58, 66, 89, 131, 153
    East India Company, 37
    Protestant, 36
    Revolt, 37
    West India Company, intro, 20, 23

East Indies, 37, 58
East Jersey, 159
Eaton, Theophilus, 128
Edam, 58
Eesanques, 58
Egg Harbor, 123
Eighty Years War, 37, 76
Eirik the Red, 1
Elizabeth I, 10, 12,
Eriksson, Leif, 1
Elbe, 84

El Dorado, 105
Elsinboro Township, intro.
Emigrant House (24
England (intro, pro., 8, 10-11, 22, 38, 74, 136, 142, 146, 154, 159
English, intro, 3, 8, 10, 33, 44, 62, 67, 74, 78, 87, 111, 128, 145, 150, 151-152, ep.
    Catholics, 134
    Men-O-War, 152
    Parliament, 168
    Separatists, 49
Eru Packen (Elupacken), 83
Esopus, 66
Estonia, 74
Erik XIV, 72
Essex House, 170
Europe, 2, 7, 36, 72, 76, (17, 21
European, pro., 4, 7, 26, 52, 74-75, 83, 85
    Golden Age, 37
Evelyn, Robert, 65

factorij, 50
Fairview, 54
falles, the, 24, 46, 66, 91, 163
Fama, 98
Farckens Kill, 130
Far East, pro., 38
Fendall, Governor, 140, 147
Fenwick, Major John, 139, 160
Fenwick's Colony, 161
Figurative Map, 46
Finland, 74, 96
Finns, 70, 86, 96, 121, 137, 155, ep.
    Forest, 96
    stray, 96
Finnish, 70, 81, (24
Finn's Point, 123
Fleming, Klas (Clas), 78, 89, 101
Flemish, 74
Florida, 8, 62, ep.
fluyt, 37, 63
Flying Deer, 88
Flying Griffin, 80
Fogel Grip, 80, 87, 89

Fort Altena, (22
Fort Beversreede, 111
Fort Casimir, 112, 137, 148, 153, 170, ep.
Fort Elfsborg, 102, 111, 115, 145, 161
Fort Myggenborgh, 102
Fort Nassau, 54, 62, 65, 85, 91, 111, ep.
Fort New Gothenburg, 103
Fort Nya Alfsbörg, 102
Fort Orange, 49, 52
Fort Trefaldighet (Trinity), 115, 153
Fortune of Amsterdam, 45
Fortune of Hoorn, 45
Fort Wilhelmus, 50
Fox, George, 159-160
France, 74, 76, 149-150, ep.
Francis Lord Plowden, Governor and Baron of Mount Royal, 143
Franklin, Benjamin, 56
Freedenburgh, 94
French, pro., 4, 8, 54, 154, ep.
Huguenot, 52
Friesland, 38, 112
Frobsisher, Martin, 10, 33
Fuchs, Leonhart, pro.

Gates, Sir Thomas, 19
Gehring, Charles, 138
"General Stijfvesandt", 120
Genesis of the United States, The, 22
German(s), 52, 81, ep.
    army, 100
Germantown (23
Germany, 74, 76, 100, 150
Chemnitz, 100
Gibbon House, 97
Gibbstown, 11, 17
Gilbert, Sir Humfrey, 11-12, 170
Gloucester City, 54
County, 123, 164
Gloria Dei Church, 123
Godspeed, 15
Godyn, Samuel, 57-58
Godyn's Bay, 58, 12
Gothenburg (Göteburg), 74, 87, 98, 124
Geoctroyeerde Westindische Compagnie, 34, 48

Golden Hind, 10
Governor Berkeley, 87
Grand Banks, 4
Greenland, 4
Great Kahn, 6
Great Lakes 94
Great Ship, 132
"greene country towne", 25
Greenwich, 97
Grenville, Sir Richard, 12
Griffen, 161
Groningen, 38
Groote Christoffel (Great Christopher), 117
Guelderland, 38
Guiana, 37
guilder(s), 53, 90
Guinea, 78, 137
Guinea, 152
Gulf of Guinea (pro.
Gulf of St. Lawrence, 1
Gunillaberg Manor, ep.
Gunnerson, Peter, 90
Gustav I, 72
Gustav II Adolph, 74
Gustavus Adolphus, 76
GWC, 48, 52
Gyllene Haj (Golden Shark), 113, 116
Gyllengren, Lieutenant Elias, 117, 122

Habsburgs, 134
hactenus inculta, 140
Hague, The, 46, 53,
Hakluyt, Richard, 10, 36
Half Moon, 33, 80
Halve Maen, 33
Hanseatic League, 72
Harlot's Creek, 63
Harmer, Gottfried, 130
Harmon, Ephraim, 170
Harriot, 12
Hartford, 111, 116
Harvey, John, 22, 63
Hawkins, John, 10
Hein, Admiral Piet, 48
Helm, Ake, 120

Hendricksen, Captain Cornelius, 46
Henry VIII, 7, 10
Heraclitus of Ephesus, pro.
Herrman, Augustine, 140, 149
Heyes, Peter, 58
Hictock, 139
High Mightinessess, 38
High Island (Metedeconck), 50, 52, 147, 159
High Street, 163
Hindloopen, 47
Hindlopen, 57
Hindricksson, Ivert, 97
Hisingen, 90
Hog's Creek (Varken's Kill), 128
Holland, 38, 45, 50, 59, 77, 89, 147, 151, 165
Holm, Thomas, 169
Holy Experiment, 160
Holy Roman Empire, 18
Hooghe Eylandt, 50
Hoorn, 63
Hoornkil (Hoerenkil, Horenkil), 63, 150, 153
Hopkins, Edward, 111
Hore, Robert, 8
Hossit, Gillis, 57
House of Commons (19
Hudde, Andreas, 106, 109, 115
Hudson, Henry, 20, 33, 80
    River, 23, 47, 55, 57, 66, 74, 159
    Strait, 7
    Valley, ep.
Hundred Year's War, 76
Huygen, Hendrick, 88, 17
Hy-Brazil, 2

Iceland, 4
Ille de Sable, 81, 86
Indian(s), 16, 20, 53, 61-62, 83, 85, 105, 109, 112, 116, 137, 139, 143, 157, 159
Kings, 142
Indonesia, 38
Ireland, 7, 134, 142
Irish, ep.
Irish Tenth, 164

Iroquois, 55
Irving, Washington, 120, ep.
Island of Brasil, 2
Isle of Jersey, 159
Italian(s), 60, pro.
Iver the Fin, 97, 112, 157

Jacobson, Marcus, 156
Jacquet, Jean Paul, 121, 137
Jamaica, 159
James River, 16
Jamestown, 16, 40, 45, 87, 136
Jansen, Captain Poewel, 89
Jansz, Jacob, 57
Jegou, Pierre, 159
Jersey Shore, 40
Jesus of Lûbeck, 10
Johan III, 72
Jönköping, 79
Jönsson, Anders, 113
Jöransen, Captain Adrian, 81
Joyful Message, 47
Juet, Robert, 33

Kalm, Peter, 29
Kalmar, 79
    harbor, 79
    Nyckel, 79, 88, 89, 96
    Key of, 79
Kanastoge, 28
Kattan, 113, 124
Kechemeche, 28
Keckquenner, 139
Keift, Governor Willem, 63, 85, 90, 106, 109, 128
Kent, 163
Kent, England, pro., 169
King Charles II, 151
King Henry VII, intro, 6
King James I, 134
King of Sweden, 156
King Phillip III, 22
Kingsessing, 103, 123
Kingston, 66
Kling, Captain Måns Nilssen, 81, 87, 90
Knickerbocker, Diedrich, ep.

Knights of Conversion, 143
Kock, Peter Larsson, 120
Königsmark, 155
Krygier, Captain Martin, 137
Kurlansky, Mark, 3

Labrador, 8
Lady Barbara, Baroness of Richneck, 143
lagom, 79
Lake Laconia, 24
Lamberton, George, 128
"lång", 156
L'Anse aux Meadows, 1
Latvia, 74
La Warr, Roger, 21
la Motte, M., ep.
Lawrie, Gawen, 161
Leeward Islands, 109
Leiby, Adrian C., ep.
Lenape, 27, 40, 55-56, 62, 65, 90, 128
Lenapehoking, 27
Lenapewihittuck, 27
Lenni-Lenâpé, 27, 55
Lewes, intro., 63
Lindström, Peter, pro., 105, 115
Lion of the North, 77
Little Prince, The, 148
Little Timber Creek, 54
livery of seisin, 11, 170
London, 36, 154, 163
    Company, 15, 163
    Bridge, 45
Longfellow, Henry Wadsworth, 132
Long Finn, Rebellion, 155
Long Island, 111, 141, 162
Long Island Sound, 132
Lord Baltimore, 50
Lord de la Warre, 18, 21
Lost Colony, 14
Louis XIV, 154, 165
Lovelace, Governor Francis, 157, ep.
Lower Counties, 168
Lowlands, 36
Lucas, Nicholas, 161
Lucassen, Andres, 83

Lützen, 76

mace, 37
Machierick, 139
Magellan, Ferdinand, pro., 37
Magellanica, 75
Mahican, 40
Maine, 1, 15, 40, 49
Malabar, pro.
Malacca, 38
Mahamen, 83
Manhattan, 45, 52-54, 101, 117, 139
Manna-hata, 42
Manhattes, 53
Manor Rensselaerswyck, 57
Manteo, 12
Mantes, 28, 62
Marlow, Godfrey 163
Markham, William, 168
Marriner, Mabel, 141
Mary Guildford, 8
Maryland, 22, 123, 136, 139, 141, 151, 156, 159, 166
Mason, Charles, 168
Massachusetts, 132
    Bay Company, 132
    Colony 128
Matanzas Bay, Cuba, 48
Matinicum, 101
Matthew, 6
Mattahorn, 83, 12
Mattsdotter, Britta, 106
Maurice River, 29
Mauritius River, 47
Mayflower, 49
Meckansio, 105
Mediterranean, 37
Mennonites, 150
Mercurius, 121-122
Metedeconk, 51, 159
Mey, Cornelius Jacobsen, 45-47, 54
Michaelius, Reverend Jonas, 78
Mingo, 55
Mingwe, 55
Minquas 55, 62, 65, 90, 103
Minquas Kill, 46, 62, 83, 110, 128, 137

Minsi, 27
Minuit, Peter, 52, 77, 83, 85, 89
Mitot Schemingh (Mitasemint), 83
Mölndal, 103
Moll, John, 169
Moluccan, pro.
Moluccas, pro.
morgens, 53
Morton, John, ep.
Mullica, Eric Pålsson, ep.
Mullica River, ep.
Mullica Hill, ep.
Mullica Township, ep.
Munsees, 40
Munsi, 27
Murderer's Island, 50
Muscovy, 18
Muscovy Company, 33, 36

Nanticoke, 28
Narriticons, 28
Narriticons Creek, 129
Nassau, Fort, 46
Navigatio Sancti Brendani Abbatis, 2
Nertunius, Reverend Mattias, 125
Neshaminy, 28
Netherlands, 38, 43-45, 63, 76, 138, 154
    United, 38, 48, 154
    Spanish, 154
New Albion, 141, 144
New Amstel, 137-138, 147, 149, 152
New Amsterdam, 52, 66, 77, 85, 90, 115, 129, 148, 152
New Beverly, 163
New Bohemia, 149
New Brunswick, 1
New Castle, pro., 154, 159, 170
New England, 18, 62, 67, 133, 134, 144, 151, 159
Newfoundland, 1, 11, 40, 134, 141
New Haven, 128, 132, 145
New Jersey, 8, 29, 45, 70, 123, 141, 159
New Korsholm, 103, 112
Newport, Captain Christopher, 15
New Netherland(s), 47, 57, 66, 77, 85,

106, 109, 128, 147, 151, ep.
   Company, 48
   Colony, 52
New Orange, 154
New Sweden, 52, 81, 83, 86, 89, 96, 110, 113, 116, 137, ep.
   Colony, ep.
   Company, 79, 13
   Restoration, 156
New World, 6, 10, 14, 44, 49, 78, 89, 134, 136, 140, 159
New York, 8, 45, 160, ep.
Bay, 6
Court of Assizes, ep.
New Wales, 166
Nieu Nederlandt, 49
Nicholson, Samuel, 161
Nicolls, Colonel Richard, 152
   Deputy Governor, 152
Nicolls, Matthias, 157
Nieuw Port Mey, 47
Noble, Richard, 163
Nonesuch House, 43
Noort Rivier, 47
Norman Conquest, 154
Norsemen, 1
Norse, 1
North America, intro, 8, 10-11, 46, 66, 81, 140, ep.
North Atlantic, 8
North Pole, 36
North River, 117
Northwest Passage, 7, 12, 37
Norway, 40, 74
Nothnagle Cabin, 70
Nova Cesarea, 159
Nova Scotia, 40, 81, ep.
Nova Zembla, 36
nutmeg, 37
Nya Sverige, 84, 105, 121
Nya Sverigekompaniet, 79
Nya Vasa, 103

Odessa, DE, 149
Old Mine Road, 66
Onrust, 45-46

Orange-Nassau, 112
Orient, 36, 6, 65
Örn, (Eagle), 113
Ottoman Empire, pro.
Outer Banks, 12
Outhout, Foppe Jansen, 138
   Meneer, 139
Oxford, 141
Oversyssel, 38
Oxenstierna, Count Axel, 77, 101
Oxenstierna, Eric, 113

Pahaquarry, 66
Papegoia, Lieutenant Johan, 106, 113, ep.
Passayunk, 15, 17
   Indians, 65
patroon, 57, 77
patroonship, 57
   -sub, 57
Peobody Museum, 51
Penn, William, intro, pro., 11, 28, 50, 63, 122, 160-162, 164-171
   Lord Proprietary, 166
Penn, Admiral Sir William, 165
Penn's Neck, 123
Pennsylvania, 29, 123, 130, 141, 25
Phantom Ship, The, 132
Philadelphia, intro, 123, (23
   International Airport, 101
Phillip II, 10
philos, 25
Pinnace, 79
Plockhoy, Peter Cornelius, 153
Plowden, Sir Edmund, 128, 141, 168
Plowden, Francis, 143
Plymouth, 8
   Colony, 49
Pocahontas, 16
Point Rosee, 1
Poland, 74
Potomac River, 136
Portsmouth Town, 133
Portugal, pro., 36
Portuguese, pro., 14, 48, 148
Powhatan, 16

Prince Maurice, 47
Prince's Island, 50
Printz, Colonel Johan Björnsson, 87, 89, 95, 98-107, 109, 111, 112-113, 130-132, 145, ep.
Printz, Gustaf, 112
Printz, Armegot, 106, 23, ep.
Printz Hall, 101
Printzhoff, 101, 113, 119
Privy Council, 134, 24
Prophet Daniel, 125
Puerto Rico, 125
Puritans, 128

Quaker(s), pro., 22, 24, 25
    Act, 159
    English (18
Fenwick, 160-161, 163-164
Irish, 164
Queen Henrietta Maria, 136
Quesquakous, 58
Quintipartite Deed, 163

Raccoon Creek, 123, 163
Raleigh, Cittie of in Virginia, 14
Raleigh, Sir Walter, 11-12
Ramberget, 90
Rambo, John, 122
Rambo, Peter Gunnerson, 90, 103, 112, 170
Rancocas, 28
Rapalje, Joris, 49
Resolution Island, 10
Restless, 45-46
Revolt of the Long Finn (Swede), 155
Ridder, Lieutenant Peter Hollander, 89-91, 100, 103, 130
Ridley Creek, 29, 103
Rink, Harry, 70-71
Rising, Johan, 113, 115, 117, 119, 121, ep.
Roanoke, 12, 14
Rocks, The, 86, 98
Romans, 45
Rose Valley, PA, 103
Rotterdam, 88
Royal Navy, 165

Royal Seal, 136
Rudders, Johan Jonsson, 126
Russia, 33, 74
Rut, John, 8

Sagas, 1
Saint Brendan, Voyage of, 2
Saint Christopher, 88
Saint Kitts, 88
Salem, 11, 21, 24
    County, intro., 20
    Oak, 24
    River, 29, 101, 128
    Towne, 161
Sampson, 8
Sandy Hook, 141
Sankikan(s), 28, 66, 91
Sanlúcar de Barrameda (pro.
Sant Hoeck (Sand Point), 112
Sassafras River, 123
Saxony, 76
Scandinavian, 1, 72
Schuylkill (River), 28, 46, 65, 85, 103, 110, ep.
    Valley, 123
Scheyechbi, 27
Schlaghen, Peter, 53
Scot(s), 81, 155, ep.
seganku, 28
sewan, sewant, 32, 56
shallop, 62
Shalom, 161
Shawnee-Minisink, 27
Shield of Stockton, 163
Siconese, 28,
    Great, 58
Sigismund III,
Skute, Sven, 102, 117-119, 122, 154
Slate Roof House, 171
Smallpox, pro.
Smith, Captain John, 16, 18, 36, 55
Smith's Island, 145
Smuggler's Path, 149
Society of Friends, 159
South America, pro., 37, 63,
South Hook, 57

Spain, pro., 37, 74, 76, 134
    King of, 140
Spanish, pro., 12, 19, 22, 87, 109, 125, 134
    Armada, 14, 37
    Catholics, 36
    Main, 37
spice(s), pro.
    Islands, pro.
Spiring, Peter, 78
(Silfverkrona), 78
Spitzbergen Island, 36
Squirrel, 62
Stalcop, Johan, 155
Staten Island, 63
States-General, 45, 53, 57, 137, 149
St. Christopher, 22, 125
St. Croix River, 151
St. Cruz, 126
Stidden, Timon, 130
Stille, Olaf, 120
St. Jacob, 150
St. John's, 11
St. Martin, 109
Stockholm, 125
Stockholm Bloodbath, 72
Streiff, 76
Stuart(s), 159
stuiver, 56
Stuyvesant, Peter, 109-111, 117-122, 137, 139, 149, 152, ep.
succotash, 30
Suriname, 154
Susan Constant, 15
Susquehanna River, 55
Susquehannock, 55
Sussex, 63
Svanen (Swan), 98
Swart, Antoni (Black Anthony), 87
Swarte Arent (Black Eagle), 117
Sweden, 72-73, 76, 78, 88, 89-91, 101, 112, 116, ep.
    New, 79, 81, 86-87, 89, 100, 103, 113, 115-116, 122, 124-125, 137
    Company, 79, 83
Swedes, intro, pro., 11, 13, 14, 15, 16, 17, 18, 20, 21, 22, 23, ep.
Swedish, intro, 12, 15, 17, 24, 25, ep.
    Nation on the Delaware, 122
    Granary, 97
    Navy, 89
Swedesboro, 123
Sylvania, 166
Symonssen, Michel, 88

Taspeemick, 139
Teencoorntgen, 59
Tempest, The, 126
Texel, 59, 81
Thames, 163
Thirty Year's War, 76
Tiger, 45
Tijger, 45
Tinicum, 101, 110, 122, ep.
Thickpenny, John, 130
Thomas Lord Plowden, High Admiral and Baron of Royalmount, 143
Thompson, Andrew, 161
three sisters, 29
T-O maps, 7
tobacco, 14, 30
Tom, Sheriff William (23
Torkillus, Reverend Reorus, 89
Town Bank, 133
Treaty of Breda, 154
Treaty of Tordesillas (pro.
Treaty of Westminster, 154
Trefaldighet, 153
Trenton, 24, 46, 91
Trico, Catalina, 49-50
Trinity College, 134
Trinity Sunday, 115
Truth, Sojourner, ep.
Turner, Nathaniel, 128
Turner, Robert, 166
Tuscany, 8

Uí Breasail, 2
Unilachtigo, 27
Union of Kalmar, 72
Unity, 78
University of Pennyslvania's Museum of

Archeology and Anthropology, 51
Upland, 123, 168
Uproar Among the Swedes, 155
Usselinx, Willem, 48, 74
Usquata, 128
Utie, Colonel Nathaniel, 140, 147
Utrecht, 38, 46

Valley of the Swans, 57
van deer Water, Captain Jan Hindricksen, 81
van den Bogaert, Joost, 94
van Dyck, Gregorius, 89, 102
van Elswyck, Hendrick, 117, 119
van der Hulst, Willem, 50, 52
van Gezel, Cornelius, 147
van Ilpendam, Jan Jansen, 106, 129
van Langdonk, Joost, 89, 91
van Meteren, Emanuel, 36, 42
Van Rappard Documents, 50
van Rensselaer, Kiliaen, 57
van Sluys, Anneka, 123
van Sweeringen, Gerrit, 147
van Winkle (Rip), 120
Varken's Kill (Varkenskill), 100, 128, 139, 145, 161
Varlo, Charles, 146
Vasa, 72, 77
Vass, Sven 105
Velasco Map, 22
Venezuela, 37
Verhulst, 50,
Verrazano, Giovanni, intro, 8-9, 22
Virginia, 12, 14, 49, 63, 67, 101, 136, 144, 151, 160, 168
Virginia Company of London, 15, 19
Virginia Company of Plymouth, 15
Virgin Queen, 12
Vespucci, Amerigo, 6
Victoria, pro.
Viking(s), 1, 72
Vinland, 1
von Twiller, Wouter, 66-67
VOC, pro., 38
Vriessendael, 63

Wade, Robert, 170
Waegh (Scales), 117
Waldron, Resolved, 140
Wallonia, 48
Walloon, 49, 147, 159
wampumpeag, (wampum), 28
Waldseemüller, 6
Walvis, 58
Wanchese, 12
Watcessit, 144
Wehenset, 128
Welcome Park, 171
Wellington's Law of Command, 147
Welcome, pro., 25, 169
Wenamink, 139
Werden, Sir John, 166
Wesel, 52, 154
West Gotha Cavalry, 100
West Indies, 48, 59, 87,
West India Company, 48
West Jersey, 159
West, Thomas, 18
White Clay Creek, 29
White, John, 12, 14
Whore Kill, 63
Wickquakinick, 28
Wickusi, 129
Wicaco, 28, 123, 25
WIC, 54, 57, 65, 77, 78, 90, 117, 137, 149
William & Nicholas, 152
William, Prince of Orange, 49
William the Silent, 49
Willing Mind, 163
Winifred, Baroness of Uvedale, 143
Winthrop, Governor, 132
Woolen, John, 130-132

Yale University, 51
Yong, Thomas, 24, 65-66

Zeeland, 38
Zuyder Zee (9
Zuyt Baye, 47
Zuyt River, 47
Zwaanendael, 57, 81, 86, 140

www.ingramcontent.com/pod-product-compliance
Lightning Source LLC
Chambersburg PA
CBHW042358280426
43661CB00096B/1152